POSITIVITY

Groundbreaking Research Reveals How to Embrace

the Hidden Strength of Positive Emotions,

Overcome Negativity, and Thrive

CROWN PUBLISHERS NEW YORK

POSITIVITY

BARBARA FREDRICKSON,
Ph.D.

All rights reserved.
Published in the United States by Crown Publishers,
an imprint of the Crown Publishing Group,
a division of Random House, Inc., New York.
www.crownpublishing.com

CROWN and the Crown colophon are registered
trademarks of Random House, Inc.

Library of Congress Cataloging-in-Publication Data
Fredrickson, Barbara.
Positivity : groundbreaking research reveals how to embrace
the hidden strength of positive emotions, overcome
negativity, and thrive / Barbara Fredrickson.
p.   cm.
Includes bibliographical references.
1. Positive psychology. I. Title.
BF204.6F74   2009
158.1—dc22   2008027683

ISBN 978-0-307-39373-9

Printed in the United States of America

DESIGN BY BARBARA STURMAN

10 9 8 7 6 5 4 3 2 1

First Edition

For

Jeff, Garrett, and Crosby,

my most cherished teachers

Contents

PART I

The Good News About Positivity

PART II

Raise Your Ratio

PART I

The Good News
About Positivity

CHAPTER 1

Waking Up to Positivity

One's own self is well hidden from one's own self:
Of all mines of treasure, one's own is the last to be dug up.
—FRIEDRICH NIETZSCHE

TAKE 1

The morning sun streams through your bedroom window and wakes you from a fitful night's sleep. After a long string of gray and rainy days, you appreciate seeing blue sky. But soon enough you realize the alarm didn't go off. You're disappointed because you've been meaning to wake up extra early so you can have time to yourself before the kids wake up and the morning race begins. With what little time there is, you decide to skip your planned exercise routine, spend some more time in bed, and write in your journal. You write,

> I can't believe I let myself down again by forgetting to set my alarm. How am I ever going to take charge of my days (and my life!) if I can't make this simple change? Without exercise, I'm going to feel like a slug today. Ugh. I'd better focus on why I write in this

journal in the first place: to think about my larger goals and
connect them to what I do each day. Is this really working? Is it
worth my time when I could be sleeping? What I really should
be doing with this extra time is checking for fires on e-mail or
reviewing my ridiculously long to-do list. Isn't our water bill past
due? Where is it anyway?

At this point you close your journal, get out of bed, go to your
computer, and open your e-mail. Sure enough, you find that your
co-worker, Sharon, needs input from you before she can submit
her proposal, and she needs it by this afternoon. You'll be stuck
spending at least part of your morning preparing forms for her.
Feeling angry at her imposition, you open the next e-mail to see
that the project you spearheaded received preliminary approval and
you've got forty-eight hours to make a final set of revisions. "Forty-
eight hours!" you say out loud. "Am I supposed to drop everything
to make these revisions?" How am I going to fit this in?" The
nanosecond of joy you felt on learning the good news is squashed
by your concerns about clearing this last hurdle.

Just then, your daughter, who's nearly four years old, wakes up
and calls, "*Mommy!*" You glance at the time: 6:42. You've told her
time and again to wait quietly in her room until you come in for
hugs and kisses at seven, and here she is, not listening, *again.* Your
frustration is growing—far too many demands both at work and at
home. Nobody understands how impossible your life has become
with this career shift. You go to your daughter's room, snap at her
about calling for you early, and then march off to make breakfast.

The whole morning is a grim race, and everybody's losing. You'd
have been out the door on time had your seven-year-old son not
misplaced his favorite shoes. Then starts the parental nagging:
"Why can't you just wear a different pair!? If those shoes are so
important to you, why don't you keep better tabs on them?" Now
all four of you—the kids, you, and your husband—are racing
around the house trying to find those @#$% shoes!

Later, having dropped the children off at school—late again—you arrive at work—also late. The first person you see is Joe, your collaborator on the project that was just accepted. He's smiling broadly. At times you appreciate Joe's good spirits, but today his smile makes you suspicious. You think, *He's trying to butter me up so I'll do all the revisions!* He approaches. "Did you hear the news? We got the money! We're set for the year!" You say, "Yeah, but did you see that list of revisions—and just forty-eight hours to make them? I've also got to deal with Sharon's proposal this morning." Joe's smile fades as he takes a moment to figure out how to respond to your negativity.

Sound familiar? If you're like most people, you probably recognize this kind of morning all too well: *Can't do anything right. Can't give myself the time I need. Can't stick with my goal of journaling. Can't stand that Sharon is making her emergency my emergency. Can't fathom how I'll meet a forty-eight-hour revision deadline. Can't get on the same page with Joe. Can't even teach my kids to stay in bed until 7:00 a.m. Can't get through the morning "race" without yelling and fussing. Can't get the kids to school on time. And if I can't get myself to work on time—how in the world am I going to meet all these demands?*

We all know negativity; it looms large and is easy to spot. Negativity pervades your self-talk and your judgments. It bleeds into your exchanges with your kids and your colleagues, eroding goodwill between you. Making matters worse, unchecked negativity breeds health-damaging negative emotions—anger, contempt, and depression—that seep into your entire body. You can feel your simmering bitterness eating away at your stomach, raising your blood pressure, and turning your shoulder and neck muscles to stone. Even your face feels hard and tight, which may be why others steer clear if they can. What's more, you move through your day as if you have blinders on. You find fault and blame everywhere. You see no solutions. Everything is painfully predictable. Negativity comes on fast and strong, hitting like a sledge-hammer. And none of us is immune to it.

So what about positivity? Compared to negativity, positivity seems pale and weak. It's hardly the mirror image of negativity. Positivity seems so puny that at times we don't even notice it.

But what if positivity matters?

And what is positivity anyway?

Let's start with what it isn't. Positivity doesn't mean we should follow the axioms "Grin and bear it" or "Don't worry, be happy." Those are simply superficial wishes. Positivity runs deeper. It consists of the whole range of positive emotions—from appreciation to love, from amusement to joy, from hope to gratitude, and then some. The term is purposely broad. It includes the positive meanings and optimistic attitudes that trigger positive emotions as well as the open minds, tender hearts, relaxed limbs, and soft faces they usher in. It even includes the long-term impact that positive emotions have on your character, relationships, communities, and environment. Although some of this may sound like the vocabulary of greeting cards, the term *positivity* points to vital human moments that have now captured the interest of science. And the new scientific discoveries about the importance of positivity are stunning.

Your mild and fleeting pleasant states are far more potent than you think. We know now that they alter your mind and body in ways that can literally help you create your best life.

So let's roll back time and do a retake on that same morning of yours, this time with positivity. Rest assured that no matter how good you are at negativity, you're also capable of positivity. As you read, keep in mind that, like negativity, positivity goes beyond self-talk. Although subtle, it too infuses your mindscape and outlook, heart rhythms and body chemistry, muscle tension and facial expressions, and your resources and relationships.

TAKE 2

You wake up to morning light streaming through your bedroom window, feeling well rested. You notice your alarm didn't go off. You're disappointed because you meant to wake up extra early so you could have time to yourself before the kids wake up. You look out the window and think, *Oh well, at least it looks like the weather's going to be beautiful.* Your disappointment melts. *I've got a little time to myself.* You decide to skip your planned exercise routine and go straight to your journal. You write,

> *My body must have known I was oversleeping and woke me up so I can take care of myself. I'll need to be creative about fitting in today's exercise . . . I know, I'll go over to the park during work and take a power walk. This new journal has been so important to me. It gives me the space to reflect on what's working well in my life—to feel grateful for all I have. It helps me keep perspective on my larger goals—making a difference with my work, helping me be more loving to my family.*

You spend the next ten minutes writing about why you work:

> *Yesterday I met a woman who benefited from last year's community project. Seeing her face light up makes me all the more certain that I picked the right career to switch to. It may keep me extraordinarily busy, but it's so clearly worth the effort when I see the difference I make in the organization's success and my colleagues' lives.*

Just then your youngest daughter, who's nearly four years old, wakes up calling for you. You glance at the time: 6:42. You've been asking her to wait quietly in her room until you come in for hugs and kisses at seven. You wonder what she needs. You get up, go to her room, and give her a long good-morning hug and kiss. "I've missed you, Mommy," she says. You lie down beside her to snuggle and talk until seven.

The morning routine is always tight on time, but you're finding that when you come to it calm and well rested, it goes much better. You can even make a family game out of finding your seven-year-old son's misplaced shoes: "Whoever finds them gets to be the middle one in a big family hug!" Now all of you are racing around the house—laughing—trying to find those shoes. You spot them on top of the refrigerator. The refrigerator! You all laugh about how they might have gotten up there, and you get the added bonus of being in the center of all those loving arms. You savor the cozy moment, knowing that all too soon your kids will be older and will find this family ritual too corny.

After dropping your kids off at school, you arrive at work. The first person you see is Joe, your collaborator on the proposal you submitted a few months back. He's smiling so broadly that you can't help smiling yourself. "Hey, good morning, Joe—what's up?" He says, "Did you hear the news? We got the money! We're set for the year!"

You raise your hand and slap him a high five, and say, "We make a pretty great team, don't we?" From the previous year's experience, you suspect you might be facing some last-minute revisions. You invite Joe to join you on your power walk to plan out the revision process . . .

At this point you may be thinking, *Not so fast!* It's not fair to compare the morning on positivity to the morning on negativity. Not all the same bad stuff happened. After all, Take 2 left out the bad night's sleep, Sharon's last-minute request, and being late for school and work. I'd agree with you on the not-so-fast statement. Let's slow down to consider how and why positivity made a difference.

Before we dig in, take a moment to notice that some bad parts of the two mornings were identical: your alarm didn't go off, your daughter woke up early, your son misplaced his favorite shoes, and you're facing a tight deadline for revisions. Positivity can't prevent all bad things from happening to you—just some of them. Let's see which. Along the way I'll point out several key differences between the two takes. These differences illustrate six vital facts about positivity.

Fact 1. Positivity feels good. My guess is that simply reading the second take was enough to make you feel noticeably better than you felt reading the first. Whereas the first was dark and heavy, the second was light and buoyant. This first fact may seem almost too obvious to mention, but it's essential. It's the sparkle of good feelings, after all, that awakens your motivation to change. You begin to yearn for more "good days" like this. The sheer obviousness of this first fact often blinds us to subtler facts about positivity. Yet when we unwrap the glittering gift of positivity—as we'll do in chapter 2—to take a first look at its inner workings, we'll find even more reason to marvel. What's more, not all positivity is alike. In chapter 3, I'll describe the forms positivity can take, ranging from joy, gratitude, serenity, and interest, to hope, pride, amusement, inspiration, awe, and, last but not least, love. Each of these ten forms of positivity can change your life—and your future.

Fact 2. Positivity changes how your mind works. Positivity doesn't just change the contents of your mind, trading bad thoughts for good ones; it also changes the scope or boundaries of your mind. It widens the span of possibilities that you see. In Take 2, you benefit from positivity's broader mindscape several times. First, you readily see a way to fit your missed morning exercise into your day later on. Second, in your journal, you maintain your focus on your larger goals. Third, you see past your daughter's early waking to be more forgiving. Fourth, you quickly spy the lost shoes in the most unusual place. Fifth, you connect with your colleague, Joe, and trust his smile. Sixth, you come up with a way to dovetail exercise and planning in your busy schedule by inviting Joe to join you on your power walk. The way positivity broadened your outlook may be subtle—even imperceptible—

but it was pivotal to the unfolding events of the morning. In chapter 4, we'll see how mind expansion happens.

Fact 3. Positivity transforms your future. Although good feelings will forever be fleeting, over time, positivity literally brings out the best in you. An underlying assumption within the second version was that this day's emotional climate was not a rare occurrence. It followed a long stretch of days—perhaps even weeks or months—that were also rich in positivity. As your positive emotions accrued, they built up your resources, leaving you better off on this particular morning than you would have been without them. In Take 2, you benefit from positivity's capacity to build multiple resources. Your repeated experiences of positivity built up at least one physical resource (you slept better); at least one mental resource (you were more mindful of current circumstances); at least two psychological resources (you were more optimistic and resilient); and several social resources (you had better connections to family and colleagues). Each of these resources, built through repeated experiences of positivity in your recent past, contributed to your having a better morning in the second rendition. In chapter 5 I'll share with you how positivity can change your future for the better.

Fact 4. Positivity puts the brakes on negativity. In a heartbeat, negativity can spike your blood pressure, but positivity can calm it. It works like a reset button. In Take 2, you benefit from this effect at least twice. While at first you were disappointed that your alarm didn't go off and that your daughter woke up early, your positivity quickly flushed this negativity out of your system. This left you in a better position to move on and make the best of the new circumstances you faced. It turns out that positivity is the secret to becoming resilient. In chapter 6 I'll reveal the science behind this secret.

Fact 5. Positivity obeys a tipping point. The most stunning and practical fact to emerge from the science of positivity is that its effects are nonlinear. This is not science-as-usual. There's no single arrow shooting from cause to effect. Arrows abound. And they bend, loop, and shoot from both ends at once. In traditional linear science, proportionality rules. No matter where you start, if you change the input by a certain amount, outputs change in proportion. Not so in nonlinear science. Where you start makes a huge difference. Effects that are virtually nonexistent at one starting point grow disproportionately large at a different starting point. A tipping point is that sweet spot in between where a small change makes a big difference.

Take 1 and Take 2 feel like different worlds altogether. They differ in more than just degree precisely because they sit on opposite sides of a tipping point. If you look back closely at Take 1, you'll see that positivity did make an appearance: at first blush you appreciated the morning sun, the good news about your project, and your colleague's smile. Yet it hardly seemed to matter; negativity carried the day. By contrast, in Take 2, positivity came around often enough to tip the scales toward extraordinary outcomes. Your morning was not just a little better, it was dramatically better. You felt alive and growing. You valued the contributions you made at home and at work. With each successive good moment, you moved upward and outward, not downward and inward. The two sides of this tipping point feel—and are—radically different. This book provides a prescription—indeed, a precise ratio—to tip your life to the flourishing side. In chapter 7 I'll describe the new, nonlinear scientific discoveries that lie beneath this prescription.

Fact 6. You can increase your positivity. If reading about these two mornings resonated with you, it's because the potential for life-draining negativity lies within you, just as does the potential for life-giving positivity. You have more say than you think about which you feel and when. The treasure of your own positivity is waiting. You can tip the scales to unleash your life's potential to flourish. That's why I devote the entire second part of this book—chapters 8 through 12—to helping you learn how.

Positivity can make an enormous difference in your life. This book unpacks that difference to reveal how and why positivity carries such potency. With positivity, you see new possibilities, bounce back from setbacks, connect with others, and become the best version of yourself. You even sleep better. How do I know this? In part, because like you and everyone else, I've experienced similar days in my own morning routines. In addition, though, I've dedicated my career to examining positivity in people's emotional lives.

While a poet seeks new metaphors to express ideas about human emotions, I'm a scientist, and I seek new ways to quantify them. Far from a dry, abstract exercise, I've found that a scientific approach to emotions reveals hidden, and perhaps universal, truths about the core nature of being human. If you've ever wondered *Why do we feel emotions?* or *What difference does it make if I look on the bright side?* I can tell you. The latest science shows how our day-to-day emotional experiences affect the very course of our lives.

My science is psychology. You might be surprised to learn that even though the science of psychology dates back to the close of the nineteenth century, for most of its history, emotions were a taboo topic, considered too slippery to be legitimate targets of study. My mentors were the first to begin the modern scientific study of human emotions. I represent the second generation of scientists working in this area. Nearly all previous efforts within the science of emotions centered on negativity—depression, aggression, anxiety, and all the ills that negative states like these can produce in people's lives. I took a different path. I've made a career out of studying the positive side— joy, serenity, interest, love, and the like. This is still rare within the science of emotions. My most widely cited scientific contribution is my "broaden-and-build" theory of positive emotions. The theory describes not only how positive emotions evolved for our human ancestors, but also the value they hold for modern-day humans. My expertise in positive emotions put me at the forefront of the new field of positive psychology at its inception in 1999. Since then, I've been recognized as one of the world's leading voices on emotional positivity.

Yet at one level, we are all already experts on emotions. We each experience them day in and day out—sadness and joy, anger and gratitude, and more. They are as common and natural as breathing. And positive emotions seem especially familiar to us. Indeed, if you're like most people, you feel good more often than you feel bad. Even though positive emotions infuse the prayers we say, the books we read, and the movies we watch, words like *love, joy, gratitude, serenity,* and *hope* are more than literary terms. They are also scientific terms that can be defined and measured with precision. I've tested these vital human states to reveal what they can do to improve people's lives.

Frankly it was hard for me to start this book. The new discoveries about positive emotions are so compelling that it was difficult to pull myself away from the laboratory and from writing scientific articles to write this book. Yet I felt called to do so. You need to know the news about positivity. It's important news about *you*.

The promise of this book: You will never look at feeling good the same way again. You'll understand and appreciate the potency of positive emotions in ways that will prove to be astonishingly useful. There's a side of positive emotions that you don't yet know. Once your eyes are opened to this side—the scientifically tested side—you'll have a fuller understanding of yourself and your potential. With this more complete self-knowledge, you'll function more fully and be empowered daily. Positivity presents an opportunity to step up to the next level of existence: to broaden your mind and build your best future.

I began investigating positivity for the simple reason that it was largely uncharted territory and I've always loved intellectual frontiers. While this spirit still guides my work to some degree, something changed a few years back. My decades of data collection were taking shape and showing me far more than I'd ever imagined or hypothesized. What I was seeing was no less than a prescription for life and how to live it. This stunned me. It still does.

These days my work is also guided by my aim to test the viability of this prescription. Is it for real? As a scientist, accepting things on faith—or on mere hints within the data—is not in my bones. My mission is to unearth, test, and then share the hidden value of positivity.

I've written this book because I suspect that you want to know what the latest science has to say about how positivity can improve your life.

Positivity can uniquely revitalize your worldview, your mental energy, your relationships, and your potential.

If you crave more life in your life, this book is for you.

CHAPTER 2

Positivity: Means, Not Ends

*There wouldn't be such a thing as counterfeit gold
if there were no real gold somewhere.*
—SUFI PROVERB

First the good news: Whatever your current circumstances, you've got what it takes to reshape your life and the world around you for the better. You have, already within you, the active ingredient that's needed to craft a happy life that's full of growth and creativity, and to be remarkably resilient in hard times.

The even better news is that this active ingredient is renewable. Any time you need more, you can get more. You have an inner well-spring you can tap anytime you want to replenish your supply.

The bad news is that if you're like most people, you're currently low on this ingredient. And you can't pull together the recipe for your best life without building a bigger supply.

The even sadder news is that, again, if you're like most people, you don't know what you possess. Your inner wellspring remains un-tapped. You stumble about, seeking what you need in all the wrong places. You're constantly looking outside yourself—to money and all that it can buy—and coming up short.

What's the active ingredient?

Positivity. Heartfelt positivity.

Among our birthrights as humans is the experience of the subtle and fleeting pleasant feelings of positivity. It comes in many forms and flavors. Think of the times you feel connected to others and loved; when you feel playful, creative, or silly; when you feel blessed and at one with your surroundings; when your soul is stirred by the sheer beauty of existence; or when you feel energized and excited by a new idea or hobby. Positivity reigns whenever positive emotions—like love, joy, gratitude, serenity, interest, and inspiration—touch and open your heart.

Whether it's fascination, laughter, or love, your moments of heartfelt positivity don't last long. Good feelings come and go, much like perfect weather. It's the way we humans were designed. Positivity fades. If it didn't, you'd have a hard time reacting to change. If positivity were permanent, you wouldn't notice the difference between good news and bad news, or between an invitation and an insult.

If you want to reshape your life for the better, the secret is not to grasp positivity too firmly, denying its transient nature. Rather, it's to seed more of it into your life—to increase your *quantity* of positivity over time. I've found that what matters most is your positivity ratio. It's a way to characterize the amount of your heartfelt positivity relative to the amount of your heart-wrenching negativity. Stated formally, your positivity ratio is your frequency of positivity over any given time span, divided by your frequency of negativity over that same time span. In mathematical terms, the ratio is captured by the simple expression P/N.

As we'll see in later chapters, a fascinating fact about people's positivity ratios is that they're subject to a tipping point. Below a certain ratio, people get pulled into a downward spiral fueled by negativity. Their behavior becomes painfully predictable—even rigid. They feel burdened—at times even lifeless. Yet above this same ratio, people seem to take off, drawn along an upward spiral energized by positivity. Their behavior becomes less predictable and more creative. They grow. They feel uplifted and alive.

Downward spiral or upward spiral. As I see it, that's your choice.

However much we resist acknowledging it, we humans are not static. We're either on a positive trajectory or a negative one. Either we're growing in goodness, becoming more creative and resilient, or we're solidifying our bad habits, becoming more stagnant and rigid. No matter how much we may want to keep things as they are, or envision our life goals as a perfect snapshot we can one day frame and preserve, time moves on. How you'll move with it is up to you. What I can tell you is that your positivity ratio makes a big difference. It forecasts whether your life trajectory is leading you to languish or flourish.

Languish or flourish? Yes. Like any other living thing, you too may either languish, barely holding on to life, or flourish, becoming ripe with possibility and remarkably resilient to hard times. People who flourish function at extraordinarily high levels—both psychologically and socially. They're not simply people who feel good. Flourishing goes beyond happiness, or satisfaction with life. True, people who flourish are happy. But that's not the half of it. Beyond feeling good, they're also *doing* good—adding value to the world. People who flourish are highly engaged with their families, work, and communities. They're driven by a sense of purpose: they know why they get up in the morning. Striving to flourish, then, is a noble goal. It's not just about making yourself happy. It's about doing something valuable with your day and with your life. Although flourishing is noble, it need not imply grand or grandiose actions. It simply requires transcending self-interest enough to share and celebrate goodness in others and in the natural world. Flourishing represents your best possible future. Positivity can help you get there.

How do I know all this about you? I know because my life's work centers on positivity. I don't just experiment with positivity in my daily life—I experiment with it in my laboratory, where I test hundreds of people each year. With each experiment, I learn more about how positivity fundamentally changes the way we humans see the world, how we think, and what we do. I'm not the sort of scientist who is bound and chained to her laboratory. My research also takes me out into the wild—into the real-world ups and downs of people's day-to-day lives. Of course, I don't do this alone, but with the help of a team of the world's best graduate students and research assistants. I have collaborated with other leading scientists who share my quest to learn more about human emotions. And, of course, I absorb the latest scientific evidence on positivity from around the world.

There's so much to discover about being human. The more we know, the better equipped we are to build the lives we want. My strong sense is that you'll want to know what your heartfelt positivity can do for you, and how it works. It's my hope that you too will be inspired to experiment with positivity to broaden your mind and build the best future for yourself and those you love.

What Good Is Feeling Good?

It seems almost foolish to ask, *What good is feeling good?* The answer seems obvious enough: pleasant feelings are valuable because we like the way they feel. Pushed further, you might say they signal that all's well. Our lives are good. We've experienced success. We're safe and satisfied.

What's more, if you tell a doctor or therapist that you feel good, he or she will take that as a sign that pain, distress, depression, and hostility are not currently taking a toll on your health and well-being. For many health professionals, "feeling good" means little more than "not feeling bad." Feeling bad is what needs monitoring. It forecasts heart attacks, strokes, eating disorders, obesity, suicide, violence, and more. Feeling good is valuable because it means that odds are you're out of the woods for those risks and troubles.

But positivity does so much more than simply signal the absence of negativity and health risks. It does more than signal the presence of safety and satisfaction, success or good health.

The latest scientific evidence tells us that positivity doesn't simply *reflect* success and health, it can also *produce* success and health. This means that even after positivity fades, we can find traces of its impact.

Beyond the present pleasant moment, your positivity has downstream consequences for the very trajectory of your life. Positivity spells the difference between whether you languish or flourish.

My most widely cited contribution to science thus far is my answer to a riddle that had stumped past scientists. My phrasing of the riddle was this: *What good are positive emotions?* There are other ways to phrase the riddle. You might ask, *Why do people experience pleasant emotions? What purpose is served by our fleeting feelings of joy, gratitude, serenity, and love?* Or, *Has positivity had any adaptive significance over the course of human evolution?* As with any good riddle, the right answer requires a big shift in perspective.

The Old View:
Positivity as Negativity Warmed Over

A bit of history regarding emotions is useful here. Past scientists tried to answer the riddle of positive emotions by resting on the assumption that all emotions, both negative and positive, were consequential to our human ancestors because they produced urges to act in particular ways. Scientists say that emotions trigger *specific action tendencies*.[1] Fear is linked with the urge to flee, anger with the urge to attack, disgust with the urge to expel, and so on.

A core idea nestled within this concept is that having these particular actions spring to mind when our ancestors felt a particular emotion is what made emotions consequential to our species. These were the actions that worked best in getting them out of life-or-death situations that occurred time and again. In other words, those who ran when they spotted the big hunter cats survived. Those who didn't were eaten. Surviving was key, because if an early human did not live long enough to have children, he or she didn't become part of our ancestral family tree.

Another core idea is that specific action tendencies "embody" emotions. Just as these urges overtake our conscious thought, they simultaneously trigger rapid changes in our bodies to support those actions. Stop for a moment to imagine a clear and immediate danger. Maybe an oncoming car is out of control and speeding toward you. Maybe you're in a long bank line and a group of armed masked men enter and chain the door. In any case, when you see danger looming, you not only experience an overwhelming urge to flee to safety, but within milliseconds your cardiovascular system switches gears to redirect oxygenated blood to your large muscles so you'll be prepared to run away.[2] Your adrenal glands also release a surge of cortisol to mobilize more energy by increasing the glucose in your bloodstream.[3] The urge to flee that comes with fear doesn't simply roll around in your head. It infuses your whole body, your entire being.

The concept of specific action tendencies made two important scientific contributions. First, to the extent that these urges helped our ancestors act quickly and decisively in life-threatening circumstances, it explained how the forces of natural selection shaped and preserved emotions as part of our universal human nature. Second, it explained why emotions could infuse both mind and body by orchestrating a cascade of physiological changes.

Within the science of emotions, the value added by the concept of specific action tendencies was huge. It's no wonder that scientists were wedded to it. The trouble came when scientists tried to pinpoint the specific action tendencies for positive emotions. One scientist linked joy with the urge to *do anything*.[4] Others linked serenity with the urge to *do nothing*.[5] These urges aren't nearly as specific as fight, flee, or spit. What's more, the physiological changes that come with positive emotions seem like nothing compared with those linked with negative emotions.[6] Positive emotions simply didn't fit the theoretical mold that worked so well to explain the value of negative emotions. Given these observations, the question *What good are positive emotions?* provoked considerable scientific curiosity.

The New View: Positivity Broadens and Builds

Working with this brain-teaser, together with other intriguing features of positivity, in the late 1990s I created the broaden-and-build theory of positive emotions to answer the riddle of positive emotions.[7]

As I developed this new theory, I challenged deeply held assumptions within my field. I went beyond what my mentors had taught me. While I agreed that the concept of specific action tendencies was useful, my sense was that it held value only for negative emotions. To fully understand the value of positive emotions, I had to chart a new course. I proposed that, unlike negative emotions, which narrow people's ideas about possible actions, positive emotions do the opposite: They *broaden* people's ideas about possible actions, opening our awareness to a wider range of thoughts and actions than is typical. Joy, for instance, sparks the urge to play and be creative. Interest sparks the urge to explore and learn, whereas serenity sparks the urge to savor our current circumstances and integrate them into a new view of ourselves and the world around us.

> Positivity opens us. The first core truth about positive emotions is that they open our hearts and our minds, making us more receptive and more creative.

Positivity opens us. The first core truth about positive emotions is that they open our hearts and our minds, making us more receptive and more creative.

Another assumption I challenged was the hidden belief that if emotions held value for our human ancestors, it was because those emotions changed their behaviors in ways that—in the emotional moment—changed their odds of survival or reproduction. While it's easy to imagine how fleeing in fear could save someone's life, it's harder to imagine how playing in joy might do so. To make sense of this, I had to look beyond the moment and identify benefits not located in the present.

What I eventually concluded was that positive and negative emotions mattered on different time scales. Whereas the narrowed mindsets sparked by negative emotions were valuable in instances that threatened our ancestors' survival in some way, the broadened mindsets sparked by positive emotions were valuable to our ancestors in different ways and over longer time scales. Broadened mindsets mattered because—over time—such expansive awareness served to *build* our human ancestors' resources, spurring on their development of assets, abilities, and useful traits. These new resources functioned as reserves, better equipping our ancestors to handle later threats to survival, which of course were inevitable.

To get a feel for the ways positive emotions can build life resources, envision for a moment something that has made you feel joyful, playful, or intensely alive—when you wanted to smile and cheer, or jump up and dance around. Maybe it was witnessing your child's delight in taking her first steps, or playing a game of chase or catch with your dog, sharing a meal and lots of laughter with a friend you haven't seen in ages, or playing touch football in the park during a family get-together. Maybe it was dancing with a group of friends as your favorite band played. Whatever comes to mind for you, take a moment to relive the experience in your mind, letting your joy rekindle. Consider how you felt and what you felt like doing. What we've learned about joyful experiences like these is that the playful urges they carry build resources, and in times of trouble, these gains in resources can spell the difference between life and death.

Seem farfetched? Let me tell you about patas monkeys. Like humans and many other mammals, when these monkeys are young, they play chase. Yet their game of chase has a twist. They run headlong into a flexible sapling or bush to catapult themselves in an unexpected direction. If you close your eyes and picture this stunt, you'll see that it would defy getting "caught." It turns out that adults of this species never pull this stunt themselves. Never, that is, unless they need to escape a predator. In play, patas monkeys develop a particular physical skill that might one day save their lives.[8]

Likewise, we've all heard the phrase "the family that plays together, stays together." The wisdom in this phrase is that social play builds ties between people that are lasting and consequential. This wisdom holds outside the human family circle as well. A fascinating example comes from a certain breed of ground squirrels. Like some other mammals, when one squirrel sees a predator in the distance, it will sound an alarm call that alerts other squirrels to run for cover. It's a risky move. In crying out, the danger-spotting squirrel draws attention to itself, which may well attract the predator. Scientists used to think that animals would risk their lives like this only for kin with whom they shared common genes. New evidence suggests, however, that squirrels also sound alarm calls for former playmates, not genetically related.[9] These squirrels developed a social resource while playing—and these buddies will put their lives on the line to save their playmates.

To illustrate resource-building with a different form of positivity, envision the intense pull you feel when you're keenly interested in a new person, place, or thing. Your mindset is open and curious. It draws you out to explore. Scientists have shown that because positive and open mindsets produce exploration and experiential learning, they also come to produce more-accurate mental maps of the world.[10] This means that, relative to times when you feel negative and rejecting (or even neutral), you learn more when you feel upbeat and interested and are acting on your curiosity. That's because negativity—and even neutrality—holds you back. Negativity and neutrality constrain your experience of the world. In consequence, they also constrain your knowledge of the world. Positivity does just the opposite. It draws you out to explore, to mix it up with the world in unexpected ways. Each time you do, you learn something. These gains in knowledge might not be revelatory today, but they'll be useful down the road. And under certain circumstances they may be life-savers.

> Positivity transforms us for the better. This is the second core truth about positive emotions. By opening our hearts and minds, positive emotions allow us to discover and build new skills, new ties, new knowledge, and new ways of being.

Positivity transforms us for the better. This is the second core truth about positive emotions. By opening our hearts and minds, positive emotions allow us to discover and build new skills, new ties, new knowledge, and new ways of being.

These two core truths about positive emotions define my broaden-and-build theory, which holds that positive emotions were consequential to our human ancestors because over time those good feelings broadened our ancestors' mindsets and built their resources for the future. Positivity transformed early humans for the better, leaving them with extra measures of physical, social, intellectual, and psychological resources. The sparkle of good feelings enticed early humans to broaden and build when they felt safe and satisfied. Those who gave in to this pull became better prepared to survive future threats to life and limb. Those who didn't fared less well. Over millennia, natural selection sculpted our ancestors' capacity to experience heartfelt positivity, creating the form and function of the positive emotions that we modern-day humans experience.

Like Ancestors, Like Us?

We can't assume that what was good for our ancestors is good for us. Think about our craving for high-fat foods. For our ancestors, high-fat foods were rare finds. Early hunters weren't successful every day, or even every week. It made sense that those who craved a fat-rich food like meat and binged on it when it was available survived. Their bodies could store fat as essential energy reserves that carried them through lean times.

Today, high-fat foods are as close as the nearest vending machine. Bingeing on junk food still builds energy reserves in terms of fat stored in the body. But because we can eat these foods all our waking hours if we choose to, our craving is not as relevant to our lives as it was to our ancestors'. The taste for high-fat foods that we inherited from our ancestors may well be a product of evolution, but it's not particularly useful in a modern world that surrounds us with choices our taste buds crave.

You're no early human. You have restaurants and twenty-four-hour food marts. And you can see more people while walking down a busy city street at lunchtime for fifteen minutes than your ancestors might have seen in their entire lives.

But maybe not everything is so different. Just like your ancestors, from birth you relied on other people for food and shelter and needed to learn and grow to make it to adulthood. And like your ancestors, you also need to make friends to build community around you, need to contribute something valuable in adulthood to be well regarded by others, and need to understand your place in the world so you can make good decisions. There's every reason to believe that moments of heartfelt positivity—like feeling grateful for your caregivers, being genuinely interested in your learning activities, feeling joyful when playing with others, feeling pride in your accomplishments or appreciation when everything seems to be going right—are as valuable to you as they were to your ancestors.

Live Longer, Live Stronger

Positivity broadens and builds. It transforms people and helps them become their best. And when at their best, people live longer. That's one fascinating implication of the broaden-and-build theory.

Consider the story of Adam, a thirty-six-year-old gay man from San Francisco. He contracted HIV in the late 1980s, as did Glen, his partner of six years. Although Glen's disease progressed to AIDS early on, Adam had many symptom-free years. One benefit of Adam's better health was that he was able to serve as caregiver when Glen's health began to falter. One weekend in April 1990, Adam was reading his favorite newspaper and noticed a small advertisement looking for HIV-positive men who were caregivers to their partners diagnosed with AIDS. He was surprised and pleased to see that scientists wanted to study someone in his shoes, so he called the number at UC San Francisco to learn more.

The study involved physical exams and lots of interviews. An interviewer came to Adam and Glen's home every two months for a few years. The interviews were pretty depressing at first. They focused on the many stresses of caregiving, what they were and how they made him feel. Sure, those stresses were part of the process, but Adam wondered why this was all the researchers cared about. After the second interview, Adam asked why the research team never asked about the good things in his life, the things he did to make the day go better for him and Glen. By the next interview, Adam was surprised and pleased again. The research team had listened. Apparently, he wasn't the only one to have complained that the interviews were so negative. Other study participants also wanted to focus on the positive, and so the research team reshaped their interviews.

Within a year, Glen was dying. Adam continued to be interviewed about his experiences even after Glen's death. A year later, Adam's HIV progressed to AIDS. When it did, his doctors told him he might have only six months to live, no more than a year at most. Adam refused to live in the shadow of this death sentence. Instead, he took the same approach that he'd taken during Glen's failing health. Each day was a blessing. Each day would offer something to celebrate: the smell of flowers from the corner store, the kindness of a longtime friend, the chance to continue to be independent despite his ailments. Focusing on the positive during each day, Adam's days added up. Three years went by and Adam was still living independently. Five years later, he and his close friends couldn't help but credit his positive approach to life with keeping him going strong. Eventually, AIDS did take him, but it was nine years after the doctors had forecast that he had less than a year to live.

Adam's story is not unique. Positivity does indeed forecast living longer, as has been supported by several scientific studies in the years since I first introduced the broaden-and-build theory. One of these studies emerged from the UC San Francisco research project that Adam was in and helped shape.[11] Others tap more general samples of the population. But the findings are the same in each: people who express more positivity than others live longer. Up to ten years longer.[12] Positivity matters. Just as our ancestors needed positivity to survive, we need it today for the same reason.

Safety in Numbers

In later chapters I'll discuss the scientific approach to positivity in greater detail. For now, I'd like to share the news of a single publication—a scholarly paper of great value because it presents a meta-analysis, or a study of studies. The authors gathered nearly 300 different scientific studies of positivity, which collectively tested more than 275,000 people. These were *all* the studies that the authors could locate in an exhaustive search of the scientific literature. Though any single study might be dismissed as flawed in some way, when you pull together all the evidence—from controlled laboratory experiments to longitudinal studies of people's lives through time—you can be far more certain of your conclusions.

What did this meta-analysis conclude? That positivity produces success in life as much as it reflects success in life. Regardless of whether success was measured as a satisfying marriage, a larger salary, or better health, positivity mattered.[13] When you take all the numbers in all of the studies as a whole, the one scientific account that stands supported is the broaden-and-build theory. It's all the more gratifying to report the news of this meta-analysis because neither I nor my students and collaborators were its authors. None of the authors had a vested interest in the broaden-and-build theory. Science advances at its best when independent researchers test the claims made by their peers. It's satisfying to know that the broaden-and-build theory has been duly tested and upheld by both data and my fellow scientists.

Positivity: Is It Un-American?

Let's stop for a minute to appreciate the shift in worldview that this new perspective on positivity may require. The United States—and much of the capitalist world—was forged under the influence of the Protestant work ethic, a philosophy that holds that enjoyment and leisure are sinful, and that only through austere work activities can people prove their true worth. This worldview produces characters who shun all pleasant impulses and activities that might generate joviality—like sport or dance—in favor of long work hours and personal thrift. It produces a culture that celebrates intensity, competition, and doggedness.

Although American society may have strayed from its early Protestant roots, many of the cultural values embedded within the Protestant work ethic are alive and kicking today. Take, for instance, our entrenched need to achieve. What else would keep Americans working more days per year than the citizens of any other nation? Or look at the common but unspoken belief that hard work pays off. If so, then those who aren't enjoying successful careers and fat brokerage accounts must be decadent, lazy, or otherwise inferior.[14] Those of us who grew up in the United States could scarcely avoid being steeped in these messages.

Despite my life's work on positivity, I'm no exception. In grade school it didn't take me long to learn how to please teachers with my focus on coursework. In college I spent long hours in the library to earn As. In graduate school I spent even longer hours in the laboratory entering and analyzing data. After I'd become a postdoc, one of my close friends (also a scientist studying emotions) sized me up by saying, "You study emotions because you don't have them." Despite this unsolicited diagnosis, as an untenured professor, I'd continue to overspend my time writing empirical articles in my chosen "publish or perish" profession. While this addiction to achievement can at times pay off, it comes at a price. We keep our noses so much to the grindstone that we literally don't see the goodness in the world, the wonder that's there to open our hearts and help us grow.

It's fair to say Americans are conflicted about positivity. Our Declaration of Independence guarantees "the pursuit of happiness" as one of our core rights. Yet when we work hard simply to acquire the material goods and services that Madison Avenue promises will make us happy, we may be missing the point of this fundamental American right. All people yearn to be happy, but many of us have been coaxed into looking for our happiness in all the wrong places. We look for happiness in higher salaries, more possessions, or higher achievements. Or we fixate on the future, holding out that "one day" our dreams will come true and make us happy. We're so wrongheaded about the sources of our positivity that we value that extra hour at work to (we hope) please our boss more than we value connecting with our kids. We unwind with martinis instead of meditation. We lift weights instead of walking through the park. We follow fad diets instead of eating smaller portions of beautiful and well-prepared food. We watch TV or surf the web instead of reading or listening to a book. We write e-mail instead of poetry. My research shows that these pursuits are misguided, and that the way to pursue happiness is to pursue positivity each day, wherever we are. Moment by moment, our daily positivity adds up, and through it we build the lives we seek.

The shift that I needed to make—and that you may need to make—is to view positivity as a wise and healthy investment in ourselves and in the world around us. Positivity is a means toward better ends, not simply an end in itself.

The old story is that anything that feels good is merely a distraction—trivial, inconsequential, and therefore expendable. The new story—backed by science—is that these same good feelings, cultivated through natural and ordinary means, are the active ingredients needed to produce an upward spiral toward flourishing. Whereas the old story leaves people feeling guilty when they "take time" for something that makes them feel good, the new story can give people the courage to cultivate, protect, and cherish moments that touch and open their hearts.

The shift for me was huge. As a young assistant professor, I overworked so thoroughly that my boyfriend (now my husband) had to work hard to convince me that we should take vacations. Although I eventually conceded, I insisted that we keep our vacations secret from my colleagues and students. I would also bring along stacks of papers to grade and a laptop so I could keep up with my e-mail. There was joy and laughter in those early vacations—but there was also frustration, guilt, shame, and red ink. Having learned from my own research, when I vacation these days, I leave papers and e-mail behind and focus on having fun with my family. I also encourage my students and junior colleagues to do the same, which is the opposite of what my own mentors had encouraged. More important, I look for mini-vacations each day—a walk through the arboretum, lunch with a friend, a dance class, or a book to read for fun. I try to balance my entrenched work ethic with a growing play ethic. I find that vacations from my strong need to achieve refuel me and add depth to my life. In an achievement-hungry workplace, my new approach can at times run against the grain and take some resolve to pull off. Even so, I find the fruits so sweet and abundant that there's no going back to my old ways.

Although worship of achievement and its dark underbelly, trivialization of positivity, form a dominant theme in modern urban life, other cultural norms do exist. We know that some groups cultivate and sustain positivity better than the rest of us do, and we can learn something from studying how they do it. Those who follow Buddhist meditation practices, for instance, experience greater positivity in daily life.[15] In later chapters I'll tell you how meditation works and how you can make it work for you. Another group particularly good at positivity may surprise you: older adults. Scientists have shown that people over seventy attend to and savor positivity more than do those with fewer years and wrinkles.[16] This may be the wisdom of old age: a focus on positivity can make late life fulfilling, despite the inevitable aches, pains, and memory loss. One side effect of reading this book may be to hasten this positive aspect of aging!

How Much Is Enough?

So far, I've sketched only a description of how positivity opens our minds and transforms our lives into something better. In the next several chapters I'll present the scientific evidence that has convinced me that there's reason to take the news about positivity to heart and experiment with it in your own life.

If you decide to do so, you'll need more than a good description. You'll need a good prescription. Because you're still reading, I'll assume that you're already on board and that you want to broaden your mind and build a better future for yourself. I'm sure you've already guessed that I'm going to suggest that you increase your positivity.

But how do you go about doing this? How much positivity is enough? And how can you tell if and when you're in the ballpark?

Here's how your day might start if you faithfully followed one possible prescription:

You wake up on a bright, sunny morning. You take a few moments to just breathe deeply and relax. When you're fully awake, you gently nudge your spouse and move closer to cuddle. You want to show your affection and your desire. Your spouse—obviously roused from a deep sleep—rolls over, elbows you sharply, and barks "Are you nuts? Let me sleep!" Smiling about your spouse's antics, you spring out of bed and hop in the shower. For some unknown reason, the water is freezing cold. Although you were looking forward to a long, warm shower, you say to yourself, *I'm so lucky to have running water! I'm so much better off than people in other parts of the world.* Smiling and singing through your shower of icicles, you later skip down the hall to check in on your kids. You see a black widow spider crawling across your sleeping toddler's face. You smile and tiptoe out of the room, not wanting to disturb the peace. You think, *Nature is so fascinating—I'll need to tell my friends about this interesting spider!* You make your way to the kitchen for breakfast. Just as you sit down with your bowl of cereal, you find that sometime during the night your aging cat, Spike, vomited on your favorite antique tablecloth. You sit down next to the mound of vomit to eat your breakfast. You say to yourself, *Poor dear old Spike. I hope you're feeling better. I guess this tablecloth wasn't going to last forever.* Then you turn on the TV. The newscaster is reporting live from the latest war zone. The footage shows civilian victims of a recent bombing, bleeding and dismembered. You think, *What a clever camera crew. They were able to take such vivid pictures! And what a pleasing voice this nice-looking newscaster has . . .*

I don't need to go on, do I? You know you hate this prescription already. You hate it for the same reason we all have universal disdain for the name Pollyanna. You know Pollyanna. She's the one with a plastered smile on her face who conveys nonstop joy. You want to shake her and say *"Get real!"*

That's precisely the problem with this prescription. It can't connect with reality. To experience 100-percent positivity defies and denies the humanness of life. It would mean that you'd buried your head in the sand, and it would eventually drive others away from you.

The prescription that I suggest you try out is more reasonable: aim for a positivity ratio of at least 3 to 1. This means that for every heart-wrenching negative emotional experience you endure, you experience at least three heartfelt positive emotional experiences that uplift you. This is the ratio that I've found to be the tipping point, predicting whether people languish or flourish.

As with any dietary guideline, I offer you this prescription as an emotional guideline. Also, as with any dietary guideline, you don't need to achieve this ratio at any given moment, or even on any given day. Strive instead to meet or exceed this ratio over a stretch of several days or even weeks.

In chapter 7, I'll describe the fascinating research that led to this prescription. I'll also discuss the science that backs it. Of course, as with any prescription or dietary guideline, this 3-to-1 positivity ratio is subject to modification. Future studies will no doubt have more to teach us. Science is never complete.

Yet we can all breathe a collective sigh of relief to learn that the prescription is not 3 to 0. Negativity is important. Nobody can flourish without it. Even the happiest people cry when they lose someone or something they cherish. They're angered by injustice and frightened by danger. Their stomachs turn when they see vomit or witness human atrocities. The beauty of the 3-to-1 positivity ratio is that it's large enough to encompass the full range of human emotions. There's no emotion that needs to be forever shunned or suppressed.

No Yellow Smiley Faces

The 3-to-1 positivity prescription should be easy enough to follow. Just throw in a few upbeat words or a smile now and then, and you'll have the life you want.

Not so fast. If you're thinking it will be that easy to change your positivity ratio, you're wrong. Simply uttering more positive words or forcing a smile might actually do you more harm than good.

By design, humans are exquisite insincerity detectors. If your positive words or upturned lip corners are devoid of sincere, heartfelt, positive feeling, you and those around you will sense it. Notice that throughout this book I refer to "heartfelt positivity" time and again. That's because science shows that sincerity counts.

Consider Jen's story. She's a thirty-eight-year-old mother of three in California, and her youngest child has autism. She recently volunteered for a study on how mothers cope with the stresses of caring for a chronically ill child, and how it affects their health. She indicated to the research team that although she found raising her youngest child to be taxing, she also found the good in her new role. In working through her difficulties, she discovered strengths she didn't know she had, and deepened her religious faith. In other words, Jen was higher than most in what scientists call *benefit finding*—she found the good that emerged from her struggles. You might suspect that this would set Jen apart and make her among the healthiest of the moms tested. It didn't. Even though Jen was quick to articulate positivity, she didn't truly *feel* it. When she was asked during the course of a few normal days how happy, excited, or content she was feeling right then, she most often admitted "not at all." It turned out that Jen was lower than most on her level of *heartfelt* positive emotions. What the research team discovered was that only the moms who both found benefit in their stressful experiences and reported experiencing positive emotions in their day-to-day experiences showed healthy fluctuations in the "stress" hormone cortisol. But Jen's positivity was not heartfelt, so her own cortisol levels were high all day long, which is not particularly healthy.[17]

Here's another illustration. Victor is a fifty-nine-year-old sales manager from North Carolina who suffered a heart attack a year ago. His doctor asked him to join a study on behavior and coronary heart disease at the Duke University Medical Center. In one part of the study, scientists used an imaging technique to watch his heart in action while an interviewer asked him some questions. The interview was videotaped. Victor found one question particularly stupid. The interviewer asked, "When you get angry or upset, do people around you know it?" "Of course they know it!" Victor burst out. "They're the ones to blame, aren't they?" He tried to be polite to the interviewer, to smile now and then to hide his growing frustration, but he found the questions to be almost idiotic.

It turns out that during the particular two-minute segment of Victor's interview when he was questioned about his anger, the imaging technique revealed that he experienced a silent ischemic episode. Although Victor felt no pain or discomfort, the left ventricle of his heart collapsed a bit, indicating that the blood supply to the muscle of his heart was dangerously restricted. This was a serious sign of Victor's heart disease that could easily bring on another heart attack, and even end his life.

Over the next several months the research team coded in detail the videotape of Victor and other study participants, all male coronary patients. They identified every facial expression of emotion that occurred during the interview that coincided with the heart imaging procedure. There was a lot to code. These men expressed about one emotion every two to three seconds. Of all these facial expressions, only two types distinguished those who showed myocardial ischemia.

The scientists conducted the study because they'd predicted that facial expressions of anger would forecast ischemia. They did. What they didn't expect was that smiles would, too. But not just any smiles—only those that scientists call "non-enjoyment smiles." All smiles involve the *zygomaticus major*, the muscle on each side of our faces that raises our lip corners. Non-enjoyment smiles stop there. They do not also involve the *orbicularis oculi*, the muscle that circles each of our eyes, which, when contracted, lifts our cheeks and creates crow's feet. It turns out that this signature action around the eyes reveals whether people really feel the positivity that they convey. This means that non-enjoyment smiles are essentially insincere positivity.

What scientists discovered in this study was that insincere positivity put these men in as much coronary danger as did anger. Mountains of research tell us that anger kills.[18] This new discovery suggests that insincere positivity may kill too.[19]

Jen's story, Victor's story, and the scientific discoveries that they represent, provide an important warning as we attempt to increase positivity in our lives. Although it might be easy to express positivity in words or with smiles, if we don't actually *feel* the positivity we express, we may actually be doing harm. In short, your body knows when you're cheating and punishes you for it.

As you begin to experiment with elevating your positivity ratio, tracking your own sincerity will be key. What you'll strive for is more frequent heartfelt moments of positivity. Not negativity—or even neutrality—masquerading as a smile. In Part II of this book, I describe a range of ways that you can find your own personalized path to meeting or exceeding the prescribed positivity ratio—all while being genuine. For now, I simply want you to recognize that it's not as simple as the ever-popular yellow smiley-face icon implies. Maybe this is why the yellow smiley face is the symbol that scientists working in positive psychology love to hate.[20] Although offered in good fun, it trivializes the effort and sincerity that it takes to invoke genuine, heartfelt positivity.

The View from Here

Now you know the good news and bad news about positivity.

The bad news is that most of us don't have enough of it in our daily lives, so we hardly benefit from the gifts that it offers. Without more positivity, we can't pull off the recipe for flourishing life success.

Sadly, most of us don't even recognize that we have ready access to more of what we need. We don't recognize that we've got an inner wellspring we can tap to generate genuine, heartfelt positivity any time we wish.

But let's focus on the good news. All of us are already familiar with positivity. We've felt it in the tenderness of our hearts, the fascination of our interests, the inspiration of our daydreams, the ease of our smiles, and the warmth of our caresses. And now you know that positivity can do more for you than simply make you feel good. It can broaden your mind and open your heart. Your moments of heartfelt gratitude, joy, and love can transform your life for the better by building your resources and strengths.

Best of all, positivity is renewable. As we'll begin to see in the next chapter, and more completely in Part II, each of us can choose to seed more of it into our lives. As these seeds grow, we flourish. We become full of possibility, remarkably resilient and happy. We contribute. With more positivity, we can create both the life we want and a world worth leaving to our children.

CHAPTER 3

What *Is* Positivity?

Know that joy is rarer, more difficult, and more beautiful than sadness. Once you make this all-important discovery, you must embrace joy as a moral obligation.

—ANDRÉ GIDE

For most of us, joy is all too rare—perhaps not literally rarer than sadness, but still too rare to tip the scales toward flourishing. Having read the headlines about positivity, it's time to dive more deeply into joy. Then into the rest of the positivity palette: gratitude, serenity, interest, hope, pride, amusement, inspiration, and awe. And, saving the best for last, we'll dive deeply into love.

Positivity comes in many shapes and sizes. You'll come to see that it encompasses far more than mere physical pleasure or a vague sense of happiness. My goals in this chapter are to introduce you to the subtleties of these distinct states and to invite you to begin exploring when and how these pleasant feelings arise for you.

You may have noticed that the term *happiness* is not in my top ten. I avoid this term because I feel it's murky and overused. Although sometimes we use the word *happy* to refer to heartfelt positivity (as in "seeing you smile makes me happy"), that same feeling is often better described by another, more-specific term, like *joy, gratitude,* or *love,* depending on the exact circumstances. We use *happy* to describe someone's personality (as in "he's a happy guy"), reflecting how a person typically reacts. Or happiness is used to describe an ultimate life goal (as in "I just want to be happy"). Still other times we use *happy* to convey simple acceptance (as in "I'd be happy to carry your umbrella"). My point is that the word *happy* is rather generic, too vague to be useful here.

What about bodily pleasures, like eating delicious foods, taking the chill off with a soft, warm blanket, or sexual stimulation? Are these positivity? No, I don't believe so. Sure, they're related. I think of them as cousins. Both classes of feelings glitter with enjoyment and undeniably draw us toward them. These are all feelings we *want* to have. A fascinating fact about bodily pleasures is that—if you're a healthy person, not suffering from addictions—they draw you to do exactly what your body needs at that moment. A cool bath, for instance, is pleasing only when you're overheated. It would be quite unpleasant if you were already chilled. The same is true of eating. Notice how good food can taste when you're hungry. After you've had your fill, though, the very same food starts to taste bad. Indeed, that's one of your cues to stop eating.[1]

Bodily pleasures and positivity influence our minds differently and operate on different time scales. In some ways, bodily pleasures are more akin to negativity than to positivity. They narrow your focus (toward the object of your desire) and help you meet a current survival need. Of course, bodily pleasures differ from negativity in that they draw you toward certain circumstances, not away from them. But their narrowed mindsets and in-the-moment payoffs set them apart from true positivity, which broadens your mind and pays off down the road.

The distinction between bodily pleasures and positivity can be hard to see at times, especially because—as cousins—you often find them hanging out together. You might take pride in the delicious meal you prepared, find serenity in the peacefulness of a warm, soothing bath, or feel overwhelming love for your partner as you enjoy sex together. In these cases the positive emotions are what matter most in the long run.

Ten Forms of Positivity

I've introduced you to ten forms of positivity: joy, gratitude, serenity, interest, hope, pride, amusement, inspiration, awe, and love. Now I want you to get to know each one personally. Discover what you and this feeling share in common. Of course, each is already familiar to you to some degree, and terms for describing them are already deeply embedded in our language. I suspect, though, you may be less aware of their full scope and beauty. You may not have previously considered the aspects of each state as scientists have investigated them. And you might not have appreciated all the moments in your life when each has entered your heart.

I focus on these ten positive emotions for two reasons. First, they are targets of a growing amount of scientific research, including my own. Second, over the years I've examined the daily emotional experiences of hundreds of people—ranging from college students to working men and women in midlife and beyond. From this I've learned that these ten forms of positivity color people's day-to-day lives the most. Other forms certainly exist.[2] Yet my research shows that these ten are the most common. With one important exception, I describe them in the order of their relative frequency, starting with the ones people feel most often, and moving on toward those felt more rarely. The exception is love, which appears to be the most frequently experienced form of positivity. I describe it last (and you'll soon see why).

As I tell you about each emotion, I'll start by describing the circumstances and patterns of thought that spark that emotion. These are the specific levers you can pull to turn positivity on, to gain control over when and how often you feel it. I'll also describe the sensations that each particular emotion brings, and what it uniquely makes you want to do and think.

The beauty of emotions is that they are highly individualized, depending more on your inner interpretations than on your outer circumstances. What makes one person awestruck with inspiration may be totally lost on another person. Likewise, what amuses one person may offend another. This means that each person's pathway to flourishing is unique. Increasing positivity in your own life, then, begins with self-study. In chapter 11, I lay out a plan for self-study you can follow to increase your positivity. In the meantime, as you read about the ten different types of positive emotions in this chapter, simply ask yourself: *When was the last time I felt this feeling? Where was I? What was I doing? What else gives me that feeling? Can I think of still more triggers? What can I do now to cultivate this feeling?*

Getting in tune with your own positivity means going beyond one-size-fits-all terms like *happy* and *good* in favor of more precisely named emotional states.[3] Even so, I encourage you to use these ten terms for positivity *softly*. Apply them lightly. Focus more on the levers that turn on the feeling that flows through you than on the label itself. Apply a label ever so gently only to see if it fits. I'm reminded here of a quote by the newspaper columnist Ann Landers. She wrote, "Rose-colored glasses are never made in bifocals. Nobody wants to read the small print in dreams." She grasped intuitively what science has since confirmed—that overanalysis kills positivity.[4] This is one of the great paradoxes of positivity. These fleeting states are remarkably fragile, and yet somehow they add up to a power to change the very course of our lives.

JOY. Visualize this: Your surroundings are safe and familiar. Things are going your way—even better than you expected. At the moment the situation requires little effort on your part. These are the circumstances that spark joy. If you had the good fortune—as I did when my second son was born—to give birth in a nurturing environment with only the most supportive people present (for me, these were my husband and—only when needed—my nurse-midwife), the first moments that you held your newborn were perhaps the most joy-filled of your life. Sadly, not all birth stories unfold as textbook cases of joy. When my first son was born, the joy I felt at finally meeting him face-to-face was sullied by painful complications and an overwhelmed nurse-midwife. And many births, especially in the United States, are too scripted, too rushed, too public, and too medicated to inspire true, heartfelt joy.

There are many other sources of joy as well. Perhaps your co-workers have just surprised you with a birthday party. Or you open a letter to find an unexpected bonus. Or you're out to dinner with new friends and delighting in their good company. Joy feels bright and light. Colors seem more vivid. There's a spring in your step. And your face lights up with a smile and an inner glow. You feel like taking it all in. You feel playful—you want to jump in and get involved.[5]

What brings you joy?

GRATITUDE. Imagine you've just realized that someone has gone out of their way to do something good for you. Your neighbor, a re-tired schoolteacher, offers to entertain your kids for a few hours one afternoon. A mentor gently steers your career in the right direction. Your spouse cleans up and makes dinner on your busiest day so you don't have to. A store clerk is especially helpful and kind as you make a complicated exchange. The neighbor kid shovels your walkway after a heavy snow. Or maybe it's not even a person who has brought you tremendous benefit. We can feel grateful for breathing clean air, hav-ing able bodies, or having a safe and comfortable place to rest when weary. In any case, gratitude comes when we appreciate something that has come our way as a gift to be treasured.

Gratitude opens your heart and carries the urge to give back—to do something good in return, either for the person who helped you or for someone else. Gratitude, though, has an evil twin: indebtedness. If you feel you have to pay someone back, then you're not feeling grate-ful, you're feeling indebted, which often feels distinctly unpleasant. In-debtedness pays back begrudgingly, as part of the economy of favors. In contrast, gratitude gives back freely and creatively. It's a truly pleas-ant feeling intermixed with joy and heartfelt appreciation. And grati-tude doesn't play by the rules. It's not the etiquette we teach our kids. Too often I find myself prodding my kids with "What do you say?" when they're silent upon receiving a gift or a kindness. When they push out a monotone "Thanks," they're only being polite, not grateful. Gratitude is not mindless manners or tit-for-tat reciprocity ("you scratch my back, I'll scratch yours"). True gratitude is heartfelt and unscripted.

The film and social movement *Pay It Forward* is a great example of gratitude in action. It started with one boy doing three good deeds for three others. The one request the young benefactor had was that instead of paying the favor back, the recipients should pay it forward, to three new people, in some creative and fitting way.[6]

When was the last time you felt grateful—not polite or indebted, but truly and openly grateful?

SERENITY. Like joy, serenity enters when your surroundings are safe and familiar and require little effort on your part. But unlike joy, serenity is much more low-key. It's when you let out that long, luxurious sigh because your current circumstances are so comfortable and so *right*. It's when you lie back in a shaded hammock after a day of strenuous and rewarding work in your garden. It's strolling down a sandy beach on a bright morning with ocean sounds filling your head and a cool breeze tingling your skin. It's curling up with a good book and a warm lap cat, with your favorite cup of tea beside you. It's that sinking-into-the-mat feeling of Savasana, the traditional closing pose in yoga practice.

Serenity makes you want to sit back and soak it in. It's a mindful state that carries the urge to savor your current circumstances and find ways to integrate them into your life more fully and more often. When you tell yourself, "I need to do *this* more often!" that's serenity. I call serenity the afterglow emotion. It often comes on the heels of other forms of positivity, like joy, pride, amusement, or awe. Just today, my four-year-old son, high on having created his first wood sculpture in preschool, expressed this afterglow quality of serenity beautifully. As he got into the car after school, he sank back into his car seat and said with a smile and a sigh, "I just love everything!" Talk about mind-broadening. Think about the last time you savored a serene moment like this.

INTEREST. Although you're feeling perfectly safe, something new or different draws your attention, filling you with a sense of possibility or mystery. Unlike joy and serenity, these circumstances call for effort and increased attention on your part. You're utterly fascinated. You're pulled to explore, to immerse yourself in what you're just now discovering. It's when you see a new path in the woods and want to find out where it leads. It's when you uncover a new set of challenges that allow you to build your skills, whether in cooking, bridge, or dancing. It's that fascinating new book that awakens you to new ideas. When you're interested, you feel open and alive. You can literally feel your horizons expanding in real time, and with them your own possibilities. The intense pull of interest beckons you to explore, to take in new ideas, and to learn more.[7]

When did interest last draw you in by the nose?

HOPE. Although most positivity arises when you feel safe and satiated, hope is an exception. If everything were already going your way, there would be little that you'd need to hope for. Hope comes into play when your circumstances are dire—things are not going well for you, or there's considerable uncertainty about how things will turn out. Hope arises precisely within those moments when hopelessness or despair seem just as likely. Perhaps you've just failed an important test, lost your job, found a lump in your breast, or scooped up your child after a bloody bike accident. Hope, in desperate situations like these, is "fearing the worst but yearning for better."[8]

Deep within the core of hope is the belief that things can change. No matter how awful or uncertain they are at the moment, things can turn out better. Possibilities exist. Hope sustains you. It keeps you from collapsing into despair. It motivates you to tap into your own capabilities and inventiveness to turn things around. It inspires you to plan for a better future.[9]

The anthropologist Lionel Tiger casts hope as the evolved antidote to our big human forebrains. Unlike any other earthly creature, we humans can envision our own futures and, in so doing, all possible calamities. Without hope, our uniquely human ability to forecast our inevitable death and demise would leave us in motionless despair. With hope, we become energized to do as much as we can to make a good life for ourselves and for others.[10] Was it hope that motivated you to read this book?

PRIDE. Pride is one of the so-called "self-conscious emotions." We all know its evil cousins, shame and guilt. These painful feelings overcome us when we're to blame for something bad. Pride is the opposite: we're "to blame" for something good. As one of the so-called seven deadly sins, pride has a mixed reputation. We say pride makes people's heads swell, or that pride comes before a fall. Any emotion can go too far, and perhaps this is especially true for pride. Unchecked, pride becomes hubris. But when specific and tempered with appropriate humility, pride is clearly a positive emotion.

Pride blooms in the wake of an achievement you can take credit for. You invested your effort and skills and succeeded. It's that good feeling you get when you put the finishing touches on a home-improvement project, whether it's fixing the washing machine, planting a garden, or redesigning your bedroom. Or when you achieve something in school or at work: aced a test, won a race, made a sale, or published your ideas. Or when you recognize that you made a difference to someone else, through your help, kindness, or guidance.

These are not just any achievements, but socially valued ones. We sense at a deep level that our actions will be valued by others. That is what makes pride a self-conscious emotion. Unless you're a sociopath, you're acutely aware of how your actions—good and bad—can be perceived by others. You feel pride when you're praiseworthy and guilt when you're blameworthy. Pride carries with it the urge to share the news of your achievements with others, either in words ("Hey, look what I did!"), gestures (upright posture, head tilted slightly back, slight smile, hands on hips, or arms raised in victory), or both.

The mindscape of pride is expansive as well. It kindles dreams of further and larger achievements in similar domains: *If I can do this, maybe I can . . . open my own business . . . landscape the front yard . . .*

redesign the living room . . . earn a scholarship . . . make the Olympic team . . . be promoted . . . make a difference in the world. In this way, pride fuels the motivation to achieve. Well-controlled laboratory experiments show that when people feel pride, they are more likely to persist on difficult tasks.[11]

What makes you proud? And what has pride inspired you to do?

AMUSEMENT. Sometimes something unexpected happens that simply makes you laugh. A friend makes a funny face after she tries your latest dinner creation. You mistakenly direct your preschooler to "use the tub and get in the toilet." A neighbor shares her latest favorite joke. ("What do you call an agnostic, dyslexic insomniac?")[12] A colleague jokes about the worst time of day to hold meetings. Not intending to wring the fun out of such silliness, social scientists describe these circumstances as "nonserious social incongruity." This label makes two important distinctions about the surprises—or incongruities—that bring amusement. First, amusement is social. Although at times we laugh alone, those laughs are only pale renditions of the laughter we share with another. In fact, like yawns, laughter is highly contagious. Second, surprises are only amusing if they are embedded within safe contexts, not if they are dangerous or threatening. If your friend makes a face because she's choking, or if your neighbor's joke is offensive, you're not amused. By definition, then, amusements are nonserious. Heartfelt amusement brings the irrepressible urge to laugh and share your joviality with others. Shared laughter signals that you find your current situation to be safe and lighthearted and that you'd like to use this blessed time to build connections with others.[13]

When was the last time you laughed?

INSPIRATION. Every so often, you come across true human excellence. You transcend the ordinary, seeing better possibilities than usual. Witnessing human nature at its very best can inspire and uplift you. Perhaps you see a colleague step away from his own pressing schedule to patiently help a disoriented older man find his way through the labyrinth of the medical center. Or you see tennis genius

Roger Federer play a flawlessly fluid game in the U.S. Open.[14] You read the work of a poet who seems to see into the core of the human soul. Or you witness one of your role models doing what she does best.

Feeling inspired rivets your attention, warms your heart, and draws you in. It's the polar opposite of feeling disgusted by human depravity, which instantly repels you. Inspiration doesn't simply feel good, it makes you want to express what's good and do good yourself. It creates the urge to do your best so that you can reach your own higher ground. Along with gratitude and awe, inspiration is considered one of the self-transcendent emotions. It's a form of positivity that pulls us out of our shell of self-absorption.

Sadly, inspiration is not the only response you might have to seeing someone else do something extraordinarily well. Like gratitude, inspiration has an evil twin. Whether you call it resentment or envy, it arises when we see human excellence and respond with negativity. We grumble, mock, tear the person down, or beat ourselves up for not doing equally well. When we compare ourselves with someone who does better than we do, sometimes we get discouraged instead of inspired. Whether you respond to human excellence with positivity or negativity is a choice. It's a choice about whether your heart is open or closed. With this choice you step onto an upward spiral or a downward spiral.[15]

Can you think of a time when you made the choice to be inspired?

AWE. Closely related to inspiration, awe happens when you come across goodness on a grand scale. You literally feel overwhelmed by greatness. By comparison, you feel small and humble. Awe makes you stop in your tracks. You are momentarily transfixed. Boundaries melt away and you feel part of something larger than yourself. Mentally, you're challenged to absorb and accommodate the sheer scale of what you've encountered. Sometimes we're awed by nature, as with stunning sunsets at the Grand Canyon, or by seeing, hearing, and feeling the power of ocean waves smashing and wearing away at the rocky cliffs of the Pacific shoreline. Other times we're awed by humanity, as when we see Neil Armstrong take his first steps on the moon or visit the cathedral of Notre Dame in Paris and stand beneath the great Rose Window aglow in the morning sun.[16]

Although a form of positivity, awe at times sits so close to the edge of safety that we get a whiff of negativity as well. Awe mixes with fear when we've witnessed a tornado or seen the World Trade Center towers collapse. Awe, like gratitude and inspiration, is a self-transcendent emotion. It compels us to see ourselves as part of something much larger, whether it's God's great creation or this nation's great progress. Awe can also bind us emotionally to powerful and charismatic leaders, who often seem larger than life.[17]

What has transfixed you with awe?

LOVE. There's a reason love is called a many-splendored thing. It's not a single kind of positivity. It's all of the above, encompassing joy, gratitude, serenity, interest, hope, pride, amusement, inspiration, and awe. What transforms these other forms of positivity into love is their context. When these good feelings stir our hearts within a safe, often close relationship, we call it love. In the early stages of a relationship, tied up within your initial attraction, you're deeply *interested* in anything and everything this new person says and does. You share *amusements* and laugh together, often as a result of the awkwardness of coming together for the first time. As your relationship builds and perhaps surpasses your expectations, it brings great *joy.* You begin to share your *hopes* and dreams for your future together. As the relationship becomes more solid, you sink back into the cozy *serenity* that comes with the security of mutual love. You're *grateful* for the joys your beloved brings into your life, as *proud* of their achievements as you are of your own, *inspired* by their good qualities, and perhaps in *awe* of the forces of the universe that brought you two together.

Each of these moments could equally be described as a moment of love. So even though love is often the most common flavor of positivity that people feel, I reserved it for last so that you could better appreciate its many facets. Viewing love in this way can also sharpen your ability to see love as a momentary state—as a surge—and not simply as a description of one of your relationships, be it with your spouse, child, parent, or sibling. These intimate relationships might best be viewed as the products of recurrent surges of love. Although multifaceted, love has a characteristic nonverbal display, as we nod our heads affirmatively toward our loved ones, and lean in toward them. Love also changes the inner chemistry of our bodies. It raises our oxytocin and progesterone levels, biological responses linked with lifelong bonds, trust, and intimacy.[18]

Think of a time when you felt love surge within you.

Thinking Makes It So

Positivity comes in many flavors. It's the longing to embrace that you experience when a loved one returns. It's the laugh you share with a neighbor as you watch your kids acting silly. It's the ease you feel when you find a comfortable spot to sit and relax. It's the fascination of watching a crackling fire, ocean waves, or human excellence in action. It's the dreams you hold for your future, or the future of your community. Positivity can be found everywhere.

Yet, in all cases, positivity is fragile. Whether it's a moment of joy, serenity, or inspiration, it can be squashed in the flash of an eye or in the firing of a few neurons. Suppose, for instance, that your loved one returns home, but you're preoccupied with your own activities. You might be so caught up in finding receipts for last year's income tax return that you scarcely notice that someone has entered the house. Or what if—at that same moment you and your neighbor's kids erupt in silliness—you were rushing to load everyone in the car to make an appointment. Or suppose you find that comfortable spot to rest, but instead of settling back, you instantly feel guilty about taking a break and anxiously spend your time updating your mental to-do list. Or when watching the fire, the waves, or a display of human talent, you take it to be rather ordinary, hardly worth your attention. Or maybe your dreams never get off the ground because you weigh them down with self-doubt and cynicism.

My point is that whether you experience positivity or not depends vitally on how you think. Positive emotions—like all emotions—arise from how you interpret events and ideas as they unfold.[19] They depend on whether you allow yourself to take a moment to find the good—and on whether, once you've found it, you pump that goodness up and let it grow. This dependence on thinking is what makes positivity so fragile. Our minds can be overstuffed with worries, doubts, and demands. Add to this the nearly continuous drip of media messages we take in from our televisions, radios, iPods, and billboards. No wonder we often don't have space in our heads to focus on others, celebrate silliness, see the extraordinary right under our noses, or let our dreams grow big.

People who enjoy the sweet fruits of positivity in their lives intuitively understand this simple truth. We all have the power to turn positivity on and off for ourselves. Experiment with this. Turn positivity on right now. Take a moment to notice your physical surroundings. Whether you are in your living room, dorm room, or bathroom, or on the bus, subway, or train, ask yourself: *What's right about my current circumstances? What makes me lucky to be here? What aspect of my current circumstances might I view as a gift to be treasured? How does it benefit me or others?* Taking time to think in this manner can ignite the inner glow of gratitude that enlivens your eyes and softens your face with a smile, however faint.

I regularly ride the bus to work. When I ride, I read. In my busy day, my bus ride is virtually the only time that I can count on to read what pleases me. So I look forward to my bus rides. Sitting on the bus, looking up from the pages of my book, I tell myself that I'm lucky that the bus route is so convenient, that in my town the bus is free, and my ride is long enough for me to finish a chapter. With a good book I can transform my daily commute into mind-expanding time to myself, and if I sit in the right spot, each day I can catch a glimpse of my favorite fountain in the center of town. These thoughts, regular as they have become, help me start my workday with heartfelt appreciation for my town, for the author of the book I'm reading, and for the conditions of my life that allow me to be on this bus, in this town, and with this author's ideas mixing it up in my head. Experiment with asking yourself questions that draw you toward the positive. Pose them to yourself right now, wherever you are. See if creating mental space for seeking out and savoring the good can warm your heart and soften your face, calling forth a just-noticeable smile.

Before reading the next paragraph, be sure to take a few moments to savor and enjoy the good feeling you've created for yourself.

Now, turn positivity off. Positivity-spoiling questions come to mind readily: *What's wrong here? What's bothering me? What could be different and better? Who's to blame?* Try asking yourself these sorts of questions. Follow your answers and the chain of thoughts they produce. Notice how quickly your positivity plummets.

My morning bus ride can quickly turn sour. If I let myself seek out what's wrong, I can find plenty. On any given morning, it may be colder than my jacket's warmth. If it's windy, my skin breaks out in uncomfortable hives. Nearly every day, about halfway along my quiet bus ride, a particular young man—always jovial—steps aboard and loudly greets whoever is near him, and I find myself rereading the same sentence over and again, trying to regain my concentration. I can find myself ruminating about the long list of things I should have done yesterday, last week, or last month, and think how much sooner I'd be in my office, catching up on work, had I only driven my car instead. I think, why did the bus driver stop here for so long? Needless to say, with these internal rants running free, there is little to no space for positivity to take root.

Oddly, even the simple act of explaining *why* a good thing is good can zap your positivity. It turns out that unexplained positivity lasts longer than positivity we analyze until we fully understand it. Scientific experiments have documented this sad paradox.[20] With my training as a scientist, this is perhaps the most frequent way I've squelched my own positivity. Too often, I've literally analyzed my budding positivity to death.

I hope this exercise has convinced you that you hold the reins to your own positivity. Although it often seems that our emotions rain down on us as unpredictably as the weather, we have a surprising amount of control over the emotions we feel. This is especially true for positive emotions. We can turn them on almost whenever we choose. And, nearly always, we can coax them to linger just a bit longer.

Although you have more control over your positivity than you may have realized, creating more positivity in your life is not simply a matter of wishful thinking. Good intentions alone won't make anyone happier. Suppose that right now you wanted to make your left shin sting with pain. Could you rouse the intended experience of pain simply by thinking about this limb and willing your body to feel pain there? Not likely. To carry out this intention, you would need to do more than apply sheer willpower. You would have to do *something*. And this something would need to be quite specific, like banging your leg against a table leg, or coaxing someone else to kick you. Those actions could be considered the levers you might pull to carry out your intention to feel pain in your shin.

By this same logic, you can't simply will yourself to feel a positive emotion. You must instead locate one of several quite specific levers to turn on your positivity. Certain forms of thought and action are these positivity levers. So just as you must do something to rouse a feeling of pain out of thin air, so too must you do something to rouse positivity where none previously existed. A fundamental difference between physical pain and emotions, however, is that the levers that turn on emotions can indeed be redirections of conscious thought. This means that you can "think something" as well as "do something" to rouse positivity.

There is particular power in the questions you ask yourself. Simply asking yourself *What's going right for me right now?* can unlock so much. If you're open and sincere as you seek meaningful, positive answers to this simple question, you prepare the soil for positivity to take root. Dewitt Jones, a photographer for *National Geographic*, stunningly illustrates the power of asking such questions in a video called *Celebrate What's Right With the World*.[21] In it, Jones tells how positivity infuses the ethic of National Geographic, and discusses how it has changed his life. Through the lens of his camera, he shows us how seemingly ordinary people and places—even disappointing ones—can radiate tremendous beauty if only we persist in asking ourselves *What's right here? What can I celebrate?* and are patient enough in letting our answers surface. The effect of this video has been powerful when I've shown it in class. One of my students told me she was always skeptical of nature photos in magazines. She assumed they were edited and wondered why she never saw pretty images when she looked at nature herself. Jones's teachings helped her realize that she never saw beauty because she didn't believe it was there. With her eyes newly opened by his compelling account, she paid more attention as she walked through campus. She told me later, "Sure enough, all of the beauty seemed to pop out when I [had] thought it didn't exist. The plants showed off their healthy green color, with rain droplets on the leaves." She said she'd never look at nature the same way again.

Similar questions form the launching point for Appreciative Inquiry (or AI), an approach to organizational change that has spread like wildfire through business consulting circles.[22] Most often, business consultants are hired to solve problems. It's no wonder, then, that most open their dialogue with you or your work group by asking you to describe the problem. You may even have scripted an answer to that question in your head before the consultant arrived. So a consultant who practices AI may take you by surprise. She'll start by asking you to "tell me about this work group at its very best." Her goal is to create a vivid and detailed image of what's working, using positivity to inspire and energize the changes that may be needed to bring out the best more often.

The View from Here

You now know ten new ways to cultivate positivity. Your positivity palette includes the distinct states of joy, gratitude, serenity, interest, hope, pride, amusement, inspiration, awe, and love. Each has its own unique levers. Making small changes in the ways you appreciate and frame the events of your day can turn positivity on.

I suspect you feel more at home with some forms of positivity than with others. This is natural. Yet I invite you to get to know each form of positivity better by studying your own experiences and locating when you've felt each of the many varieties of positivity. In chapter 11, I'll encourage you to expand this self-study by making your own personalized portfolio for each of the ten states you encountered here.

Although each type of positivity arises for different reasons and feels somewhat unique, my laboratory studies show that they all share a common core. Each holds the ability to broaden and build your life. Each lays a pathway toward your higher ground. And as your positivity ratio reaches its tipping point, each helps you to flourish.

In the next four chapters I'll tell you about the scientific evidence that justifies my bold claims for positivity. My hope is that once you appreciate the depth of this evidence, you'll come to feel even more confident and hopeful. So much so that you'll be inspired to begin experimenting with your own sources of positivity. Even more than all the exciting new science, your own experimentation will launch you on a path of understanding and flourishing.

CHAPTER 4

Broaden Your Mind

*There is a way of breathing
that's a shame and a suffocation.*

*And there's another way of expiring,
a love breath, that lets you open infinitely.*

—RUMI

Positivity—whether it blooms as joy, serenity, or any other hue on your positivity palette—literally gives you a new outlook on life. This, as I've mentioned, is the first core truth about positive emotions: they open us.

Imagine yourself as a flower in springtime, your petals drawn in tightly around your face. If you can see out at all, it's only a speck of light. You can't appreciate much of what goes on around you. Yet once you feel the warmth of the sun, things change. You begin to soften. Your petals loosen and begin to stretch outward, exposing your face, and removing your delicate blinders. You see more and more. Your world quite literally expands. Possibilities unfold.

Some flowers bloom just once. Other flowers, like day lilies, close up every evening and bloom again every time they see the sun. Sunlight is essential to the growth of all green plants. Plants know this.

They turn toward the light, stretching themselves open to take in as much as they can. Scientists call this the heliotropic effect.

A similar heliotropic effect has been described in people.[1] Positivity is essential to the growth of all humans. We know this instinctively. We turn toward positivity, stretching our minds open to take in as much as we can. I call this the *broaden effect*.

Positivity broadens our minds and expands our range of vision. The effect is temporary. Just as day lilies retract when sunlight fades, so do our minds when positivity fades. Threatened with negativity, our minds constrict even further. There's no limit to how often our minds can cycle through these moments of expanded and retracted awareness. As positivity and negativity flow through us, the scope of our awareness blooms and retracts accordingly.

Here, I've borrowed metaphors from the poet's toolkit to convey how readily positivity broadens our minds. For two decades I've tested the broaden effect with the tools of science. My scientific investigations of positivity give me the confidence to make the claims that I do. The news I share is not simply poetic, based only on my own life experience. In fact it is based on the actions and experiences of hundreds of thousands of people, volunteers tested in my laboratory and those of other scientists around the world. These people were tested in experiments that attempted to debunk the broaden effect, to prove it wrong. Yet, time and again, against the odds, evidence emerged that positivity broadens us. I've become convinced that it's a core truth about being human.

You can play around with these ideas yourself. You'll need a sheet of scrap paper and something to write with. Set them aside for the moment, but have them handy. When you're ready, I invite you to study the back of your hand. You may have heard someone say they know a place like the back of their hand. But how well do any of us really know the backs of our hands? Look, now, at the back of your hand. Describe to yourself everything you see: the textures and colors of your skin; the topography of your bones and veins; the patterns within each of your knuckles. Take a minute or so to simply study the back of your hand. Get to know it like never before.

Now get your pen and paper and make a list of what you want to do right now. Assume you've got a free half hour with no pressing demands. Consider the feeling you got while examining your hand, and write down what this feeling makes you want to do.

Got your list? Good. For the moment, set it aside.

Let's move on to something different. When you're ready, I invite you to imagine and relive a joyful moment, one in which everything's going your way and you can scarcely hold back a smile. You're simply beaming. Sit with this joyful feeling for a few moments, imagining all aspects of your surroundings and sensations. Let your good feelings grow. Appreciate them like never before.

Now go back to your pen and paper. Make a new list. What does this new, joyful feeling make you want to do right now? Again, assume you've got a free half hour with no pressing demands. Consider the feeling you get when reliving your joy, and write down everything that this feeling makes you want to do.

Got your second list? Good. Now compare. Count the ideas that came to mind after studying your hand. Compare that with the number that came to mind when you felt joyful. Which list is longer?

If you're like most people, your list was longer with positivity. This is one way positivity broadens us. It calls forth more possibilities from within us than we typically see—and certainly more than we see under the influence of negativity.

Together with Christine Branigan, a former doctoral student, I conducted an experiment not too different from this exercise.[2] One by one, we tested a sample of 104 people, some of whom we randomly assigned to experience either amusement or serenity, and others to experience either anger or fear. Still others were assigned to experience neutrality—no particular feeling at all.[3]

We then posed a question: *Given this feeling, make a list of what you want to do right now.* Those who felt either amused or serene came up with the longest lists. Their lists were longer than those who felt neutral, and longer than those who felt angry or scared. Positivity unlocked more possibilities for them.

The exercise I invited you to play with was different. My aim was

to have you experience two different states—one neutral and one joyful. Having you study the back of your hand was my way to put you
temporarily in a somewhat neutral mood. Only you can decide
whether it really worked. Similarly, only you can decide whether your
efforts to rekindle joy worked. If these thought exercises worked for
you, odds are that your joyful list was longer, reflecting broadened
possibilities. Positivity opens us. It allows us to consider possibilities
that are otherwise hidden from view.

Positivity broadens at abstract levels as well. Consider the figure
below.

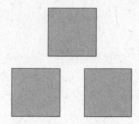

Would you say it's a triangle? Or would you say it's a group of squares?
Clearly it's both. There's no right or wrong answer. To infer the scope
of people's attention, we ask them to pick out a similar arrangement of
shapes. Do they see this arrangement as more similar to a triangle
made up of smaller triangles, or to a square made up of smaller
squares. In conducting experiments with images like these, I've discovered that whether people see the big picture—the triangle in this
case—depends on their current emotional state.[4] When we inject
people with positivity, their outlook expands. They see the big picture.
When we inject them with neutrality or negativity, their peripheral vision shrinks. There is no big picture, no dots to connect.

Through experiments like this, I learned I could broaden the very
scope of people's attention simply by making them feel good. Our
emotions are connected to our outlooks via a simple cause-and-effect
relationship. As positivity flows through our hearts, it simultaneously
broadens our minds, allowing us to see *both* the forest *and* the trees.

The effect is exquisitely subtle. Some of our laboratory experiments assess people's positivity by tracking the electrical signals within certain muscles of their faces. Remember, when your positivity is genuine, it draws smiling eyes together with a smiling mouth. With precisely placed sensors we can measure tiny electrical signals in the zygomaticus major, the muscle that pulls your lip corners up, and the orbicularis oculi, the muscle that crinkles the skin around your eyes, long before they're strong enough to create any recognizable facial expression.[5] My students and I discovered that when firing in tandem, these two facial muscles forecast flexible and broadened attention captured by computerized tests that measure people's responses in milliseconds. Your smile, then, quite literally opens you. In the moment you're smiling, you're more receptive, more able to see the big picture.[6]

Scientists at Brandeis University, using sophisticated eye-tracking technology, have replicated my discovery that positive emotions broaden people's attention. Volunteers viewed pictures on a computer screen while a camera recorded their eye movements sixty times a second, compensating for any movements their heads made.[7] By random assignment, volunteers were injected with positivity or not.[8] The picture groupings included three photographs each, always arranged with one in the center and two at the periphery. Volunteers viewed the slide show naturally, looking at whatever interested them, as if they were watching television. By tracking where they directed their eyes, these scientists confirmed that, under the influence of positivity, people looked around more, and more frequently fixed their gaze on peripheral photos. Quite literally, then, positivity changes your outlook on life. It expands your worldview. You take more in.

The one exception was when the pictures were aversive. In an instant, negativity zapped broadened attention. Going back to that day lily analogy, if the sky darkens, the day lily closes. I suspect our minds are even faster to close than day lilies—yet another demonstration of the fragility of positivity. But so long as your surroundings are benign, when positivity flows through you, the scope of your awareness blooms.

What a Difference a Broadened Mind Makes

One practical consequence of positivity's mind-broadening powers is enhanced creativity. A broad mind changes the way you think and act in a wide range of circumstances. When you see more, more ideas come to mind, more actions become possible.

This fact was demonstrated by a team of scientists at the University of Toronto.[9] They injected volunteers with positivity, negativity, or utter neutrality[10] and tested them on two very different tasks. One task measured the scope of visual attention, by tracking the influence of peripherally presented information. The other task measured verbal creativity, by asking volunteers to come up with a single word that related to three given words (for instance, *mower, atomic,* and *foreign*).[11] The researchers learned that when people felt positive, their performance on the two tasks changed in tandem: the broader the scope of their visual attention, the more creative they became on the verbal task. This is an important linkage because it documents that positivity broadens minds in multiple, interrelated ways. At a fundamental level, then, positivity alters your brain and changes the way you interact with the world.[12]

Positivity is an especially good investment when you need creative solutions fast. Indeed, students do better on standardized tests when they enter them having self-generated a positive emotion.[13] But suppose you're not a student and you no longer take exams? Odds are that scientists have studied people like you as well. The evidence shows that simply imagining a joyful memory or receiving a small kindness can make a difference in the ease with which people locate creative and optimal solutions to the problems they face on a daily basis.

Scientists at Cornell University examined the ways physicians make medical diagnoses by having them think aloud while they solved the case of a patient with liver disease.[14] Astonishingly, this research team found that when they gave physicians a small gift—simply a bag of candy—those physicians were better at integrating case information and less likely to become fixated on their initial ideas, coming to premature closure in their diagnosis. Whether you're the physician or the patient, I think you'd agree that better clinical reasoning is a good thing. Perhaps alongside the list of physical complaints we bring to our doctor's office, we should also bring small gifts or kindnesses.

Likewise, scientists at UC Berkeley Haas School of Business examined how positivity affects managers.[15] They found that managers with greater positivity were more accurate and careful in making their decisions, and were more effective interpersonally. Other studies show that managers with greater positivity infect their work groups with greater positivity as well, which in turn produces better coordination among team members and reduces the effort needed to get their work done.[16]

A different team of scientists, from the Kellogg School of Management at Northwestern University, learned that when people negotiate complex bargains, positivity again makes a difference. Participants in their experiments were MBA students enrolled in negotiation courses. It's safe to assume these were success-driven people, highly invested in negotiating winning contracts. At random, the research team assigned some negotiators to display positivity, and others to display negativity or neutrality. In each case they did this by sharing "expert advice" that displaying such emotions (or a non-emotional "poker face") would improve their bargaining style. They then let these budding entrepreneurs loose with a bargaining partner and a dispute to settle. Negotiators who strategically displayed positivity were more likely to gain concessions, close deals, and incorporate future business relationships into the contracts they forged. Common wisdom tells us that deal makers should be rational, even-tempered—unflappably neutral—or perhaps tough, committed, and hotheaded—seething negativity. These are myths. Scientific experiments confirm that people who come to the bargaining table with a cooperative and friendly spirit—riding on positivity—strike the best business deals.[17]

So, whether you're in business, or simply deal with businesses, this scientific research can serve as a powerful reminder that leading with positivity is not simply about being nice, giving in, or giving away the store. Rather, positivity broadens your outlook, bringing more possibilities into view. With positivity, your thoughts and actions surface more spontaneously; you're better able to envision future prospects and win-win solutions. You become more apt to build lasting relationships, attracting loyalty instead of bitterness.

Upward Spirals Within You

As you've seen, most research on the broaden effect takes place in laboratories. In controlled laboratory settings, scientists are able to zoom in on the immediate effects positivity produces on people's vision, attention, thinking, choices, and behavior. Building on this work, scientists have also widened their lens to include the real-life, downstream repercussions of broadened thinking. This work uniquely reveals the paths that positivity cuts in our lives.

Let me describe a study on mind-broadening that examined a wider stretch of time. This is work I did in collaboration with Thomas Joiner, a leading scientist of mood disorders and the director of the Psychology Clinic at Florida State Univerisity. We surveyed a large group of university students, and then surveyed them again five weeks later. Each time we measured their degree of positivity as well as their tendency to handle stresses in an open-minded manner. This boiled down to whether they agreed with survey items asking them whether, when they faced problems, they stepped back from the situation to envision a wide range of possible solutions.

We discovered that people who enjoyed more positivity in their lives were more able to cope with adversity in an open-minded way. They saw more solutions. This may not be surprising to you, given the evidence I've already shared about the broaden effect. More inspiring yet was the discovery of how this unfolded over time. The most positive people in the sample became even more positive five weeks later, precisely because their minds became increasingly open when they faced problems. Their openness allowed them to find solutions that not only helped them cope with troubles they faced, but also strengthened their positivity. When we sliced the data in a different way, we discovered that the most open-minded people became even more open-minded five weeks later, precisely because they experienced increasing amounts of positivity.[18] Another way to say this is that positivity and openness feed on each other, each reinforcing and catalyzing the other. This is the upward spiral that positivity triggers within you. It opens pathways that lead to growth. It epitomizes flourishing. Just imagine the possibilities that positivity might hold for your own life.

In more recent work, Joiner's students and I have replicated the evidence for upward spirals—fueled by positivity—and linked them not only to changes in open-minded coping, but also to changes in all kinds of effective ways to cope with trying times. Additionally, we found that another form of openness—trust in others—works in the same way. Positivity and trust feed on each other. As our positivity grows, so does our trust in others, and vice versa.[19] And this is just the beginning. The social repercussions of positivity run even deeper. The next section tells how.

From Me to We

The news from a great variety of experiments is that positivity broadens your outlook. It literally expands your mindscape, bringing new possibilities into view. Although this effect is subtle—at times totally imperceptible—the implications for your relationships are enormous. My students and I have discovered that positivity even broadens people's views of themselves. This is pivotal for relationships. The often well-guarded boundaries that separate "me" from "you" begin to fade from view. As they do, new possibilities for connection emerge.

Take a quick look at the series of overlapping circles below.

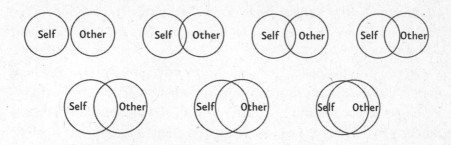

Now, for just a moment, call to mind the most recent argument you had with your spouse, romantic partner, or best friend. Where were you? What were you fighting about? Who said what? At that moment, what were you feeling? With this heated argument firmly in mind, which pair of circles best represents how you then felt about your relationship?

Now set aside that unsettling fight. Call to mind the most tender and warmhearted moments in this same relationship. Where were you? What was happening? What did you do or say? At that cozy moment, what were you feeling? Now, with this loving moment infusing you, which pair of circles best depicts how you feel about your relationship? Did the circles get closer?

This way of representing the quality of relationships was introduced by Art Aron, one of the world's leading scientists studying human relationships. Aron and his colleagues have asked thousands of romantically involved people to use this set of overlapping circles to represent how they feel about their relationships. This simple measure is so powerful it outperforms lengthier surveys and interviews when it comes to forecasting which couples stay together and which couples break up. The more overlap you see between you and your partner, the better odds your relationship faces in the long run.

Aron and colleagues call this concept self-expansion, and define it as incorporating the other person's skills, traits, and resources as one's own.[20] Interestingly, they identify self-expansion as a key trigger of positivity. Extraordinarily rapid self-expansion, according to these researchers, is what makes falling in love so exhilarating. My students and I turned Aron's logic upside down. Stepping off from our earlier evidence that positivity broadens, we predicted that positivity would expand people's self views.

We first asked college students to use the circles to convey how they felt about their relationship with their best friend. Next we injected positivity, negativity, or utter neutrality. We then gave them another set of overlapping circles, and asked them to again select a pair of circles that reflected how they felt about their best friend.[21] Doing experiments like these, we found that a temporary boost in positivity allowed people to see more overlap between themselves and others. With positivity, people feel closer and more connected to the important people in their lives.

This change occurs at a very basic perceptual level within our minds. We know this because participants in our study were not hanging out with their best friends, being warm and enjoying their good company. They were simply thinking about their best friends—and feeling closer. As positivity broadens your mind, it shifts your core view of people and relationships, bringing them closer to your center, to your heart. With positivity, you go from classifying people as separate "me" and "you," to seeing more interconnection, as in "we" and "us." The effect is so reliable that we've found it cross-culturally.

As a scientist, I've been extraordinarily lucky because my ideas and experiments have drawn the interest and curiosity of other scientists from around the world. Some have even followed their curiosity all the way to my research lab and taken up residence as visiting scholars. These scientists' openness to explore ideas and travel the world has been a true gift. They've become invaluable collaborators who have expanded the impact and reach of my ideas. This is yet another example of how positivity—this time in the form of intellectual curiosity—broadens exposure and builds both strategic alliances and globe-spanning friendships.

The year my students and I were first investigating the effects of positivity on self-other overlap, I was doubly blessed. Ahalya Hejmadi, a scientist from India (trained in the United States), joined our ongoing conversations about this line of research. Later that same year, Keiko Otake, a scientist from Japan (trained in Japan), arrived as well. Each independently decided to test our hypothesis in her own home country.[22] Their results were strikingly similar to ours. Whether in the city of Pune, in the state of Maharashtra within India, the cities of Kobe or Nishinomiya in Japan, or in Ann Arbor, Michigan, in the United States, positivity made people see more overlap between themselves and their best friends.

I'm particularly excited about these cross-cultural data because India and Japan differ from the United States in deep ways. Scientists have identified these cultures as ones that, relative to the United States, foster more-connected and more-interdependent views of self. Compared with North Americans, most people in India and Japan already see more overlap between themselves and closely connected others. Could positivity boost perceptions of self-other overlap even when self-other overlap is the cultural norm? Yes, it could.

The evidence suggests that no matter what your cultural background, feelings of openness and connection with others ebb and flow. These changes are not random. Positivity drives the effect. It opens our eyes and allows us to see our oneness with others.

We All Look the Same to Me

The news from this series of experiments is that heartfelt positivity allows you to grasp your basic oneness with close others. Feelings of oneness come and go, not at random, but in step with your feelings of joy, gratitude, love, and the like. But what about strangers? Can positivity alter your view of people you don't even know?

The answer is a resounding *yes!* My guess is that you'll be as amazed as I was (and still am) when you learn just how positivity matters here. Throughout this book, my goal has been to share with you my scientific findings. Every one of those findings was one we predicted—except this one. I jokingly refer to these results as "the finding that found us."

It started when Kareem Johnson, then a doctoral student working with me (now an assistant professor at Temple University), reasoned that if positive emotions broadened the scope of people's attention, allowing them to see the big picture—holistically—then positivity should also improve people's ability to recognize faces. This prediction follows a long line of experiments that had already documented that people recognized faces differently from, and far better than, they recognized common objects.

When you need to decide whether you've seen a given object before, you examine its features. You might ask yourself, *Did the coffee mug I used yesterday have a handle of that shape? Did it have a chip on the bottom? Was it thinner than this mug?* By contrast, evidence suggests that when you need to decide whether you've seen a specific face before, you don't examine features. You don't ask yourself, *Have I seen this nose before? Is this the same eye color that I remember? Were her lips thinner than these?* No. Instead you take in someone's face as a whole. In a fraction of a second, you match the entire configuration of a person's face to what's stored in your memory. All people become expert at recognizing human faces. Scientists have even identified specific brain areas that underlie this remarkable ability. Although we may not always remember a person's name, or where we met her, we're usually pretty good at knowing whether we've seen that person before.

Based on these past findings, Kareem predicted that if we injected people with positivity, their temporarily broadened minds would allow them to "see the whole" of a person's face even faster, making them even better at recognizing strangers.

Kareem conducted his first experiment by injecting research participants—tested one by one—with positivity, negativity, or neutrality.[23] He then showed them a series of twenty-eight faces, very quickly, for just half a second each, with a two-second delay between photos. Later he tested their recognition of these faces by showing a series of fifty-six faces in random order. Half of those faces had been shown previously, half had not. Study participants could examine the faces as long as they needed. Their job was to decide whether they'd seen that face before.

When Kareem came to our lab meeting with his data in hand, it was clear he was frustrated. His plots of face-recognition rates by experimental condition looked close to what we had predicted. Yet the statistical tests were all non-significant, suggesting the pattern we saw might well have occurred by chance alone. We puzzled about this for days, plotting the data in different ways. We broke it down to look at male and female faces and male and female participants separately. By chance, Kareem had used a set of faces that included both white and Asian faces—half of each—so we broke the data down that way as well. That's when it popped: positivity improved face recognition only for the Asian faces. Looking closer, we saw that the effect was stronger still when we zeroed in on our white participants, which were the majority of our sample.

Completely by surprise, we found ourselves contributing to the scientific discussion of racial bias. A long series of experiments had already confirmed that people are notoriously bad at recognizing individuals across racial lines. Whereas a bigot might say, "they all look the same to me," scientists call this phenomenon the "own-race bias in face recognition." Not much seems to budge this entrenched bias—not even years spent in ethnically diverse schools and job sites.[24] One suggestion—heart-wrenching in its implications—is that when you try to figure out whether you've previously seen the face of someone whose race differs from your own, you adopt the same mental strategy that you use for recognizing objects: you examine features.[25] *Have I seen those eyes before? Is that nose the same shape?* Another suggestion is that people are so busy classifying others by race that they miss the chance to see the person behind the racial label. Indeed, scientists have discovered that the first thing we notice about another person is their race.[26] We notice a person's race within about 100 milliseconds. By comparison, we notice their sex within about 150 milliseconds. When you see someone of your own race, race may well seem invisible to you. You know in an instant that "he's one of us," which leaves room to absorb and appreciate his uniqueness.

Because Kareem's finding was unexpected, it was critical to replicate it. We needed to be sure it wasn't a fluke, that one-in-a-hundred chance that the data pointed to something that wasn't real. Kareem went back to the lab and tested our newfound hypothesis, that positive emotions improved people's recognition of cross-race faces. To be especially rigorous, he did this in many different ways. He used black faces instead of Asian faces. He injected emotions immediately before the recognition test, instead of before they saw the faces for the first time. Each time, the same finding surfaced again. So the effect was reliable, making us certain that it pointed to something real. Also, the effect was utterly complete. Positive emotions didn't simply diminish the entrenched racial bias, it eliminated it altogether: under the influence of positivity, people become just as good at recognizing individuals of another race as they are at recognizing individuals of their own race.[27]

Even things that tend to divide people—like racial differences—seem to melt away when our hearts are warmed by positivity. As I said, this finding found us; we didn't seek it. By chance, we discovered that the oneness that you feel with others when positivity runs through you extends to strangers, even those you may otherwise perceive as very different from you. Instead of resorting to "they all look the same to me," under the influence of positivity you recognize that "we all look the same to me." We're all human, we're all "one of us."

Kareem's experiments are extraordinarily valuable—so much so that my colleagues at the University of Michigan honored him with an award for the best dissertation of the year in 2005. I see his work as further evidence that positivity broadens our minds. Just as it broadens your view of "me" to include other people, it broadens your view of "us" to include all of us. This idea is compatible with the work of other scientists who have found that when people find themselves in diverse groups, positivity inspires them to set aside divisive group identities ("we're Michigan Wolverines, and we hate Ohio State Buckeyes") and instead forge inclusive group identities ("we're all students, let's work together").[28]

Upward Spirals Surround You

If moments of heartfelt positivity uniquely allow you to see your oneness with others—both with people you're already close to and with complete strangers—then it stands to reason that positivity also changes the way you interact with others. A mountain of evidence confirms that it does. Some of the earliest experiments on positivity, conducted some thirty-five years ago by the pioneering psychologist Alice Isen, showed that when people feel good, they are more likely to be kind and offer help to strangers. In Isen's classic experiments, she'd make one set of participants feel good by giving them unexpected gifts—a cookie, a package of stationery—or causing them to receive a small windfall, such as a dime found in a pay phone.[29] Afterward, compared to those who didn't receive gifts, these people were more likely to spontaneously help a stranger pick up a pile of dropped papers, volunteer their time to help others, or make a phone call on someone else's behalf.[30] More recent experiments confirm that our sense of oneness is what drives our willingness to help others in need.[31]

When you act on your sense of oneness with others and lend a helping hand, you externalize your positivity. It's moved from your own heart and mind into the space between you and another person. And, just like negativity, positivity is remarkably contagious. Once "out there," it spreads. In part, it spreads because people unconsciously mimic the emotional gestures and facial expressions of those around them.[32] But that's only a small part of the story. Positivity also spreads because it sets off a chain of events that carry positive meaning for you and those around you. That classic work by Isen tells us that positivity breeds helpful, compassionate acts. Sadly, most scientific investigations have stopped there. What those early accounts missed is that helpful, compassionate acts in themselves breed positivity, and in several intertwined ways.

When you truly help someone else, there's a good chance that you feel gratified and, in a core sense, proud of what you did—proud that you chose to act generously to the other person's benefit. As we saw in chapter 3, pride broadens your mindset by igniting your visions about other and larger ways in which you might be helpful. The lofty dreams that pride inspires may at times seem misplaced, but there's a good chance that they'll move you to help again when the circumstances are right because you now see yourself as someone who takes action.

Now consider the same situation from the eyes of the person you helped. Odds are, she feels good too. She may well feel grateful for the unexpected kindness she received. And gratitude, we've seen, broadens her mindset as she gets creative about how she might either pay it back (to you) or pay it forward (to someone else). Either way, she's inclined to externalize her own positivity, adding more goodness to the social world.

Beyond the dance of positivity between you and the person you helped, those who witness your good deed may well feel inspired, their hearts uplifted and elevated. This hue of positivity also makes people want to do good themselves. They're not passive bystanders. Their hearts are moved. When those onlookers act on these feelings, they too add more goodness to the social world.

So, just as positivity stokes upward spirals within you—allowing you to see more possibilities that in turn keep you buoyed up with increasing positivity—so too does positivity stoke upward spirals all around you. Once you let your positivity out, once you let it change the way you act toward others, it sparks these spirals between and within people. As this cycle continues, you and others are inspired to act on your good feelings further and repeatedly, turning them into additional good deeds. In this way, positivity can change whole communities. It can create more compassion and harmony where we need it most.

Connecting to Something Larger

At such moments, you realize that you and the other are,
in fact, one. It's a big realization. Survival is the second law
of life. The first is that we are all one.
—Joseph Campbell

The scientific evidence that I've shared so far tells us that the moments Joseph Campbell had in mind in the passage above were ones infused with positivity—moments of deep gratitude, true inspiration, heart-felt joy, or heart-stopping awe. At such moments your mind is wide open, like the feeling you experience when you roll the top and windows down on the convertible car you've just rented. You notice more of what's out there. You appreciate the great mysteries of life. You can newly see the ways in which you are part of something much larger than yourself.

Feelings of oneness are often tied to other people—but not always. We can also feel oneness with nature. Let me tell you about a powerful sense of oneness I experienced. It happened during the most awe-filled week of my life to date, when I attended a seven-day meditation retreat, held exclusively for scientists using meditation to investigate the mind and consciousness.[33] Virtually the entire retreat was held in silence. All activities were carried out without words—not just the meditations (both sitting and walking), but also eating, working, and gathering. All silent. I was shocked at how delicious the silence was. Without distractions, my senses were heightened. I could hear tiny birds fly that I'd once thought were soundless. I saw beauty in the most unexpected places. Each morning I hiked through the woods. It was January in Massachusetts, cold and snowy. My most stunning moments of oneness with nature were during those walks. One morning I came across a huge upended tree. The exposed underside was a gnarled tangle of roots, dirt, rocks, and plant life, about eight to ten feet across. I realized for the first time how rigid my views of "earth" and "tree" had been. Earth was one thing, and trees were another. That morning I could see how wrong my thinking had been. Earth was tree, and tree was the earth. Earth, which moments ago had seemed so solid and distinct—the very ground beneath my feet—was actually a wild mix of stones, dead plants, and more. That fallen tree would soon be the earth. And the earth was not solid. It was teeming with life and former life, constantly changing.

Later that week, I saw myself in this great mix of life. Nearly all the trees were bare, and the trails I was navigating had a fresh cover of snow. Deep in the forest I came across an impossibly bright patch of green moss, all but hidden beneath a blanket of white. Almost before I had the chance to recognize what I was seeing, a thought popped into my head: *We're everywhere!* I knew instantly that "we" was life itself. Life is everywhere. And I'm a part of it. The moss and I were one. This realization still delights me. I'm not the detached scientific observer that I once fancied myself to be. I'm it. You're it. Moss is it. We're everywhere.

That week I came to believe that oneness isn't merely a perception. It's what is. Positivity opens your mind and allows you to appreciate what is. Other moments—neutral ones and especially negative ones—hide "what is" from us. They have their own agenda that takes us away from the truth of oneness. By design, negativity inspires you to protect yourself, which often means pulling back and separating yourself from others. Also by design, positivity tells you that it's safe to recognize that you are not separate after all.

The View from Here

You've now toured some of the basic science of positivity. The first core truth I've shared with you is that positivity opens us. Now you know—despite the often flowery language of emotions—this isn't simply a metaphor. Data from a wide range of experiments show clear causal connections between people's emotional states and their outlooks on life. The more positivity courses through your neural circuits and your veins, the broader your mind will be. Positivity literally expands your peripheral vision, allowing you to see more than you typically do.

As positivity expands the scope of your visual attention, it also expands the conceptual connections you make. You come up with more and better ideas. And when you face problems, positivity makes your solutions better. What's more, your positivity and your openness feed on and reinforce each other, creating a buoyant upward spiral within you.

Positivity also alters how you see your connections with others. You think *we* instead of *me.* You look past things that separate you from others—like racial difference—to appreciate the uniqueness of strangers.

The sense of oneness that positivity brings also inspires you to do what's right for others. You break out of your cocoon to lend a helping hand. As you do so, your positivity begets further positivity, in you and in those around you, creating even larger upward spirals that surround you and infuse your community.

Positivity connects you to your full humanity, the full humanity of others, and the great mysteries of life itself.

Positivity opens us. With a new appreciation for the science that backs up this bold claim, you can have more faith in the value of your efforts to cultivate heartfelt positivity in your own life.

The next chapter describes the science that backs up the second core truth about positivity: that it transforms us for the better. This, I sense, you'll find even more inspiring.

CHAPTER 5

Build Your Best Future

*Things that are good are good, and if one is
responding to that goodness one is in contact
with a truth from which one is getting something.*

—Thomas Merton

You are constantly changing—not just your clothes or your hairstyle, but your inner core, the very essence of your being. Change is the rule, constancy the rare exception.

Consider the change under way within you at this very moment. What you know as "you" is actually trillions of cells living and working together. Most only live for a few weeks or months. When they die, they are replaced by new cells. This cycle continues for as long as you live.

The pace of cell renewal varies by body part. Your taste buds live only a few hours. Your white blood cells live about ten days. Your muscle cells live about three months. Even your bones are made anew time and again. Considering these differences, scientists have suggested that you replace about 1 percent of your cells each day.[1] That's 1 percent today, another 1 percent tomorrow, amounting to roughly 30 percent by next month, and 100 percent by next season. Seeing yourself and your cells in this way, every three months you get a whole new you. Perhaps it's no coincidence that it takes around three months to learn a new habit or make a lifestyle change.[2] Perhaps we can't teach an old cell new tricks. Perhaps our best hope lies in teaching our new cells.

At one time scientists thought that your brain cells were different, that they didn't change. Perhaps they even orchestrated the cycle of cell death and rebirth elsewhere in your body. Not so. Even key brain cells wither away and are reborn. Every part of you can change, and your brain is no exception.[3]

More fascinating still is the discovery that the pace of cell renewal doesn't simply follow some predetermined script. It varies depending on what you do and how you feel. A key signal that tells your cells whether to decay or grow, for instance, is movement. A sedentary lifestyle hastens cell decay. An active lifestyle hastens cell renewal. This is true for both your body and your brain.[4]

Your emotions are thought to be another key signal. Negativity prompts cell decay. Positivity prompts cell growth.[5] At a very basic biological level, then, positivity is life-giving.

These scientific discoveries about the ever-changing nature of your body and brain are fully consistent with the second core truth about positivity: it transforms us for the better. Let's see how.

Nina's Transformation

I met Nina when she was in her mid-thirties. By then she'd been married fifteen years and had a seven-year-old daughter. She's a technical analyst at a large computer company in Detroit—a full-time job. When I first met her, she described her life as full of stress. Her job was especially challenging. When anyone in the company had a problem with their computer, they'd call the "help desk." If the help desk couldn't help, someone on Nina's team was called. Her job was to work on unsolved problems until they were solved. She told me that her stress at work could get so bad that at times she just wanted to go home and bang her head against the wall.

Then there was her mother. Nina's mother had recently been diagnosed with a brain tumor. It was stressful because the doctors couldn't figure out what was going on, how bad it was, or what would happen next.

On top of all this, for years Nina had longed to be pregnant. She and her husband desperately wanted a larger family, but month after month she'd find that their efforts had failed. She blamed herself. She had no self-confidence. She felt depressed and lonely most of the time. She cried a lot. She'd get terrible headaches. She told me her headaches were like someone had hit her in the back of the head with a baseball bat. She also had frequent stomach pains.

That's where Nina was when I met her. Like countless others, she described her life as "in a rut." As she put it, she felt that "there's nothing to life . . . I just exist. I exist with the rest of the world . . . I'm just struggling a lot . . . there [is] no growth for me." At her best, she was languishing, just trying to get by. At her worst, she was depressed. Indeed, she'd struggled with depression on and off for years. My guess is that you can resonate with Nina's situation. You've been there— stressed, overwhelmed, spread too thin. Like Nina, perhaps you too have at times felt stuck, wondering if there was more to life. Perhaps you too have longed for something better.

I met Nina because she volunteered for a study of mine, one that happened to be hosted by her employer. In August of 2005, Nina (and everyone else who worked at the company) got an e-mail message announcing that their Wellness Program was sponsoring a seven-week meditation workshop to help employees better manage stress. It was even offered for free. Nina jumped at the chance to sign up. She thought, *Oh, I've got to be a part of that, that might help me!*

This free workshop was part of a research study I conducted. Together with Michael Cohn, a former doctoral student, I was testing the "build" part of my broaden-and-build theory in a controlled experiment. At random, we assigned one group of volunteers to adopt a daily habit intended to increase positivity. A comparison group continued to live as usual.[6] Both groups completed web-based surveys. We wanted to learn whether a particular form of meditation—crafted over centuries and specifically intended to increase heartfelt positivity—would, in some manner, change people's lives for the better.

We collected a massive amount of data from Nina and her co-workers. Yet even within this heap of numbers, Nina's entries stood out. Her transformation was especially inspiring—so much so that when the study was over, I wrote to her and asked to interview her. That was something I'd never done before. I'm a quantitative researcher; numbers are my life's work. Yet I knew in my bones that to hear her story face-to-face would mean so much more. I asked Nina for her story because I wanted to share it with you. I sensed that her words might help me better describe what's at stake for you, and why you might want to experiment with positivity in your own life. Indeed, Nina's transformation may well pave the way for the transformation that matters most: your own.

Given how Nina's life was going when the study started, it's not surprising to learn that her positivity ratio was seriously low, at about 1 to 1. We've seen that this is a typical ratio for people struggling with depression. Luckily for her—and completely by chance—Nina landed in our experimental group. She was thrilled to be picked. This meant that instead of simply completing our web-based surveys, she also got to join a meditation class, held at work over the lunch hour.

Going to the first workshop session, she thought, *Okay, this is silly.* One of her colleagues who went to the workshop with her arrived cynical, saying, "I see it as a free hour of sleeping!" Nina was more open. She urged her colleague, "You've got to really listen to what [the teacher] is saying—really listen—and let yourself go a little bit, just let yourself go." Her friend continued to view the class as nap time. Nina thought, *Okay, whatever. I'm going to do it, you do your own thing. I'm here for me.*

Nina's meditation teacher was Sandra Finkel, who has a degree in public health and had been teaching meditation for more than twenty years. Sandra introduced basic principles of meditation, guided workshop participants through group meditations right in class, and answered any questions that Nina and others had for her. And to help them establish their own daily meditation practice, Sandra gave all workshop participants a CD on which she had recorded a series of guided meditations that they could follow at home. The guided meditations were about twenty minutes long. They didn't demand a huge time commitment. But Nina didn't always use the CD to meditate; she found the mix of silence and speaking to be too abrupt. So she listened enough to get the gist of the meditation, and then meditated on her own, while listening to her favorite calming music.

The meditations taught in this course were different from those Nina had come across before, in that they aimed to cultivate feelings of love and kindness. With them, Nina found that her body relaxed. She'd get a soft, tingling feeling. It felt wonderful to get to this peaceful place within her. Before the study began, if she came home from work and found her husband sitting down, she'd question him: "How can you sit down when there are things to be done?" She described herself as "just run, run, run, run." During the study she realized,

> You know what? There are always going to be dishes to be done. Why do I have to do them now? No, I'm going to sit and relax because I love the way my legs feel when I relax. Physically, I feel a lot better now. I don't have as many headaches anymore. I don't have the stomach pains. I've learned how to relax . . . I know how to do it now. It feels great. I never knew how to relax before, and now I can just really let go.

She described her experience with meditation as "finding myself again." Yet at the same time she came to recognize that life's "not all about me anymore." She realized that life's about working together and connecting with others: "We all want the same things," she told me. "Everyone wants to be happy. Everyone wants to be loved." Sure enough, the one-minute web surveys that Nina completed every day at the end of her workday documented these changes in her emotional outlook. Slowly, as she began to meditate more regularly, Nina's positivity ratio rose, eventually to about 6 to 1.

I checked in with Nina about three months later, to see what difference her increase in positivity had made. The good news was that she hardly ever felt depressed, lonely, and teary-eyed anymore. And she had no more headaches and no more stomach pain.

Yet, far beyond these reductions in distress and pain, Nina had changed for the better. She was far more optimistic and confident than she'd been three months earlier. She was better able to keep her mind focused on what she was doing. And when she faced setbacks, she bounced back more quickly. She'd become resilient.

Within three months, Nina truly went from languishing in life to flourishing. True, she felt better emotionally and had a more positive outlook on life. But her transformation didn't end there. Nina's new positivity energized her with a renewed sense of direction and purpose. She found her everyday conversations with family and friends to be more enjoyable and more meaningful. Now, and for the first time, she felt like an important part of her community. She felt she was making a positive difference in the world.

These positive changes showed up loud and clear in Nina's survey responses. When I compared her responses at the end of the study to her responses three months earlier, it was obvious to me that she'd grown in important ways. When we finish up experiments like this, we routinely ask participants what they've noticed. In our final surveys we ask what changes they have seen over the past few months. Here's what Nina wrote:

I feel more confident with myself and with people around me. I am not so hard on myself. I have been able to forgive things easier than before. I am not so hard on myself or others. Some particular things tend to just "roll" off my shoulders now, as opposed to letting them bother me throughout the day. I am able to find peace within myself and I am able to share more positive thoughts with those around me. Thanks for bringing this study in to my workplace. I am really glad that I had the opportunity to do this. I feel that I have gained much knowledge out of this session with your team. I will not stop meditating. It is a wonderful feeling of relaxing, peacefulness in my soul.

Nina recognized and appreciated many of the same changes that our surveys had picked up. And she valued these changes tremendously. In our follow-up survey she described them as significant and pervasive, affecting many different aspects of her life. She saw her transformation as both mental, affecting her image of herself and others, and practical, affecting how she acted and interacted with others on a daily basis.

When we checked in with Nina more than a year later, she reported that these profound changes in her life had persisted. In fact, she saw them as permanent. She continued to meditate regularly. When we asked her why she thought her changes continued, here's what she wrote:

> I feel that I grew spiritually. I feel more at peace with myself. I am not as stressed as I was before I began the study. I look at people's personalities differently and empathize with them more. My husband and I tried for two years to have another baby. After the study, I continued to meditate. My feelings of self-love and kindness toward myself and the world around me continued to grow, and we conceived. I believe that this study has not only helped my life, it has helped my soul to grow. I feel so much love for my family and friends. I enjoy the little things more today than I did before I began to meditate. I notice things that most people tend to overlook: sunrises in the morning, beautiful sunsets in the evening, the beauty in a snowflake. Meditation has made a great impact on my life and soul. I rekindled old relationships, forgave those who hurt me in bad relationships and made peace with them. Now I enjoy life more with my husband, daughter, and twin babies. I look forward to my happy life with them and watching my children grow and learn. Peace and loving-kindness—Nina.

Reading Nina's entry in our follow-up survey gave me goosebumps. I wept with joy as I told my husband about Nina's efforts to conceive, and the twin babies that were born out of positivity. He knew what her story meant to me. Years ago, he and I had also struggled to conceive. As a scientist to my core, I had adopted a very data-driven approach to conception. I charted my temperature. I read books on the science of fertility. Taking that approach, I'd been on that same emotional roller coaster Nina had been. Each month when I failed to conceive, I was devastated.

Then something hit me. If positivity broadens and builds, then we were going about it all wrong. I didn't need to create charts and learn facts. I needed to cultivate love and enjoy my relationship with my husband. After all, positivity changes the particular hormone cocktail in which we're steeped. Were those changes enough to make an egg cell more permeable to sperm, increasing the odds of conception? Did the "oneness" that positivity can create between two people have a physical basis that could literally "build" new life? Someday I'll team up with a reproductive scientist to test these hypotheses empirically. But I wasn't going to wait a decade for the results of that experiment. I was ready to experiment with my own life. After all, I had nothing to lose.

And, sure enough, the very month my husband and I decided to let go of the numbers and rediscover our love for each other, we conceived. I know the exact days on which both of my boys were conceived—both were days that my husband and I were tripping on love and savoring every minute. Of course, my experiences here provide no scientific evidence. Indeed, fertility specialists have long advised couples struggling to conceive to reduce their stress. Stacks of scientific studies suggest that stress and negativity cut a woman's odds of conceiving. But is eliminating negativity really enough? Maybe positivity is what makes the difference. After all, my first data-driven approach to conception wasn't particularly negative. But it was hardly joyful, either.

With my own sweet babies born out of positivity, I've found myself advising friends facing fertility issues to cultivate their own heartfelt love and joy with their partners. Each friend soon conceived. Again, this is no scientific evidence. Perhaps these couples would have conceived without my sage advice. One day, as I said, I'll find a collaborator who can test this hypothesis with me. Until then, cultivating positivity—coupled with an openness to accept whatever happens—can certainly do no harm.

Nina's story highlights how acceptance—how being open—builds positivity and triggers upward spirals. When I later interviewed her, she told me that before the study began, she'd tried to control everything. And she was very hard on herself when things didn't work out: "When that time of the month would roll around, I'd find myself crying in the bathroom. It's just awful . . . It always came down to 'What am I doing wrong?'" Being in our study helped her to learn about herself. She told me that by the time the study ended in November, "I just decided it's not meant to be. We are meant to be a family of three. I just let go of it, I just let it go . . . By meditating, I have a place to go. I can find some peace . . . at the end of December we found out we were pregnant."

Beyond being blessed with her new babies, Nina described other dramatic changes in her life. At work, she used to avoid certain calls, either because the problem was too difficult or the particular person who needed help drove her "up a wall." All her life she'd been "the shy one." But after the study, she found herself taking more-challenging calls and being more open to difficult problems and difficult people. She figured she might learn something. She talks to people more and makes herself more present. Instead of connecting to people's machines remotely, she'll go find them and sit down in their cubicle. She'll connect with the person, not just the machine. This was totally new for her. "I used to sit down at their desk and say, 'Okay, fixed, I'm out of here.' Now I take the time. I do a lot more connecting with people now than I ever used to."

Nina told me she also felt closer to her family. Sure, they still argued, but she'd learned to be less reactive and self-centered. She was more able to see things from their perspective. She'd even mended a severed friendship with a woman she'd known for twenty-five years and who'd been maid of honor at her wedding. Somehow, nine years before, they'd gotten into a huge argument and just stopped talking to each other. She said, "It was almost like she died." But shortly after being in the study, her old friend sent her an e-mail. At first Nina was suspicious. Over coffee, she recounted to me her first reaction to her friend's initiative.

"What is she contacting me for? I thought she'd died!" I was very standoffish at first because of the situation that happened so long ago. Then I said, "You know what? Just meet with her." If it's not meant to be, if we've no longer got the same things going on, it's not meant for us to be. Oh my God! It has been awesome! I met with her, and both of us—in the parking lot—we just cried! And we both had things in common. She has three kids, I have three kids. And we just connected. It's almost like she did some growing up, and I did some growing up. I felt better about myself, I felt that I could reach out to her . . . I wish I'd had these tools so long ago. Maybe we didn't have to spend nine years apart. But that's another thing that came out of this study. I've got my great friend back! . . . I'm just thankful that we have each other again!

Because Nina's survey responses had indicated that the study helped her find her purpose in life, I asked her to tell me more. How did she phrase that purpose to herself? She paused for a moment. Then, quietly and with great reverence, she told me, "I have been trying to spread the love, spread the peace. I try to pick people up from feeling down." Whether with the cashier at the grocery store, clients at work, or her family and friends, Nina had stories to tell of how she reached out to others during ordinary encounters and tried to lift their spirits, tried to help them in whatever small ways she could. Because of our study, she now tries to live her life with positivity each day—to live in the moment. "I honestly believe the meditations made a huge impact on my life . . . My soul grew. I just feel more peace. I think that's how a person can have their soul grow—by feeling more peace. I wish the wars would stop, but people need to find peace within themselves before they can spread the peace out to others."

It's gratifying beyond words for me to learn that—using the tools we gave her to increase her positivity—Nina turned her life around. She transformed herself for the better, going from a sad state of languishing to an inspiring state of flourishing. She dug in and invested her time and energy in positivity. And her efforts paid off in a big way. In the space of three months, she literally changed her life and became a beacon of positivity. Her transformation was nothing short of stunning.

If you're like most people, you can identify with the emptiness Nina felt at the start. You can identify with the stress, the struggle, the rut, the stagnant pool of languishing. Maybe you're wading through it now, going through the motions of life, but hardly feeling alive. Now think about your own story, three months from now. Suppose that you, like Nina, decide to experiment with positivity. Suppose you commit to changing your daily routine in ways that seed more joy, more serenity, and more love. Meditation is not the only way. Many paths can lead to the same outcome. Indeed, Part II of this book describes dozens of strategies for increasing your positivity ratio. Suppose that for the next three months you experiment with them. In what ways will your story be the same as Nina's? In what ways will it be unique? How might you use the story of Nina's turnaround to catapult yourself toward your best future, toward your own stunning turnaround?

Nina's story excites me all the more because she's just one of many whom we've helped. Like Nina, hundreds of people have participated in my positivity-boosting studies—women and men juggling the demands of work and family, some younger than Nina, some older, some earning more, some less, some investing as much or more time in learning how to be more positive, and some less. Success stories abound.

Safety in Numbers: The Open Heart Study

Some 200 of Nina's co-workers volunteered for the same study in which Nina took part. Though originally the study was advertised as an investigation of how meditation reduced stress, we've come to call it the Open Heart Study. We didn't open hearts the way cardiac surgeons do, but with positivity. From the data we gathered at Nina's workplace, we learned that our non-surgical intervention is an extraordinarily efficient and effective way to jump-start positive life changes.

Analyzing the data for this large field experiment brought us many "Eureka!" moments. For years we'd had the evidence that positivity and flourishing go hand-in-hand, but our past data did not allow us to untangle cause and effect. To do that, we needed a true experiment—an intervention study in which one randomly assigned group of people increased their daily diet of positivity, and another didn't.

I can't overemphasize the importance of random assignment. Without it, you'd never know whether some other characteristic of the people who stepped up their positivity was the true source of their good outcomes. Maybe people who start a meditation practice are more conscientious or curious than those who don't. Maybe they're more spiritual. By assigning people to groups at random, as a scientist I can be certain that any consequential differences between people "come out in the wash"—that is, different types of people are equally represented in each group. Using random assignment is a key way scientists go out of their way to make their tests as fair and unambiguous as possible. With it, the odds that increased positivity is the source of good outcomes in this study skyrocket.

Another way that I safeguard the conclusions I draw from an experiment like this is to gather boatloads of numbers. As you know by now, I'm a measurement junkie. Whereas another spouse might ask, "Honey, how are you feeling today?" when I want to know how much pain my husband is experiencing, I simply ask, "Zero to ten?" This is a tried-and-true measurement tool that pain researchers developed long ago: zero means no pain, and ten means the worst pain you've ever experienced. In this context, the number six means more to me than a mumbled "not so good." Likewise, Nina and the other employees who took part in this experiment gave daily numeric ratings to their emotions on a measurement tool much like the one I'll introduce you to in chapter 8. They also completed longer surveys to assess a range of personal resources—things we can all draw on to manage the ups and downs of daily living. With these measurement tools, we took a "snapshot" of where each person stood as the experiment began. A few weeks after the meditation workshop ended, we took another snapshot using these same measures, to assess whether and how people had changed over the preceding three months.

We also zoomed in to take a very detailed snapshot of the emotions people experienced on an ordinary workday. For this we used a measurement tool called the Day Reconstruction Method. (Because I think this might be useful for you too, I'll describe it in more detail in chapter 8.[7]) For this, Nina and our other study participants divided their day into a series of episodes—like the scenes of a movie—typically lasting anywhere between ten minutes and two hours. A first episode might be "lying in bed before getting up—twenty minutes." A second might be "getting ready—thirty minutes," followed by "eating breakfast with family—twenty minutes" and "commuting to work—twenty-five minutes." For each and every episode, we asked people a standard set of questions, including *What were you doing? Were you interacting with anyone?* and *What were you feeling?*

Gathering all these numbers allowed us to test a very specific hypothesis about a chain of causal events.[8] We predicted that practicing this way of meditating with an open heart would cause people to experience more positive emotions in their daily lives. In turn, we predicted that any increases in positivity that people experienced would cause them to grow—by building their personal resources. And, finally, we predicted that any growth in resources would matter, that people's growth would cause them to experience their lives as more fulfilling and reduce signs of depression. In testing this hypothesis—this psychological chain reaction—we tested the second core truth about positivity: that it transforms us for the better. I call this transformation the build effect.

Even though I'd predicted it, I still find the degree of the support the numbers held for the build effect stunning. I still wonder, could this really be true? My job is to keep testing this idea in different ways, looking deeper and at different facets of people's lives. I continue to design and conduct experiments that create every opportunity to reject the theory. So far, none of them do. So far, the numbers tell a story much like Nina's.

POSITIVITY RISES. Nina and her fellow volunteer co-workers dug in and practiced this new way of meditating. On average, they spent about eighty to ninety minutes of their valuable time each week listening to our guided meditations or practicing on their own. Little by little, the practice opened their hearts. The shift was subtle. It was also slow to emerge. On average, people didn't report any reliable increases in their positive emotions until their third week of meditation practice. Even so, positivity continued to rise steadily throughout the study. I find this profile of change fascinating. First, it's distinct from what you'd expect from placebo effects, which tend to be large and immediate. Second, it tells me that even small shifts in our daily diets of positivity—if enduring—can change our lives for the better.

We learned that all kinds of positivity steadily rose. Even though the meditations themselves centered on feelings of love, the benefits to positivity were not confined to this emotion. We saw the same subtle upward shift for joy, gratitude, serenity, interest, hope, pride, amusement, and awe as we did for love.[9] Intriguingly, we saw no changes whatsoever in people's reports of their negativity. It neither rose nor fell in any reliable way. So this open-heart intervention appeared to strike positivity surgically, causing it alone to rise. This is an important find. Scientists who investigate emotions often wonder whether effects attributed to increases in positivity might follow solely from decreases in negativity. Having observed no change in negativity in this study, we could rule out this concern.

IT GETS BETTER WITH TIME. If you don't already love the particular marriage of science and positivity that I'm offering, here's something that might win you over. It's something we would have never discovered had we not asked Nina and her colleagues to rate their emotions day in and day out on our five-point numeric scale. Having done so, we could examine the relationship between the amount of time people devoted to meditation practice each week and the amount of increase in positivity they enjoyed. Over the course of just nine weeks, this "dose-response" relationship *tripled*. Think of this as getting better and better at squeezing the juice out of an orange. At your first attempt, you extract only so much juice. Then you learn how to make the most of that orange and find ways to extract even more juice from it. Over time, the people in our study got better and better at extracting the "joy juice" from the time they devoted to their meditation practice.

This finding is especially fascinating because past scientists had discovered that most changes in emotions don't last: whether you win the lottery or become paraplegic, odds are that at a shockingly fast pace your emotional life will soon be back where it was before your lucky (or unlucky) day. That is, people adapt. Big emotional changes soon evaporate. Scientists have called this the *hedonic treadmill effect*.[10] Just as if you were on a treadmill, you may think you're going forward emotionally, but in fact you end up in the same place you started. What the numbers in the Open Heart Study suggest is that the slow and steady rise in positivity we observed actually outpaces the hedonic treadmill. It's like stepping off the treadmill and onto a moving walkway—you get more forward progress out of each step. The key may well be that this meditation practice is both routine and ever-changing. People can intentionally return to it time and again, but as they do so, they never find or do exactly the same thing. They can choose to deepen their practice, focus on new challenges, or tailor it to fit the needs of the day. The freshness it brings regenerates positivity time and again.

IT MAKES LIFE MORE ENJOYABLE. The daily emotion reports we solicited from Nina and her colleagues revealed that this particular meditation practice did indeed inject people's lives with more positivity, and that with continued practice people got an even bigger "bang for their buck" in terms of the positivity yield they extracted from their time spent meditating. When we zoomed in and asked our participants to give us episode-by-episode reports of their emotions on one particular morning we learned even more.[11]

When we examined the more than 900 episodes that Nina and her colleagues collectively described, we discovered that the amount of time people devoted to practicing meditation over the preceding three months continued to predict their positivity. Yet this was not because people had meditated on the particular morning we surveyed them. In fact, surprisingly few had. Certainly, positivity was higher during meditation times, and—for those few who happened to meditate that day—it was higher over the whole morning. But, even taking these momentary and same-day boosts in positivity into account, those who had devoted some time to meditation over the preceding three months had more positivity than those who had devoted little or no time to meditation. So, even on an ordinary morning some two weeks after Nina and her colleagues completed our meditation workshop, they were better off emotionally. That's how powerful and enduring this lifestyle change is. Like a time-release capsule, it keeps producing positivity even when people aren't meditating daily.

This made us wonder: When exactly *are* people reaping the benefits of their meditation practice? What are they doing? We knew from past research that positivity springs up especially when people interact with others. Given the clear focus on social connections within the meditations, we wondered whether boosts in positivity were experienced across the board, or only when people were interacting with others. The answer was both. Meditation produced more positivity regardless of whether people were alone or with others, yet the boosts in positivity were especially large during social interactions. Meditation brings out not only the best in you, but in others as well. At the very least, it helps you more fully enjoy their company.

OPEN HEARTS BUILD LIVES. Having established that starting a meditation practice indeed boosts people's daily diets of positivity, my students and I looked to the numbers to ask the question every scientist loves to ask: "So what?" What difference does boosting positivity make for people? We looked at how people had changed over the three months of the study. While I find Nina's personal story of transformation stunning, even more remarkable to me is the reliability of the build effect. The same pattern of growth emerged across Nina's colleagues: the slow and steady increases in positivity—induced by meditation practice—got people to grow. After learning this form of meditation, they had more resources at their disposal than they'd had three months earlier. Also, we saw evidence of growth across a wide range of resources, spanning four distinct areas of functioning. First, our participants gained mental resources, becoming better able to attend mindfully to the present and to savor upcoming pleasant events. Second, they gained psychological resources, becoming more accepting of themselves and seeing their lives as more purposeful. Third, they gained social resources, forging deeper and more trusting relationships and feeling more support from close others. And, fourth, they gained physical resources: they were healthier.

We then asked the numbers "So what?" again. What difference did all this growth in resources make for people? Plenty. People judged life to be more satisfying and fullfulling, and they experienced fewer signs of depression. Keep in mind that all these benefits sprang from spending just eighty to ninety minutes a week meditating with an open heart. More remarkable still was that we could statistically isolate that *all* of these benefits of meditation were caused by increases in positivity. Positivity was the active ingredient, the engine of change. In other words, if meditation didn't budge positivity, it built nothing. If Nina's colleague slept through the meditations, feeling nothing, then it's unlikely that they did her any good. People's lives changed only when positivity rose.

The great news here is that you can know whether or not your life is on the right track, whether or not you're on a path of growth. Put simply, if your heart is moved with positivity, you are moving toward growth. You're building a better life.

What Are You Gaining?

What might this better life entail for you? What gets built? In my scholarly work, I use the all-encompassing term *resources* to describe what's gained. By this I mean your reserves—any enduring part of yourself that you might draw on later, when you face challenges, setbacks, or new opportunities. They are the tools in your toolbox, the resources at your disposal. The beauty of this term is that it is broad and flexible enough to cover the diverse range of human qualities that are touched by positivity. Positivity can help you grow psychologically, mentally, socially, and physically.

POSITIVITY BUILDS PSYCHOLOGICAL STRENGTHS. There's a lot of talk these days about character. Where does it come from? Were you born with it? Did your parents give it to you, or was it your schooling? The downside of typical discussions about character is the assumption that your strengths are immutable, fixed in stone. Yet, given the ever-changing nature of our bodies and brains, I think it's more reasonable to think of psychological strengths as habits. Whereas some of your habits seem lifelong, others change over time. Picture yourself changing a habit. My guess is that you'll picture putting in concerted effort, deliberate thinking, even training. In other words, you'll plan out a formal process to turn your bad habit into a good one. But your habits can also change incidentally, without effort, thought, or plan. Your habits can change with the accumulation of negativity or positivity in your life.

Consider Nina's transformation. All her life, she was the shy one. She lacked confidence. She dwelled on her failings. She felt she merely existed. Now she's the one who reaches out to others, who accepts the challenging service calls. Now difficulties just roll off her shoulders. For the first time her life has purpose. Positivity built these psychological strengths in her. She didn't take assertiveness training or go to resilience school, she simply became more open. And over time this newfound openness transformed her life.

I've seen this pattern of growth many times in my scientific data. People who experience more positivity in their lives grow psychologically. They become more optimistic, more resilient, more open, more accepting, and more driven by purpose.[12] Certainly, having all these good qualities can bring on positive feelings. Yet the Open Heart Study confirms that the causal arrow can also run in the other direction. Positivity can build these good qualities—in all of us.

POSITIVITY BUILDS GOOD MENTAL HABITS. What about your habits of mind? How often do you find yourself doing one thing but thinking about another? Do you ever get so wrapped up in your own head that you fail to fully appreciate the beauty of nature that surrounds you, your children's laughter, or the good smells coming from the kitchen as your partner cooks you dinner? From the research described in chapter 4, we know that positivity opens us to the moment, allowing us to take in and appreciate more of our surroundings. From the Open Heart Study we also know that positivity can build enduring mental habits of openness. In other words, when our participants cultivated these open-hearted moments through meditation, they elevated their daily intake of positivity. Fast-forwarding three months, we find that this greater positivity has created more open-minded mental habits. Our participants became habitually more aware of their surroundings, more mindful. They got better at savoring what was good in their lives. They even got better at considering many different ways to reach their goals. They could find multiple pathways around their problems. These changes didn't reflect only the momentary effects of positivity, but were enduring mental shifts. Over time, and with repeated experience, positivity can create in you these same mental habits.

POSITIVITY BUILDS SOCIAL CONNECTIONS. The greater openness that positivity creates has some surprising interpersonal implications. First and foremost, your positivity is energizing to those around you. It's a large measure of what makes you attractive. Also, it's contagious. When you share your own joy, it ignites joy in others, a process that can forge lasting social ties.[13] The more you open up and share your heartfelt positivity with others, the stronger your connections to others become.[14] This was certainly true for Nina. After being in our study, she connected better with clients, family, and friends—even strangers.

The emotion of gratitude illustrates this nicely. As gratitude opens your heart, it creates the urge to do something kind for the person who was kind to you. Scientists have carefully studied the downstream effects of expressing heartfelt gratitude. The evidence shows that when we share our gratitude—whether in words, kindnesses, or gifts—we fertilize our relationships, helping them grow stronger and closer. Indeed, the degree of appreciation young people show to a romantic partner after receiving a thoughtful Valentine's Day gift can forecast how long the relationship lasts. When brand-new college roommates are coaxed to express their appreciation to each other, they become closer friends.[15]

Even within long-standing intimate relationships, the impact of positivity is huge. Scientific studies show that shared moments of laughter and joviality between partners deepen their relationship, making it more satisfying to both.[16] Other studies show that couples who express high levels of positivity to each other build up important reserves that help them weather the inevitable hardships they will face. Statistically, they are far less likely to get divorced.[17] In sharing your positivity with others—whether through laughter, kindness, or genuine smiles—you convey "let's build something together." And whether you build a temporary connection or a lasting bond, these ties create the social fabric that weaves you into the social world that surrounds you.

POSITIVITY BUILDS PHYSICAL HEALTH. Consider your physical health. Although it's easy to see that becoming healthier can be a cause for joy—or that getting sick can spoil positivity—scientists are beginning to appreciate much deeper connections between positivity and health.[18] Remember Nina's headaches and stomach pain? When she finally learned how to relax deeply into positivity, her pains melted away. We saw similar health improvements across her colleagues in the Open Heart Study. On increasing their daily diets of positivity, people found themselves healthier. They reported fewer sore throats, less nausea, even less acne.

This isn't just a matter of perception. Positivity is now linked to solid and objective biological markers of health. For instance, people's positivity predicts lower levels of stress-related hormones[19] and higher levels of growth-related[20] and bond-related hormones.[21] Positivity also sends out more dopamine[22] and opioids,[23] enhances immune system functioning,[24] and diminishes inflammatory responses to stress.[25] With positivity you are literally steeped in a different biochemical stew. Perhaps it's not surprising, then, that positivity brings lower blood pressure,[26] less pain,[27] fewer colds,[28] and better sleep.[29] People high on positivity also have lower disease risks. They are less likely to have hypertension,[30] diabetes,[31] or a stroke.[32] Scientists have already confirmed that positivity predicts longer lives. Uncovering the health consequences of positivity begins to tell the story of how this happens.

Let's talk about love. How do you know your partner loves you? Words can tell, but don't you find that hugs tell more? Think of the last time you had a long, close hug from your partner. Not that quick hug you use to say hello or good-bye. That's merely the full-body equivalent of a peck on the cheek. I mean a real heart-to-heart hug. You and your partner wrap your arms around each other and hold on tight. This kind of hug lasts closer to a minute than a second. When I need a hug like this, I tell my husband, "I need to be plugged in." That's how reenergizing I find our real heart-to-heart hugs to be. Maybe you've felt that too.

I had lunch recently with Kathleen Light, an internationally acclaimed scientist who has done groundbreaking work on how hugs and other forms of physical affection affect our health. What she's discovered is that loving touch does all kinds of good for your body. And the effects are not just momentary. Any single hug is unlikely to change your physical makeup. Rather, people who get hugs like this often—every day—actually have higher circulating levels of oxytocin (a healthy neuropeptide) and lower blood pressure than everybody else.[33] These findings are fully compatible with experimental studies of animals, and now of humans too. Animals stroked lovingly on their bellies over a stretch of days come to have higher oxytocin and lower blood pressure compared with untouched animals.[34] So do husbands and wives whose spouses have learned how to touch their partners' head, neck, and shoulders in loving ways.[35]

Through frequent close body contact, then, love literally gets under your skin, making you healthier. What I love about Kathy

Light's findings about hugs is that they mirror the build effect of positivity. Although any single hug—or moment of positivity—is unlikely to change your life, the slow and steady accumulation of hugs—or positivity—makes a huge difference. So find a way to increase your daily dose of genuine, heart-to-heart, hang-on-tight hugs. You will not only give and receive good feelings, but over time, you'll give and receive good health.

The View from Here

My guess is that for about as long as you can remember, you've heard marketers claim that their particular product or service will "change your life." I certainly have. And if you're like me, the result of this relentless collective effort to influence your consumer choices is well-founded cynicism. You come to distrust such sweeping claims. Why should you buy it? Where's the proof that life will change?

But I'm a scientist, not a marketer. I choose my words very carefully. My claims are evidence-based. I have more than twenty years of on-the-job training in honing down my words to prevent overstatements.

But from here, surveying the landscape of the latest scientific evidence for the build effect, I say with confidence: *positivity can change your life.*

Nina's account of her own transformation is riveting. For some of you, her words will be enough to inspire you to experiment with positivity.

But she's just one person. Maybe you're not at all like Nina. Or maybe you've become jaded to testimonials. If so, perhaps—like me—you'll find comfort in the numbers. That's what the Open Heart Study offers: more than a hundred stories of personal change, gathered numerically and with scientific rigor. The evidence confirms that when people increase their daily diets of positivity, they change their lives.

Some of you may need this kind of proof before you take note, before you're inspired to cultivate more positivity in your own life.

Either way, you now know that the effects of positivity are not random or isolated. They are predictable and sweeping. Your life is a complex tapestry of your psychological strengths, mental habits, social connections, physical health, and more. In the span of three months, positivity can change these various parts of you in beautiful synchrony. At a deep level, positivity changes who you are. And those changes can make life itself more fulfilling.

This is the second core truth about positivity: it transforms us for the better. And the better you are, the better you're able to face the challenges of life. Hardships are inevitable; they won't disappear just because you raise your positivity ratio. But they can be easier to handle. The next chapter shows how.

CHAPTER 6

Bounce Back from Life's Challenges

What is to give light must endure burning.
—Victor Frankl[1]

Bad things happen to all of us. When they do, many of us crumble or grumble, but others bounce right back to face the world again, often even stronger than before. Have you ever wondered what makes the difference? My studies suggest that positivity is perhaps the best-kept secret of people who, against all odds, keep on bouncing back.

I grew up hearing people say, "Everyone remembers where they were the day JFK was shot." I didn't. I had just graduated from embryo to fetus.

For many Americans, 9/11 is their landmark event, like the JFK assassination.

I was at my sister's home in Minneapolis. I'd flown in the night before to attend the funeral of my cousin, who had died after a long battle with cancer. His death was hard on me. We were about the same age. He was married, with two young kids. And he was a scientist and a professor, too. Oddly, we'd really only just gotten to know each other through sharing ideas at a family gathering about our respective research programs. The last time I'd seen him, he'd given me some useful leads on work in his field (kinesiology) that connected to my own work. He was a generous spirit. I was going to miss him.

So, that morning, as we were getting ready for the midday funeral, my sister received a call from her husband on his way to work, saying, "Turn on the television." We did. The first tower had been hit. Weakened already from grief, we slumped into the couch in confusion. *Was that an accident?* we wondered. Then the second tower was struck. This was no accident. In a heartbeat, my entire world no longer felt safe.

As we drove to the funeral, several towns away, my sister and I were numb. Yet the moment I entered the church for this sad ritual, I began to feel reassured. The world would go on. People would still come together when loved ones died, to comfort one another with hugs and kind words, to give and receive love, despite the grief and confusion of larger-scale tragedies. My heart went out to my cousin's two boys. If my world no longer felt safe under this new shadow of terrorism, I could only imagine what they felt.

We turned on the radio as we drove from the church to the cemetery and learned that all flights were canceled until further notice. My heart sank. I was supposed to fly home to my own boys (my husband and firstborn) that evening. As we walked to the grave site, the skies were strangely silent. Even though I was surrounded by my family, I felt stranded. I needed to find a way back to my home. I yearned to hold my baby and feel the reassurance of my husband's arms.

Several confusing hours passed. I called every car-rental agency, but none were accepting one-way bookings. Finally, I called Amtrak. Thank God for Amtrak. I got the last ticket for the September 12 train from Minneapolis to Ann Arbor. With the transfer in Chicago, it would be nearly a seventeen-hour trip, but worth it!

That September 12 train was full of displaced airline passengers. And that day this group of strangers was talking. They shared their own all-too-fresh 9/11 stories and their concerns about friends and family who lived or worked near the towers. Everyone seemed to have a tie to New York. All hearts were tender with a fusion of empathy, vulnerability, and more.

The man sitting next to me and I shared our stories and concerns with each other like long-lost friends. *What would the United States be like from now on? What would it feel like to fly next time?* Deep into our hours-long friendship, he asked me if I thought people would ever be the same. I thought for a moment. I heard the buzz of conversation and connection all around us on the train. Every so often, a peal of laughter would erupt somewhere in the car. "Do you hear that?" I asked my companion. "People are laughing. I think they are already the same." Hurt, yes, but still the same.

Trying times almost inevitably bring negativity. Unchecked, the narrowed mindsets of negativity can pull you on a downward spiral and drain the very life out of you. Yet even while unseen forces pull you down, you can choose a different course. You can put the brakes on negativity's downward spiral and rebound. The key is to uncover your inner wellspring of heartfelt positivity. Positivity can loosen negativity's grip on your mental outlook. It opens your heart and your mind to a broader range of possibilities. As it does, it sets you on an upward spiral, a positive trajectory that cuts through dark times and leads you back to higher ground, stronger than ever.

Yes, we can all be astonishingly resilient. Indeed, this is your birthright as a human being. You can bend without breaking. And even when you least suspect it, you can rebound. The good news is that you already have what it takes to bounce back, untold reserves in your inner wellspring of positivity. By helping you regain your perspective, moments of joy, love, gratitude, and inspiration remove negativity's blinders and put the brakes on downward spirals. Positivity, I've discovered, is at the heart of human resilience.

Serendipitous Science

I arrived back in Ann Arbor near midnight on September 12, 2001. After a day or two of simply holding my family tight, I got back to work. I was on sabbatical and thick into writing about what I know best: positive emotions. It wasn't easy. I was plagued by doubt. I wondered, *Who will care?* I honestly felt that the science of positivity was no longer relevant in this new era of terrorism. For the first time, I questioned the relevance of my life's work. My mission was unraveling into a lifeless heap of numbers and words.

About a day into this gloomy funk, somehow I recognized that the sudden pessimism about my work was depression talking. Like most Americans, I was feeling distraught about world events and the tragedies of 9/11. True to form, my distress was pulling me down into a negativity abyss.

Then I remembered those people who'd been laughing on the train a few days earlier. Was their laughter irrelevant? My past work told me it wasn't. Data from my published studies suggested that positivity could be a lifeline—an important way of coping with adversity. I regrouped and began to wonder how I could best test the idea that *even now,* in the midst of this national tragedy, positive emotions were still valuable. I was instantly reenergized.

Then it hit me. We had just completed a large study in which we'd measured the purported resilience levels of more than 100 college students using a simple survey. Perhaps we could find those folks again to investigate resilience in action in the wake of 9/11. Did their ranking on the resilience survey predict correctly how they were doing during these trying times? If so, were positive emotions central to their ability to rebound? Within days we had the approvals we needed to recontact those students.[2] We invited them back to complete additional surveys.

I'd estimated these college students' odds of being resilient with a survey developed by psychology pioneer Jack Block of the University of California, Berkeley, and his then graduate student, Adam Kremen. With items like "I enjoy trying new foods I have never tasted before," "I like to take different paths to familiar places," and "Most people I meet are likeable," it's hard to see at first blush how these traits add up to resilience. Yet, over his long career, Jack Block had amassed a mountain of data—gathered over five decades—on how ordinary people fared through life's ups and downs, twists and turns. Some of these people crumbled after hardships, whereas others bounced back. What personality styles made the difference? Which inner resources forecast people's ability to bounce back from adversity and meet the ever-shifting demands of daily life? Pursuing questions like these, Block and Kremen distilled their insights into the fourteen items of their Ego-Resiliency Scale.[3] This is the tool I used to predict which people had personality styles that equipped them to bounce back from hard times. I didn't know in advance whether these students would actually show resilient outcomes. Whether they did—or, more precisely, *how* they did—was what I was after.

When we reconnected with the folks who'd earlier taken Block and Kremen's resiliency measure, we asked them many things. We asked them to describe the most stressful situation they'd experienced since 9/11 that was in some way related to the attacks. We asked them how often they'd been feeling each of several discernible positive and negative emotions. We also measured their psychological strengths, including their optimism, tranquillity, and life satisfaction. Finally, we asked them to report any symptoms of depression they'd experienced in the days since 9/11.

These college students lived in Ann Arbor, Michigan, safely removed from Ground Zero. Even so, like most Americans, they experienced considerable stress after 9/11. They were worried about friends and family who lived or worked in New York City or Washington, D.C. They were afraid of future terrorist attacks and the possibility of war. Some were afraid to fly. Others were afraid to go to a football game. If you follow Big Ten football, you know that Michigan Stadium is the largest open-air sports arena in the United States. And on game days it's always filled to capacity, seating more than 110,000 fans. Some of those fans feared that their beloved "Big House" was now a conspicuous terrorist target. On game days, dozens of banner-pulling planes circle the stadium. Blimps too. That season, all game-day flights were banned.

We learned a lot from these students about how resilience works. The ones who scored high on the survey, suggesting they had a resilient personality style, did indeed show resilient outcomes. They bounced back faster than those who scored low. After 9/11, feeling depressed was the norm. Yet those with a resilient personality style showed the fewest signs of clinical depression. They even grew psychologically stronger in some respects: compared with their pre-9/11 responses, they became even more optimistic, more tranquil, and more fulfilled with their lives. People with resilient personalities were clearly coping better than the rest.

The most pivotal difference, though, between those with and without resilient personality styles was their positivity. It was the secret of their success. It was the mechanism behind their lesser depression and their greater psychological growth. In short, we discovered that resilience and positivity go hand-in-hand. Without positivity, there is no rebound.

At first blush, you might wonder, "What was there to feel good about? Did these people have their heads in the sand?" These are good questions. What if people bounced back by denying reality? Or by selfishly considering only their own well-being? If that were the case, then resilience would come at the price of truth and compassion.

Our data suggested otherwise. In fact, those with more or less resilient personality styles reported similar stresses following the attacks. According to national polls, after 9/11 virtually everyone felt angry, sad, and fearful. Our study participants were no different. Whether they scored high or low on the resilience survey, negative emotions ran high. They also felt concern and sympathy for those newly suffering, and their compassion outpaced all other emotions— even anger, sadness, and fear.

People who bounced back were not in denial or selfish. Like everyone else, they were pained by negativity and moved by compassion. Mixed in with their suffering and concern, they also experienced positive emotions. Perhaps like my fellow passengers on that Amtrak train, these resilient students felt joy, love, and gratitude when connecting with others. Perhaps they were inspired and awed by the groundswell of unity and compassion both within their local community and around the globe. Perhaps they were deeply curious about the unfolding world events, and hopeful about the future despite the grim reality of this trying time. Whatever the source, moments of positivity like these were what made the difference. Positivity put the brakes on depression's downward spiral and set these people on an upward spiral of growth.

The events of 9/11 shocked the world. Serendipitously, I had data in hand that ranked a large group of students by their resilient personality styles. Impressively, that pre-crisis measure of resiliency could forecast the degree of positivity people experienced during the uncertain and troubling weeks after the terrorist attacks. And positive emotions turned out to be the active ingredient that enabled certain people to bounce back and grow stronger. I'm thankful that I regained my own faith in positivity in time to gather these eye-opening data. Positivity matters. And it especially matters during trying times.[4]

In the years since I published these results, other researchers have independently tested my claim that positivity is the active ingredient that enables certain people to attain resilient outcomes. Whereas we tested young adults, another notable series of studies tested adults over sixty. We tracked people's responses after a national crisis, but these studies tracked people's responses after personal crises, ranging from minor, everyday stressors to major life events, like losing a spouse.[5] In study after study, just as we found, researchers found that people who bounce back show more emotional complexity when facing stressors.

When stress arrives at your doorstep, does positivity fly out the window? For many people, it does. But not for those who score high on resiliency surveys. Instead of simply succumbing to negativity, these folks also retain their positivity. Their emotions are more complex because their positivity sits side by side with their negativity. They don't deny the reality of negativity, but they don't wallow in it, either. Just as I saw in my study after 9/11, this ability to tap into positivity spells the difference between stress reactions that escalate and endure for days and those that dissipate more quickly. So, whether you're young, old, or in between, positivity may well be your best resource in a crisis. It's what you need to reverse the course of a downward spiral and spring back.

The Heart of Resilience

Let's zoom in and take a close look at the heart of resilience. I mean that literally: How do the physical hearts of people with resilient and less resilient personality styles react differently to stress? In my early laboratory studies, I took a close look at the underlying mechanics of resilience by examining the ups and downs of people's emotions and blood pressure. It's no surprise that when you feel anxious your blood pressure rises. What may be surprising is that you have a hidden "reset" button for these spikes in blood pressure: your own positive emotions. Good feelings not only flush out bad feelings, they also quiet your heart and quickly bring your blood pressure back to normal.[6]

Here's how we discovered this. Volunteers visited my laboratory to participate in a study of emotions and cardiovascular reactivity. They'd sit in a comfortable chair while one of my graduate students attached tiny sensors to their skin to track moment-by-moment changes in their heart rate, blood pressure, and the constriction within their blood vessels. After participants got used to this somewhat strange situation, we tracked these cardiovascular measures at rest for a few minutes. We wanted to know how each person's heart pumped when they weren't feeling anything in particular. Then, applying considerable time pressure, we asked these volunteers to prepare a speech on "Why you are a good friend." To build the psychological pressure even further, we told them that we'd videotape their speech and have it evaluated by their peers. As you can imagine, this surprise public-speaking assignment made people anxious. Indeed, that was our goal—to make everyone who participated in this study anxious. And we thoroughly succeeded! We know this from the verbal reports we gathered from our participants later on, and also from looking at changes in the cardiovascular measures we were tracking. Heart rates shot up. Blood pressures rose. Veins and arteries constricted.

Having met our goal of making everyone anxious, the real experimenting could begin. At the height of this laboratory-induced negativity, participants switched their attention away from the speech task and toward something else: a short film clip. We randomly assigned one of four different film clips, of which two were positive, one evoking serenity by showing ocean waves and the other mild amusement, by showing a puppy playing with a flower. One clip was negative, evoking sadness by showing a young boy crying at the death of someone he loved. The last was neutral, simply an old-fashioned computer screen saver that showed an abstract display of colored sticks piling up.

What you need to appreciate about the two positive film clips we used in this experiment was how extraordinarily mild they were. When people view them under normal viewing conditions—that is, when they aren't anxious about public speaking—they evoke no changes whatsoever in the cardiovascular measures we tracked.

Here you also need to know that we told participants in advance that if "by chance" they were shown a film clip, this meant that "the computer" had placed them in the "no speech" condition. That is, the start of the film clip signaled that they were off the hook for delivering the dreaded speech.[7] The very moment that the film clip started, we began to track the effects of positivity. We tracked how long it took—in seconds—for each person's cardiovascular reactions to the speech task to return to their own baseline resting levels. Some hearts, we learned, were quelled within a few seconds, while others took more than a minute to calm down. Here again, positivity made the difference. Participants who were selected at random to view one of the two positive clips—the ocean waves or the playing puppy—had the fastest cardiovascular recovery. Those who saw either the neutral or negative clips had the slowest recovery.

I've called this the "undo effect" of positive emotions. Positivity can quell or "undo" the cardiovascular aftereffects of negativity. This is your hidden reset button. You can hardly stop your heart from beating faster and harder when you face stress and negativity. But, with positivity, you can rein in those reactions and regain a calm heart.

Recall, too, that the positive clips we used didn't even budge people's heart rates and blood pressures under normal viewing conditions. So even though positive emotions may not "do" anything to your heart, they can "undo" the excursions it takes with negativity. At this core bodily level, positivity puts the brakes on negativity and equips you to rebound, both physically and emotionally. Knowing that prolonged cardiovascular reactivity to stress may pave the way to heart disease,[8] this undo effect may be one key way that positivity keeps us healthy.

My early experiments on the ability of positivity to "undo" negativity were important because they demonstrated that positivity held a key to recovery. There was nothing special about the particular people who showed the fastest cardiovascular recovery in these experiments. Indeed, they had been assigned to view the positive films completely at random. Also, two different forms of positivity—serenity and amusement—appeared equally good at hastening recovery, making me more confident that it wasn't something unique to ocean waves or cute animals at work here. What mattered were the good feelings that these different sorts of images created.

We know that when stress levels run high, some people are more likely than others to self-generate positivity. In the 9/11 study, it was those with resilient personality styles who reported the most positivity. Their positivity was what helped them bounce back. So we decided to explore the heart of the resilient personality style in the laboratory. We tested whether people with resilient personality styles "bounce back" at a physical level as well.

One of my former doctoral students, Michele Tugade (now an assistant professor at Vassar College), tackled this question in her dissertation. Michele invited people with more or less resilient personality styles to visit our laboratory, where she tested them one by one. Using our same cardiovascular measures and speech task, she built people's anxiety and then suddenly let them off the hook. We then counted how many seconds it took for each participant to return to his or her own resting levels of heart rate, blood pressure, etc.

This time there *was* something special about the people who showed the fastest cardiovascular recovery. They were the ones who scored highest on Block and Kremen's measure of resilient personality styles. They were also the ones who walked into our laboratory with more positivity. They even told us later that although the speech task made them anxious, they also found it to be somewhat positive as well. It was an interesting challenge that they were happy to take on. Here again, positive feelings turned out to be pivotal. People with resilient personality styles rebounded fast only to the extent that they experienced higher than average positivity.[9]

When we peered into the heart of resilience—tracking heart rate, blood pressure, and constriction of blood vessels before, during, and after the public speaking task—we saw that even though these physiological measures spiked just as high for people with more and less resilient personality styles, they came down faster for those with the most resilient traits. Within seconds, their hearts had calmed. By contrast, the hearts of others remained perturbed. This pattern of data tells us people with resilient personality styles are indeed emotionally responsive. They are not disconnected, head-in-sand, unflappable robots. They are moved just like the rest of us. But when circumstances suddenly change for the better, they are quick to move on. They let go.

Positivity is what makes them nimble. More than others, people with resilient personality styles put the "undo effect" of positivity to work. They bounce back—even at a core physiological level—because their inner wellspring of positive emotions bubbles over. Positivity serves as their secret "reset" button.

The Brain of Resilience

Another of my former doctoral students, Christian Waugh (now a postdoctoral research fellow at Stanford University), probed the inner workings of resilience even further. For his dissertation, Christian used a brain imaging technique called functional magnetic resonance imaging (or fMRI) together with a cleverly designed experiment. His aim was to create a new window onto understanding how those with varying resilient personality styles differed. His findings have been turning heads at neuroscience meetings ever since. They illuminate the unique thinking styles that underlie the ability to bounce back from bad events.[10]

The clever laboratory task that Christian designed involved gently "threatening" people that they might have to face something noxious, and then tracking their reactions over time. The "threat" came as a simple visual cue—either a circle or a triangle. Participants learned that one cue signaled that an upcoming photograph might or might not present some disturbing image, like a burn victim or a disgustingly filthy toilet. About half the time it did. The rest of the time this same cue was followed by a completely harmless photograph, of a light switch, for example, or a chair. The other cue, by contrast, always signaled that the upcoming photograph would be neutral.[11] This is how one simple shape—say the triangle—came to mean "threat," whereas the other—the circle—came to mean "safety." Christian's goal was to examine resiliency before and after anticipated negativity.

Three findings stood out. First, just as Michele Tugade found that people with resilient personality styles showed faster cardiovascular recovery from anticipated negativity, Christian found that these people showed faster recovery from anticipated negativity in the insula, a brain area linked to conscious feeling states.

Second, during the cue phases of the study, when participants simply viewed the triangle or the circle, those with resilient personality styles showed *less* brain activity in a region known as the orbitofrontal cortex (or OFC). Scientists had previously linked this region with "worrying." The more you worry about what-ifs, the more your neurons in this area fire.

Third, Christian's brain scans suggested that the more people worked themselves up into a worried tizzy in anticipation of possible negativity, the slower they were to appreciate that they had in fact dodged a bullet. For people with resilient personality styles, less worry meant faster relief.

These were the three most compelling differences in brain activity between people with resilient personality styles and those without them. Also telling was when these two groups showed *no* differences in brain activity. For instance, no neural differences emerged when people viewed the noxious pictures. As in our previous studies, everyone was just as moved by actual negativity. Nothing suggests that resilience comes with emotional disengagement. On the contrary, resilience is marked by exquisite emotional agility.

The results of Christian's neuroimaging study bring new insights into the mental habits of resilient people. By tracking the patterns of blood flow in the brain, Christian discovered that when faced with threats, people with resilient personality styles worry less and rebound quicker.[12] This neural portrait of resilience resonates with the behavioral portrait of resilience that has emerged from decades of past studies. Both suggest that resilient people are highly attuned to the ever-changing circumstances in which they find themselves. They are emotionally nimble. They react to what is happening now, not to what-ifs. They don't spend energy worrying about the future. Instead, perhaps appreciating that they can cope with whatever comes their way, they adopt a wait-and-see attitude. They're also quick to tell the difference between good and bad—they don't overgeneralize or overreact. They minimize their angst by cutting out advance worry and afterglow obsessions, focusing instead on the reality of the present moment.

These mental habits are what you'd expect from mindfulness, a form of open-minded awareness marked by its focus on the present moment coupled with a nonjudgmental attitude. In chapter 4, I showed how openness and positivity feed on each other, each catalyzing the other in an upward spiral. Here we find openness going hand-in-hand with resilience. More than others, people with resilient personality styles make use of both positivity and openness. The openness that comes with positivity is what enables them to see the big picture, appreciate the now, and find the good within the bad. Openness is what dissolves negativity and enables people to make a strong comeback.[13]

Building Resilience

Worried that you may not be one of the lucky few who were born re-silient?[14] Don't be. You can build your own resilience levels. Perhaps you've already guessed how: by raising your positivity ratio. Resilience is an inner resource that grows over time. Positive emotions fertilize this growth.

In part, we drew this conclusion based on a study in which we measured people's resiliency levels at the start of the study, and again one month later. In between, we tracked the day-by-day ups and downs of their emotions. Once again we found that those who scored high on Block and Kremen's scale reported experiencing more positive emotions (there was no link to negative emotions). In addition, we found that the more positive emotions people experienced, the more their resilience levels grew over the month.[15] Resilience is a resource you can build.

We've put this idea to test in our laboratory. Again we called into service that dreaded public-speaking task and tracked moment-by-moment changes in heart rates and blood pressures. This time we tested what would happen if we shared the secret of resilient people with those who scored low on Block and Kremen's prescient survey, the ones without a resilient personality style. We told one randomly selected set of participants to try their best to get "psyched up" for the speech task, to think of it as a challenge they could meet and overcome. We reasoned that thinking about the task in this way would allow people to tap into their positive emotions. For the rest, we simply ratcheted up the anxiety as usual.

It turned out that telling people to get psyched up for the speech made all the difference for those who lacked a resilient personality style. The suggestion to be more open-minded in the face of hardship was all it took to unleash their positivity. And positivity was all it took to calm their soaring heart rates and blood pressures.[16]

To illustrate how positivity can build resilience, I'll use the story of one of my former doctoral students, Wendy Treynor. After she received her Ph.D., Wendy faced a job market that was not ready for her talents. As if being unemployed after investing years in advanced scientific training weren't burdensome enough, she got cancer.

Early in 2006, I caught up with her at one of the yearly scientific meetings we both attend. She was understandably fragile, unsure of what her future would hold. I knew her to be a great scholar. Her talent for thinking and writing surpassed that of most of her peers. She so clearly deserved to live and to work in her chosen field. Moved by her current condition and concerned about her health and livelihood, I offered what advice I could.

In the summer of 2006, the very week I was outlining this chapter, I received a letter from Wendy. After telling me that she'd finally found a postdoctoral position, she wrote:

> I have been thinking about what you told me—about maintaining that ratio of positive to negative emotions . . . and I've been actively doing it. Since I saw you I've been doing yoga every day and [taking] morning walks, as well as afternoon walks and evening swims. And my well-being is skyrocketing, my mood is almost consistently joyful and peaceful (even when things get rough). And most important of all, I feel actualized, fulfilled. I feel like I am flourishing, finally, for the first time in my life ever! And I thank you and all the other emotions researchers who have brought me to this place, either through their scientific knowledge and/or love and support . . . I'm so alive, Barb; I wish you could see me now. You would be so proud of me! I can't wait to see you and tell you about my new, wonderful life! Thank you for all your love and support!

At the next year's scientific meeting (in early 2007) I finally had my chance to "see her now." Her transformation was nothing short of stunning. Wendy—who I'd long known as an exceptionally bright and considerate, albeit sober, young woman—was absolutely radiant. Her warmth was palpable. Her smiles were frequent, genuine, and uninhibited. She told me about her new position. As it turned out, it wasn't the ideal position for her. Yet she was appreciating the best of what it offered. The difference between the Wendy I'd known and the one who sat across from me at breakfast on this day lay in her newfound efforts to cultivate her own positivity. For years she had ignored her creative side. Now, on evenings and weekends, beyond engaging in the physical joys of yoga, swimming, and walking, she was learning screenwriting, singing with other local singers, and writing a (soon to be published) book on what she'd learned about life and love from her cancer—which was now completely gone. She took responsibility for her own positivity, and her payoff was huge.

As you might imagine, Wendy's deep transformation touched my heart. Knowing the heart-wrenching setbacks she'd faced, I was overjoyed to see that she'd begun experimenting with positivity in her daily life with such clear and inspiring results. She was flourishing, better equipped to rebound "even when things get rough." Just like Nina and the others who took part in my Open Heart Study, Wendy's efforts to cultivate more joy, serenity, inspiration, and pride in her daily life helped her to grow, to change for the better. Also like Nina, Wendy discovered a new purpose to her life. She founded Healing Consulting, an organization that weaves together her scientific expertise and life experience to share what she's learned with others. Through her journey, Wendy has come to view self-generating positive emotions as a form of self-love, and she has developed her own theory to explain how people can achieve an enduring sense of harmony through this form of self-love.[17] Like all who truly flourish, Wendy is now driven to make a difference in the lives of others. I'm deeply gratified to know that the scientific understanding of positivity that I can share truly helps those I cherish when it matters most.

Up Close and Personal

Life was good when I began writing this chapter. I faced the usual ups and downs of juggling my career and a young family (my boys are now four and seven years old), but nothing major.

Then, in the midst of pulling my words together on resilience, the unthinkable happened. My husband developed serious and enormously painful complications following a routine outpatient surgery for an abdominal hernia. After a grueling day in the ER with tubes inserted virtually everywhere, he was admitted to the hospital. We were told he could come home when his GI tract "woke up" and could once again handle food. Until then, he'd be on an IV. Nobody could tell us how long this would be. The situation taught me a thing or two about resilience.

As if being in pain, in the ER, and, ultimately, confined to the hospital weren't bad enough, the room my husband was assigned to was drab and dreadful. Traction bars encaged his bed. The sole window provided a view of a brick wall. It broke my heart to leave him there alone, but with two young kids at home, I had no choice. Rather than accept his sentence to these depressing environs, I vowed to transform his space. My husband and I both knew the scientific evidence about the impact of views from hospital windows; hospitalized patients whose windows looked out onto nature's greenery had shorter hospital stays than those with views devoid of nature.[18] The first thing I brought from home was one of my husband's own cherished house plants. If the window wasn't going to supply him with the solace of nature, I'd bring nature into the room. In time, thanks to family, friends, and the farmer's market, his room was brimming with fresh-cut flowers and potted plants.

I also brought pictures of the people and places he loved: a recent eight-by-ten black-and-white portrait of me and our boys that my husband had framed for me for Mother's Day, a picture of our home, and pictures of his favorite spots on the beach. I remade the walls nearest his bedside with visual reminders of the people and places awaiting his return. I encouraged our two boys to think of what they might bring to lift their papa's spirits. They shared their artwork, soccer medals, marbles, and most treasured rocks. I brought my husband's down-filled pillow from home to replace the stiff, rubberized pillow the hospital supplied. I brought in his iPod. Now he had more than 5,000 songs at his fingertips, plus a handful of guided meditations. With the pleasures of taste unavailable to my husband for the time being, I sought to enliven all four of his remaining senses.

Days passed. We had no signs that this hospital stay would end anytime soon. Thanks to schools and childcare, I was able to be at the hospital from 10:00 a.m. to 5:00 p.m. each weekday. But I was stretched thin. I was suddenly a solo parent, trying to meet everyone's needs, not to mention my own. Making matters worse, I'd gone into this ordeal with a slight cold. With all the added strain, it developed into a sinus infection. It pained me to leave the hospital each evening. In the car, as I drove home by myself, I'd cry. When I got home I'd quickly pull myself together to parent my boys, hug them, feed them, and get them to bed. But my own bed was a sad place to go—too wide and too lonely without my husband. I couldn't enjoy its comforts, knowing the discomfort my husband endured in the narrow hospital bed he couldn't escape. This dreadful downward spiral tugged at me every night.

My aim throughout these difficult days was simply to *be* with my husband. To have him know, deep down, that no matter how painful or frightening this trial was, he was not alone. Although his nurses were great, it's not surprising that they too were stretched thin. So each day I would wash his hair and bathe his skin, working gingerly so as not to cause him undue pain or disturb the collection of medical paraphernalia that now draped his body. This could take an hour or more.

Several times each day I would walk with him, very slowly, with his IV pole as his walking stick. Walking was the only thing his doctors thought might bring his GI tract back to normal sooner. So, despite the pain and the difficulty, we walked. I also did the things he wanted to do, but couldn't: fluffed his pillow, kept his books and iPod within arm's reach, helped him sit up. When there was downtime, I simply held his hand, stroked his hair, or massaged his legs, watchful for signs that my touch was received as pleasant and not painful or irritating.

Seven days after his ill-fated surgery, my husband and I were both growing frustrated. When would this hospital stay end? Why weren't we hearing explanations from his doctor for all his symptoms, tests, and results? The days were molasses-slow. And somehow, although I'd spent whole days at the hospital, every single morning I missed his doctor's rounds. When I finally had a chance to speak with the doctor face to face, late that afternoon, we got more bad news. My husband had developed a life-threatening intestinal blockage. He needed emergency surgery that evening.

Once the news sunk in, I made one quick phone call to alert Julie, my friend and neighbor. When I called her back scarcely an hour later, she'd arranged what seemed to me a miracle. My boys would have dinner with her and her family. (She too has two young boys, so my boys thought it was a great playdate.) Our mutual neighbor, a high school student (who'd frequently babysat both for Julie's boys and my own), would put my kids to bed that night. The babysitter's father, a mutual friend, would spend the night at our house. And Julie herself would come to the hospital to bring me dinner and wait with me during the surgery. In the end, Julie's time with me in the hospital stretched to the wee hours of the morning.

I was moved to tears of gratitude by the fast-acting compassion of our whole neighborhood network. Their gifts of kindness provided exactly what I needed, both instrumentally and emotionally. With their help, I was freed up and fueled up to step up the care I offered my husband.

The second surgery was a success, thank goodness, but recovery was slow. My husband, traumatized by all that he'd endured, couldn't sleep. His pain wore on. He had recurring nightmares. At times he grew despondent and slipped into his own downward spiral. I continued to draw support from others so that I could support him. After eleven long days in the hospital on IV nutrients, he tasted solid food again for the first time. After twelve days they removed the IV and let him go home. He was in constant pain, nearly twenty pounds lighter, and extraordinarily weak, and his recovery was still slow. But I was so thankful to have him recuperating in our own bed at home.

My connections to others were what kept me from succumbing to the downward spiral that threatened to swallow me up each evening. The most cherished lesson I learned from this ordeal was how deep our support was from our new neighbors and friends. We'd moved to North Carolina scarcely more than a year earlier, but even so, neighbors delivered home-cooked meals to our door nearly every evening. Parents of our kids' friends invited our boys for extended weekend playdates—and fed them dinner—so that I could spend more time at the hospital with my husband. Sincere offers to help came from all corners. The flow of goodwill and kind actions touched my heart with bone-deep gratitude every day.

And for the first time in my life I learned to truly receive those kind actions and offers of help. Moved in a heartfelt way, I was able to be more fully open. Sure, I'd known for years and from volumes of data that positivity opens us. But my experiences during this time were neither subtle nor abstract. I could feel the hinges of my heart and mind give. I became so open that for the first time I fully trusted that people *wanted* to help. I even let others know what they could do that would be the most helpful. I needed milk, bread, and lunch box items, and felt free to ask, "Could you pick some up for me the next time you're at the grocery store?" I knew that evenings were long and lonely for my husband. "Do you think you could babysit for a few hours after my boys are in bed so I can make one last visit to the hospital today?" I longed to take my husband a selection of comedy DVDs, but couldn't find the time. "Could you find me the best all-time comedies?" Beyond what I ever had imagined, our neighbors and friends were spontaneously thoughtful and responsive to my expressed needs. Many, many times their compassionate acts brought tears of gratitude to my eyes.

Reflecting back on this surprise lesson in resilience convinces me that there's something missing from the portrait of resilience my work and writing has painted for you thus far—something important. The focus has been too narrow. Not simply a property of individuals, resilience runs through the social fabric of communities. This is because positivity knows no boundaries. It runs *between* us as much as it runs *within* us. My neighbors and friends opened their hearts and shared with me the gifts of their compassion and time. Their words and deeds touched and opened my heart, and unleashed more positivity within me, just when I needed it most. With their love and generosity permeating me, I was able to avert the downward tug of negativity that recurred each evening. It gave me fuel to bring love and generosity to my husband's hospital room each morning, to keep him buoyed up and afloat. Refueled as I was by others' positivity each day, I could better help my husband avert his own downward spiral. Day by day, he and I became closer and more attuned to each other. A oneness blossomed between us like never before.

Because negative emotions narrow your range of vision, a downward spiral cuts a dark and lonely path that insulates you further and further from the healing touch of community. Upward spirals are altogether different. Because positive emotions expand your range of vision, upward spirals are by design more social. That's what's missing from the old portrait of resilience. As an upward spiral clears your path, your mind and your heart become more fully open to connect with caring others. And each connection supplies its own positivity that refuels and opens you even further. The secret of resilience, then, is going beyond tapping your own well of heartfelt positivity and being open to drink from what springs from others.

Years earlier, my husband had given me a six-inch-long antique key. He called it the key to his heart. For twelve days I wore that key on a necklace as a reminder of the love I shared with him. Strangers would remark on the size of the key. After explaining the symbolic meaning it held for me, I'd say, "Big heart, big key." Long before we were married, I'd known that my husband had a big heart. Countless times, I'd received or witnessed his big, compassionate heart in action. By contrast, I was known for my big thoughts—and my big data sets! Yet, like the Grinch on Christmas morning, I felt my heart grow three sizes during those two weeks. I thank my community of neighbors, family, and friends for this palpable growth. Although I'd long known the benefits of positive emotions in a scholarly way, I felt those benefits now more intensely and poignantly than ever before. Just as science is never complete, neither is my own or anyone's heartfelt and firsthand appreciation for the wonders of this human life.

My bigger heart had room for many emotions, a wide fusion of negativity and positivity. This poignant mix helped me carry on. It allowed me to meet the demands of each moment without losing sight of the big picture. It allowed me to receive and enact compassion. And it allowed me to bounce back to writing this chapter—more resilient than ever before.

The View from Here

Hardships are inevitable, as I learned all too well from my husband's sudden plunge into hospital living.

As I see it, there are two basic responses to hardship. Despair or hope.

In despair, you multiply your negativity. Your fear and uncertainty can turn into stress. Your stress can morph into hopeless sadness, which in turn can breed shame. Worse than this mushrooming negativity, despair smothers and snuffs out all forms of positivity. With positivity extinguished, all possibilities for genuine connections with others are lost. Despair opens the gate to a downward spiral that may well lead you to rock bottom.

Hope is different. It's not the mirror reflection of despair. Your hope, in fact, acknowledges negativity with clear eyes. More important, though, your hope kindles further positivity within you. Even the most subtle shades of hope can be a springboard for you to feel love, gratitude, inspiration, and more. And these warm and tender feelings open your mind and your heart and allow you to connect with others.

So hope opens the gate to an upward spiral that empowers you to bounce back from hardship and emerge even stronger and more resourceful than before.

Some people—either genetically or intuitively—seem to understand the gifts of positivity better than the rest of us. We call those people *resilient*. They are the ones who smile in the face of adversity, reframe bad events as opportunities, and adopt a wait-and-see attitude about future threats. This doesn't mean that they never feel bad. They bleed just like everyone else. Yet because they also find ways to cultivate good feelings—even in the midst of crises—their bad feelings don't last as long. They rebound.

We can all become resilient. Positivity is your birthright. It's part of the complex mix of humanness that you inherited from a long line of ancestors. Resilience is not just for the chosen few. It's for the masses. It's ordinary magic.[19]

Now that you know the benefits of positivity—benefits that still pay out even in dire circumstances—you have more reason than ever to open your heart to genuine positivity. Welcome positivity even when you fear the worst. And when your world seems too bleak for positivity, turn to your neighbors, your loved ones, and your cherished memories. Be open to positivity wherever it springs forth. Let it revive and renew you. You too will bounce back.

So positivity bounces. Indeed, I see no straight lines here. Instead, I see bounces and spirals, twists and turns. Positivity's dynamic and complex range of motion demands an equally dynamic and complex approach to science. In the next chapter you'll see how this new approach emerged for me.

CHAPTER 7

The Positivity Ratio

People think angels fly because they have wings.
Angels fly because they take themselves lightly.
—ANONYMOUS

In chapter 1, when I introduced the positivity ratio, I said it had a "tipping point." What exactly does this mean? What's a tipping point?

The best way to explain it might be to remind you of a tipping point you know well already. Consider ice and water. Look at these familiar and indispensable substances of life with fresh eyes. At one level they seem dramatically different. Ice is solid, rigid, and immobile. Water is liquid, flowing, flexible, and dynamic. Yet here's the marvel: to change one into the other simply requires a change in temperature. If you raise the ambient temperature above zero degrees Celsius, rigid ice melts into flowing water.

It's hardly magic, at least to most grown-ups. We know ice and water are chemically the same. Both are H_2O, two parts hydrogen and one part oxygen. But this common chemical compound is subject to a simple tipping point. You can change it from one state to another—from solid to liquid—by changing its temperature.

The differences between languishing and flourishing seem to show similar properties. If we "warm up" the emotional climate of your life by increasing your positivity ratio above the critical tipping point, you'll begin to flourish. Just as zero degrees Celsius is a special number in thermodynamics, the 3-to-1 positivity ratio may well be a magic number in human psychology.

Of course, there's nothing supernatural here, no real "magic." Even so, I do see reason for awe. The world obeys universal natural laws, and sometimes these laws are shockingly simple. Human psychology—complex as it is—may be no different. Perhaps we too are subject to universal laws that have never before been articulated. These laws may map out an escape from the rigid and confining ice block of languishing. They may equip us to find our way to the more flowing, flexible, and dynamic life of flourishing.

I'm not asking you to accept my claim on faith. Instead, I'd like you to appreciate it based on the supporting scientific evidence. In this chapter, I describe how that evidence came together for me.

Match Made

The origin of the positivity ratio begins with my good friend and University of Michigan colleague, Jane Dutton, an endowed professor at Michigan's Ross School of Business. Jane, a cutting-edge scholar of relationships in the workplace,[1] is also a self-described matchmaker, but she doesn't connect lonely hearts; she connects people with promising, interrelated ideas. She'd connected me to soon-to-be collaborators in the past, so I'd come to trust her intuition.

Early in 2003 I received an e-mail from Marcial Losada. He said he'd developed a mathematical model—based on nonlinear dynamics—of my broaden-and-build theory and that we should talk. It turned out that Jane, having seen several possible points of connection between his work and mine, had suggested he read my work. I was a bit slow to respond. My second son had been born just weeks earlier, and I was dedicating my energies to my newly expanded family.

Fortunately, Marcial was persistent. He sent me an article he was writing. In it he made the case for how his past mathematical work fit with the ideas in my broaden-and-build theory. I was sufficiently intrigued to take an afternoon off from nesting with my family to meet with him.

Born and raised in Chile, Marcial was not a typical collaborator for me. At the time, he wasn't even an academic. Although he'd received his Ph.D. from my own department of psychology at the University of Michigan, he'd done so decades before I'd joined the faculty there. In the interim, he'd had a long career in industry. Recently retired and working as a business consultant, he'd begun to dabble again in what had become his passion: mathematical modeling of group behavior.

That first meeting was electric. Having read his then-unpublished paper,[2] I had a series of pressing questions for him. I wanted to understand the data that inspired his mathematical work. I wanted to learn more about the math itself. Sitting at his dining room table in front of his laptop—what he called his portable laboratory—we talked for hours. He shared the dynamic displays of the mathematical models that fit his data on business teams. I shared the connections I saw, not only to my past work on positivity and resilience, but also to my growing interests in human flourishing.

Hours into our lively discussion, he made a bold claim: based on his mathematical work, he could locate the exact positivity ratio that would distinguish those who flourished from those who didn't. I countered with an offer: if he could find that ratio, I'd test it against data on the day-to-day emotional lives of people who I knew could be classified as flourishing or not. Both sensing that this could be a huge discovery, we vowed to collaborate. Our mutual aim was to discover and test this ratio, and, if the data held up, write a paper together.

As the weeks unfolded, the match between Marcial's mathematics and my theory and data continued to amaze me. I needed to clear the decks to make room for this sudden new turn in my research program. I wanted to do it justice. Thanks to the John Templeton Foundation, I arranged a mini-sabbatical for the following semester. I was released from my teaching duties so I could immerse myself in the science of dynamic systems that Marcial had introduced me to. I took on the task of introducing this perspective to the science of positive psychology. Having done so,[3] I'd now like to share it with you. You already know that positivity broadens your mind (chapter 4), builds your best future (chapter 5), and fuels your resilience (chapter 6). Now let's explore how positivity and negativity work together to tip your life toward flourishing. I'll start by describing Marcial's discovery about positivity.

The Butterfly in the Boardroom

For years, Losada[4] had worked in industry studying the characteristics of high-performing business teams. His mission was to help business teams with poor performance records become more successful. As part of this work, he built a laboratory room specially designed to capture the behavior of business teams in action. The room looked like any ordinary boardroom. It had the usual large table surrounded by executive-style chairs. A range of corporate teams had used this room to do their business—to craft their business missions and strategic plans. But the walls of this boardroom were different in that they sported one-way mirrors. Behind these sat Losada's team of research assistants, equipped with video cameras and specially programmed computers. He had trained these assistants to use this equipment to code every single statement—large and small—made by every single team member during the hour-long business meetings they observed. In particular, Losada tracked three dimensions: whether people's statements were (1) *positive* or *negative*, (2) *self-focused* or *other-focused*, and (3) based on *inquiry* (asking questions) or *advocacy* (defending a point of view).[5]

By the mid-1990s, sixty different business teams had been observed and coded by Losada's team. Later, based on independent data, Losada identified which of those teams could be classified as high-performing. Twenty-five percent met the criteria. These teams scored high on three distinct business indicators: profitability, customer satisfaction ratings, and evaluations by superiors, peers, and subordinates. By all accounts these teams were doing amazingly well—they were flourishing. They turned profits and were well regarded by all with whom they did business.

By sharp contrast, about 30 percent scored uniformly low on all three business indicators. These teams were clearly floundering—not making money and leaving dissatisfaction in their wake. The rest had a mixed profile, doing well on some indicators and poorly on others. Perhaps not surprisingly, "mixed-success" characterized the majority of teams that Losada encountered.

Losada painstakingly plotted his data moment by moment over the course of the meetings. He also quantified how much each team member influenced the behavior of others and called this new variable the team's connectivity. Connectivity reflects how attuned or responsive team members were to one another.

When he later divided the teams into high-, low-, and mixed-performance teams, striking differences emerged. High-performance teams stood out with their unusually high positivity ratios, at about 6 to 1. By contrast, low-performance teams had ratios well below 1 to 1, and mixed-performance teams sat just above that, at around 2 to 1.

High-performance teams also had higher connectivity and an interesting balance on other dimensions. They asked questions as much as they defended their own views, and cast their attention outward as much as inward. Low-performance teams, however, had far lower connectivity, asked almost no questions, and showed almost no outward focus. Again, mixed-performance teams sat in between.

Carefully observing the intertwined relationships in his data plotted over time, Losada noticed which of his measures forecast later changes in other measures. He eventually wrote a set of mathematical equations to capture the different dynamics he'd observed.[6]

Losada's equations demonstrated that the unfolding behavior of these business teams reflected a complex system—more specifically a *nonlinear dynamic system* (see the notes section for an explanation of these terms).[7] A hallmark feature of nonlinear dynamic systems is reflected in the term commonly known as the "butterfly effect," in which seemingly trivial inputs—like the flapping of a butterfly's wings in one location—can disproportionately determine later conditions elsewhere.[8] I've come to think of positivity as that flapping of the butterfly's wing. Like the fluttering butterfly, positivity can produce astonishingly disproportionate outcomes. How else might today's subtle and fleeting heartfelt sense of goodness launch a positivity cascade that reshapes the very course of your life and forecasts how long you live?

The butterfly showed up elsewhere as well. When Losada ran his mathematical model using the coordinates of high-performance teams, the resulting trajectory spiraled, bounced, twisted, and turned following the classic "butterfly-shaped" attractor familiar to those who have studied complex systems.[9]

So the butterfly landed in Losada's boardroom as well. It represented the dynamics of those flourishing, high-performing business teams. The "wings" of this butterfly were tall. Their height reflected the high positivity ratios that Losada had uncovered in these high-performance teams. The butterfly "wings" were also stretched wide open. Their span reflected the broad range these high-performing teams showed in both inquiry and advocacy. The overall structure of the butterfly was richly original; its trajectory never retraced its steps. You might say the behavior of these high-performing teams was always fresh and creative. In physics and mathematics, this trajectory is known as a chaotic attractor. Yet it's not "chaotic" in the colloquial sense of being random or completely unpredictable. It has a clear order. It's just a very complex order.[10]

Something altogether different emerged when Losada ran his model using the coordinates of mixed-performance teams. Although their trajectory began with a structure that mirrored the model for flourishing teams, their "butterfly" was much smaller, its wings not nearly as tall. This diminished stature reflected the lower positivity ratios Losada had uncovered in these teams. Nor did its wings span as great a distance. This lesser span reflected the narrower range of inquiry and advocacy that Losada had spotted in the mixed-performance teams. More telling, though, this smaller butterfly was not resilient. It didn't last. In fact, following an encounter with extreme negativity, the butterfly devolved into what physicists and mathematicians call a limit cycle. In other words, the trajectory got stuck in a rut. Also, the location of this rut revealed where mixed-performance teams got stuck—in negative, self-absorbed advocacy. This suggests that extreme negativity caused these teams to lose their good cheer, their flexibility, and their ability to question; they languished in an endless loop in which each person simply defended their own position and became critical of all else. You might say that people in these team meetings were no longer truly listening to one another. They were simply waiting to talk, to defend their own view. When that becomes everyone's goal, it's no wonder that the team meeting goes nowhere. Keep in mind that this was the most common type of team dynamic. I'm sure we can all recognize meetings like this—with a shudder.

Something different still emerged when Losada ran his model using the coordinates of low-performance teams. There was no butterfly at all. They showed none of the butterfly's complex and generative dynamics evident in high-performance teams. In fact, low-performance teams started where mixed-performance teams ended up—entrenched in negative, self-absorbed advocacy—simply defending their own views and critical of all else. After all, Losada had found that these teams had the lowest positivity ratios and almost no tendency to question or focus outward. But, worse than being stuck in an endless loop, the dynamics of low-performance teams showed the properties of what physicists and mathematicians call a fixed-point attractor. They spiraled down to a static point. This suggests that low-performance teams eventually lose flexibility altogether. They spiral down to a dead end—a stalemate.

The very same set of mathematical equations, depending on the input, resulted in three very different structures, or fates. Only one structure—the one depicting high-performance teams—held complexity and infinite flexibility. The others did not. Another way to appreciate the value of nonlinear dynamic systems is to say that they capture differences in kind, not just in degree. High-performance teams were not simply "more and better" than low-performance teams. Their collective synergy gave them a different fate altogether. Whereas other teams crumbled under pressure, these teams carried on. They bounced back with new questions and ideas. They remained buoyed by their high positivity ratio. Although butterflies may seem fragile, this one was remarkably resilient.

What I love about Losada's work is that it translates the two core truths in my broaden-and-build theory into the language of mathematics. The first core truth, detailed in chapter 4, holds that positivity opens us—it broadens our minds and our hearts. Resonating with this core truth, Losada's math shows how positivity goes hand-in-hand with asking questions and focusing outward. That is, it was Losada's high-performing teams who were most open to new ideas. They were a testament to what a synergistic group of open minds might accomplish. The second core truth of my broaden-and-build theory, showcased in chapter 5, is that positivity transforms us for the better—it builds our resources. Aligned with this core truth, Losada's math shows how positivity comes with greater social resources. That is, as positivity increased, so did the connectivity or attunement within the team itself. When positivity was high, team members were more responsive to one another. Also aligned with this second core truth, Losada's math shows how positivity links up with doing well, with business success. And, as icing on the cake, my work, described in chapter 6, shows how positivity helps you bounce back from adversity. Losada's math shows this, too. Teams with higher positivity were more flexible and resilient—they never got stuck in critical, self-absorbed advocacy.

So Losada's life's work and mine complement each other with stunning beauty. Losada's work on positivity was richly descriptive and distilled into mathematics. By contrast, my own work on positivity was grounded in evolutionary theory and supported by experiments. Whereas Losada's work could not support causal claims about positivity, mine could. That's the difference between descriptive and experimental research. Even so, Losada's work broke new ground beyond what I could have imagined from my theory and data alone. That's what's unique about mathematical modeling. Weaving our two scientific strands together, Losada and I created a whole new portrait of positivity.

Math Takes the Driver's Seat

To further appreciate the value added by Losada's mathematical work, you need to know about what physicists and mathematicians call the *control parameter*. The control parameter is the key that determines the fate of the system. Just as ambient temperature holds the key to whether H_2O is stuck in ice or flowing as water, Losada's control parameter determined the fate of his business teams. It determined whether they'd be stuck in a rut or enjoying flourishing success.

Here's where that butterfly makes a huge difference. Losada wasn't the first to discover a butterfly-shaped trajectory. This butterfly had been spotted in physics and math journals for more than forty years. Scores of scientists and mathematicians have devoted at least part of their careers to understanding the mathematical system that the butterfly represents. For instance, a precise numerical tipping point within this system had been discovered.[11] Below this number, you reach ruts (limit cycles) and deadlocks (fixed-point attractors). Above this number, the butterfly pops out, with all its glorious complexity. It's stunningly simple. Fate lies in a simple number. This is the power of a tipping point.

Losada's control parameter was the connectivity he'd observed among team members—their degree of attunement with one another. Through simple algebra he translated this into the positivity ratio teams expressed.[12] This is how he pinpointed the exact positivity ratio that marked the fork in the road. Above this particular ratio, the complex dynamics of flourishing would emerge. Below this ratio lay the limit cycles of languishing and the fixed-point attractors of failure—territory we'd all wish to avoid. According to Losada's math, the magic positivity ratio is 2.9013 to 1.

To those of us who are not mathematicians, this number seems absurdly precise. For sheer practicality, I prefer to say 3 to 1. It's true that, mathematically, the microscopic difference between 2.9012 and 2.9013 is consequential. In the world of math, tipping points are beyond razor-thin. Yet we live in a world of impurity and imprecision. In theory, for instance, the melting point of ice is zero degrees Celsius. But as anyone who's cleared their winter walkway of this slippery danger knows, the exact melting point of ice can reflect both local impurities (i.e., rock salt) and imprecision in our measurement devices (i.e., home-quality thermometers). Although scientists like me have worked to refine measures of emotions, it's fair to say that we have nothing as precise as a cooking thermometer to offer you for home use. So I think you'll agree, for practical purposes, as you try this at home, thinking of 3 to 1 as the tipping point is more than good enough.

Putting Math to the Test

Losada's math led to his bold prediction that only when positivity ratios are higher than 3 to 1 is positivity in sufficient supply to seed human flourishing.[13] My contribution was to take this number and run with it, and provide independent tests of this newly discovered tipping point. Losada made his discovery with business teams—groups of people working together, for better or worse. I wondered whether this tipping point would apply to individuals as well. Would people who I could identify as flourishing have positivity ratios greater than 3 to 1? Would the ratios for those who were languishing fall below 3 to 1?

I had on hand two different data sets that would allow me to test this tipping point. In each study, I had first asked people to complete an initial survey, from which I could "diagnose" flourishing mental health.[14] (Keep in mind that people who flourish are somewhat rare. Only about one in five people tested meet the criteria.[15]) Then I'd asked everyone to report their emotional experiences daily for the next four weeks. Each night they completed a twenty-item "Positivity Self Test" much like the one I'll share later in this book.

For each day, I tallied the number of positive emotions that people experienced at least moderately. I also tallied the number of negative emotions that they experienced at least a little bit. To respect core differences between positivity and negativity, I needed to use different cut-offs. One difference that research has thoroughly documented— and that I'll bet you can appreciate from your own experience—is that bad is stronger than good. Scientists call this *negativity bias*.[16] Yet, side by side with this difference in potency sits an equally drastic difference in frequency. Unless you're mentally ill, most moments in your life are at least mildly good. Perhaps surprisingly, feeling bad is relatively rare. Scientists call this asymmetry *positivity offset*.[17]

At this point I could have computed each person's daily positivity ratio and averaged them over the month. Yet, much like dietary guidelines, I think what matters most is the positivity ratio people achieve not within a single day, but over time. To honor this view, I divided each person's positivity tally for the entire month by their negativity tally for the entire month. This approach has the added advantage of eliminating the unsolvable can't-divide-by-zero problem. Though it's possible for a person to have no noticeable negativity on a given day (making it impossible to compute their positivity ratio for that day), I've never seen anyone who has no noticeable negativity over a whole month.

What I found astonishing was that across two different sets of data, the average ratio for people who flourished was above 3 to 1, whereas that for those who were languishing was below 3 to 1. To be exact, in one data set the positivity ratio for flourishing people was 3.2 to 1 and in the other data set it was 3.4 to 1. By contrast, for the rest of the people, positivity ratios were 2.3 to 1 in one data set and 2.1 to 1 in the other. In each, positivity ratios were on either side of the tipping point, just as Losada's math had predicted.[18] For the vast majority of people, positivity ratios reflected the standard positivity offset, that is, they hovered around 2 to 1. Most moments were indeed positive. But this didn't seem to be enough to seed flourishing. For the few who flourished, positivity ratios stepped up beyond 3 to 1.

More Data, More Support

My research doesn't stand alone in supporting Losada's math. It gets even better. Take, for instance, the work of John Gottman, the world's leading expert on the science of marriage.[19] Gottman has devoted his career to studying the emotional dynamics in married couples, pin-pointing patterns that make marriages mutually satisfying and endur-ing, as well as those that begin cascades toward divorce. Early in my career, I got to know Gottman's research program well. I even collabo-rated on a small piece of it in the early 1990s, when I was a postdoc-toral fellow at UC Berkeley.[20]

Gottman's signature way to gather data on marriages was to invite couples to visit his laboratory. Whereas Losada's laboratory felt like a boardroom, Gottman's felt like a living room. Here he'd ask couples to get comfortable and talk with each other as they would at home. Eventually, he'd coax them to talk about the hard stuff—any issue that currently caused them considerable disagreement. For some couples the discussion centered on money, for others it was how to raise their kids. For still others, it was how to deal with extended family. Each couple picked their own "hot" issue.

Like the very best emotion researchers, Gottman collected a wide range of data. He used tiny sensors to measure people's heart rates, sweat gland activity, and other physiological changes during the con-versations. He used carefully placed video cameras to unobtrusively capture the verbal and nonverbal communications between the mar-riage partners. He complemented these with a wide range of surveys from each person. And, ultimately, he stayed in touch with these couples and tracked which marriages lived on "happily ever after" and which ones eventually dissolved. Surveying this mass of data, Gottman developed several ways to compute the positivity ratio of a marriage. Sometimes, like Losada, he had trained coders classify everything that partners said to each other. At other times he had his coders consider observable gestures and facial expressions as well.

Gottman eventually divided the marriages into two groups. One group was made up of marriages that lasted and that both partners found to be satisfying. I call those flourishing marriages. The other group was made up of marriages that had fallen apart. The partners had become dissatisfied, estranged, separated, or divorced. At best, these marriages were languishing; at worst, they were total failures. What he found was remarkable. Among flourishing marriages, positivity ratios were about 5 to 1. By sharp contrast, languishing and failed marriages had positivity ratios lower than 1 to 1. Although Gottman was not working to test Losada's math, his data nonetheless supports it.

But wait, there's more. This time the evidence comes from a scientist named Robert Schwartz. A practicing clinical psychologist, Schwartz had developed his own mathematical model, rooted in Boolean algebra, to suggest that optimal positivity ratios are about 4 to 1. He compares these to "normal" positivity ratios—the ones most people have—which are about 2 to 1. By contrast, he suggests that pathological positivity ratios—for example, those of depressed people—are lower than 1 to 1.[21]

To test whether his own math-derived numbers fit real-world data, Schwartz and colleagues tracked the outcomes of a large set of patients undergoing treatment for depression. They received either cognitive-behavioral therapy (CBT) or drug treatment, each of which is soundly supported by scientific evidence. Each week, before and during treatment, these patients completed a survey about their emotions. Patients were also evaluated every two weeks by an independent team of clinicians to assess quantitatively their progress in treatment. It's important to note that the researchers who did these assessments had no involvement in the patients' treatment or care.

Schwartz and his colleagues agreed in advance on which scores would indicate average and which would show optimal relief from depression. To be considered in any kind of remission, patients would need to show relief from their depressive symptoms for at least four weeks in a row. To meet the more stringent criteria for optimal re- mission, patients would need to show virtually no signs of depres- sion plus clear signs of superior functioning in life. In short, they'd need to embody what the American Psychiatric Association de- scribes as optimal human functioning: "Superior functioning in a wide range of activities, life's problems never seem to get out of hand, is sought out by others because of his or her many positive qualities, no symptoms."[22]

Not surprisingly, before treatment began, Schwartz and colleagues found patients' positivity ratios to be quite low, at 0.5 to 1. Among the subset of patients who showed optimal remission, ratios rose to 4.3 to 1. Compare this to the ratios for the larger subset of patients who merely showed average remission: 2.3 to 1. Sadly, a still larger sub- set of patients showed no relief from their depression whatsoever. Positivity ratios for these folks barely budged to 0.7 to 1. Again, al- though Schwartz collected data to test his own math, his data undeni- ably support Losada's math as well.[23]

The consistency here is extraordinary. For individuals, marriages, and business teams, flourishing—or doing remarkably well—comes with positivity ratios above 3 to 1. By contrast, those who don't over- come their depression, couples who fail in their marriages, and busi- ness teams that are unpopular and unprofitable each have ratios in the gutter, below 1 to 1.

The association between positivity ratios and flourishing is so ro- bust that it emerges even though Losada, Gottman, Schwartz, and I each gathered our data totally independent of one another, using very different measures and approaches. What I find most exciting is that the connection between positivity ratios and flourishing is evident at three very different levels of human experience. Whether you're one person, two partners, or an eight-person team, positivity ratios are worth your attention. I can't help wondering whether human flourishing at still larger scales—in organizations like schools and companies, in governing bodies like the U.S. Congress and the United Nations, or in vehicles of culture like television and the Internet—will also obey this apparent law for the positivity ratio tipping point.

Now You See It, Now You Don't

Seeing positivity ratios as subject to a tipping point is a powerful idea. It can explain why the effects of positivity are at times so hard to locate. By now, scientists know well that the effects of positivity are subtle, especially in comparison to those of negativity. But what has long vexed me is that even though I know I'm looking for subtle effects, at times I find no effects whatsoever. I also face a legion of grim-faced critics at times who are convinced that positivity is useless. It's as if positivity has been playing an elaborate shell game with scientists, taunting us with "Now you see it, now you don't!"

The tipping point reveals the trick to this vexing shell game. Below 3 to 1, positivity may well be inert, swamped as it is by the greater potency of negativity. Perhaps only above 3 to 1 do the underdogs of positivity gain adequate strength in numbers to stand up to and overcome negativity. Positivity may need to accumulate and compound to a certain degree before it reaches the crucial tipping point. Only then will the broaden-and-build effects of positivity emerge. Only then will people see the astonishing benefits of positivity blossom in their own lives.

My students and I have tested this idea by flipping the questions we asked about positivity ratios. Instead of dividing people by whether they had good outcomes (like flourishing) and then looking at their ratios, we divided people by their ratios, then looked at whether they showed good outcomes. Even I was surprised by the resulting bar charts. For those with positivity ratios below 3 to 1, the bars indicating good outcomes—like broad thinking or built resources—hovered near zero. For them, positivity was inert, useless. Yet for those with positivity ratios exceeding 3 to 1, the bars rose dramatically. For them, positivity forecast both openness and growth.[24] Only these people truly enjoyed the sweet fruits of positivity. The data told a clear story: now you see it, now you don't.

11 to 1: Another Tipping Point?

Back in chapter 2, I introduced the 3-to-1 positivity ratio as my prescription for how you can lead a flourishing life, full of expansive possibilities and lifelong growth. If 3-to-1, 4-to-1, and 5-to-1 ratios each describe the good life, why have any negativity at all? Why not shoot for 100 to 1? Here we all might protest that a life without suffering is hardly possible, hardly human. Could any person, marriage, or team ever achieve a state of pure positivity? I don't think so. But even so, perhaps being negativity-free is an ideal worthy of our strivings. Could there be a level of flourishing beyond what's currently imaginable?

The beauty of having a mathematical model—like Losada's—in your scientific toolkit is that even if you can't locate that one-in-a-million person, marriage, or team that experiences no negativity at all, you can still take a stab at answering questions about pure positivity. The math tells us that the upper bound for flourishing is around 11 to 1.[25]

Although this second tipping point has yet to be tested against real-life data, you may well wish to steer clear of positivity ratios above 11 to 1. I wonder, though, whether this prescription has practical value. My friend and collaborator Michael Cohen, an endowed professor at the University of Michigan's School of Information, had a clever way of phrasing this concern. As we were discussing this idea at the corner coffee shop, he said, "It's true that you'd hit your head on the ceiling if you jumped *really* high in the gymnasium."

Whether we seek it or not, negativity has a way of finding us. Even when we jump our highest, we most often find ourselves closer to the floor than to the ceiling in the gymnasium of life.

As is true in many realms of life, more is not always better. Problems may well occur with too much positivity. Yet I see a more useful lesson hidden in the upper limit to flourishing: negativity is also a necessary ingredient in the recipe for a flourishing life. Go figure. A book about positivity also endorses negativity. Perhaps not *all* negativity, but rather *appropriate* negativity.

In making this qualification, I follow the lead of John Gottman. From decades of studying what makes marriages work, he concludes that anger and engagement in conflict can be healthy and productive forms of negativity, whereas expressions of disgust and contempt are more corrosive.[26] I also see a big difference between guilt and shame. Guilt stems from seeing something you did as wrong or immoral. There's a clear way to resolve it: you make amends and find a better, more considerate way to behave. For shame, though, it's not just something you did that's wrong or immoral; it seems as if you yourself are wrong or immoral. You just don't measure up. How do you overcome that? So anger and guilt deliver surgical strikes of negativity. They are specific and spawn remedial actions. They can be resolved. Contempt and shame, by contrast, deliver much larger blows. Their negativity mushrooms and clouds your vision. They're all-encompassing and difficult to overcome. Negativity that is appropriate is specific and correctable. Negativity that is inappropriate is more often gratuitous and global. Gottman calls the latter sort of negativity an absorbing state. It seeps into and comes to dominate the whole emotional texture of life. It creates that dreaded downward spiral.

So knowing that positivity is life-giving doesn't mean that negativity needs to be forever banished. It can't be. Life gives us plenty of reasons to be afraid, angry, sad, and then some. Without negativity you become Pollyanna, with a forced clown smile painted on your face. You lose touch with reality. You're not genuine. In time, you drive others away.

I've come to see the ratio of positivity to negativity as the uncanny balance between levity and gravity. Levity is that unseen force that lifts you skyward, whereas gravity is the opposing force that pulls you earthward. Unchecked levity leaves you flighty, ungrounded, and unreal. Unchecked gravity leaves you collapsed in a heap of misery. Yet when properly combined, these two opposing forces leave you buoyant, dynamic, realistic, and ready for anything. Appropriate negativity delivers the promise of gravity. It grounds you in reality. Heartfelt positivity, by contrast, provides the lift that makes you buoyant and ready to flourish.

Consider a sailboat. Rising from a sailboat is an enormous mast that allows the sail to catch the wind. Below the waterline is the keel, which can weigh tons. You can take the mast going up as positivity, and the keel down below as negativity. If you've ever sailed, you know that you can't get anywhere without the keel. If you tried, at best you'd slide aimlessly across the water, or at worst you'd capsize. Although it's the sail hanging on the mast of positivity that catches the wind and gives you fuel, it's the keel of negativity that keeps the boat on course and manageable. And just as the keel matters most when you're going upwind, appropriate negativity matters most in hard times.

When I first shared this analogy with Marcial Losada at his dining room table, he appreciated it immediately. He jumped up to get his well-worn *Encyclopaedia Britannica* to look up "sailboat." Just as he'd hoped, it included a small picture of a sailboat (out of the water). He found a ruler and measured the mast. Then he measured the keel. He computed the ratio. It was above 3 to 1. We looked up at each other and laughed, knowing full well that, however pleasing it was, we could never publish this particular "finding" in a scientific journal.

The View from Here

In collaboration with Marcial Losada I discovered and tested the 3-to-1 positivity ratio, the tipping point that is our gateway to flourishing.

Losada's math is fully consistent with my broaden-and-build theory, and also fully consistent with heaps of data. It also takes us further, shedding light on when positivity is inert and when negativity is vital.

The consistency here reflects what scientists have called consilience, or unity of knowledge.[27] It gets me thinking in terms of core truths about being human—about universal human attributes we all share. It also gets me out of bed each day and lures me back to my research laboratory. Back to the data. Back to devise further experiments to test positivity.

Science is never complete. The stakes in terms of human welfare are too high for me to rest easy in the belief that clever theory or fancy math alone can provide the answers we so desperately seek.

How do we best overcome adversity? How do we best flourish?

You may well decide, now that you've read what science says about positivity, that it's time to begin experimenting with it in your own life, to raise your own positivity ratio and locate your own buoyancy. I've written Part II of this book to help you achieve just that.

PART II

Raise Your Ratio

CHAPTER 8

Where Are You Now?

If you want to know the taste of a pear,
you must change the pear by eating it yourself.
—Mao Tse-tung

So where do you stand today? How do you measure up with respect to positivity? Let's find out. Take my "Positivity Self Test" now to estimate your current positivity ratio.

POSITIVITY SELF TEST

How have you felt over the past twenty-four hours? Look back over the past day and, using the 0–4 scale below, indicate the *greatest amount* that you've experienced each of the following feelings.

0 = not at all
1 = a little bit
2 = moderately
3 = quite a bit
4 = extremely

1. What is the most **amused, fun-loving,** or **silly** you felt? ____

2. What is the most **angry, irritated,** or **annoyed** you felt? ____

3. What is the most **ashamed, humiliated,** or **disgraced** you felt? ____

4. What is the most **awe, wonder,** or **amazement** you felt? ____

5. What is the most **contemptuous, scornful,** or **disdainful** you felt? ____

6. What is the most **disgust, distaste,** or **revulsion** you felt? ____

7. What is the most **embarrassed, self-conscious,** or **blushing** you felt? ____

8. What is the most **grateful, appreciative,** or **thankful** you felt? ____

9. What is the most **guilty, repentant,** or **blame-worthy** you felt? ____

10. What is the most **hate, distrust,** or **suspicion** you felt? ____

11. What is the most **hopeful, optimistic,** or **encouraged** you felt? ____

12. What is the most **inspired, uplifted,** or **elevated** you felt? ____

13. What is the most **interested, alert,** or **curious** you felt? ____

14. What is the most **joyful, glad,** or **happy** you felt? ____

15. What is the most **love, closeness,** or **trust** you felt? ____

16. What is the most **proud, confident,** or **self-assured** you felt? ____

17. What is the most **sad, downhearted,** or **unhappy** you felt? ____

18. What is the most **scared, fearful,** or **afraid** you felt? ____

19. What is the most **serene, content,** or **peaceful** you felt? ____

20. What is the most **stressed, nervous,** or **over-whelmed** you felt? ____

Scoring

You'll notice that each item within the Positivity Self Test casts a wide net. Each includes a trio of words that are related, but not quite the same.[1] With this strategy, each item captures a set of emotions that share a key resemblance and this short test becomes that much more accurate. And remember, people typically experience positive and negative emotional states at different intensities and frequencies. Negativity feels more intense, an asymmetry that scientists call *negativity bias*. Positivity comes around more frequently, an asymmetry that scientists call *positivity offset*. Any comparison of positivity to negativity needs to take these core differences into account. To compute your positivity ratio for the past day, follow these five simple steps:

1. Go back and circle the ten items that reflect positivity. These are the ones that begin with the words **amused, awe, grateful, hopeful, inspired, interested, joyful, love, proud,** and **serene.**
2. Go back and underline the ten items that reflect negativity. These begin with the words **angry, ashamed, contemptuous, disgust, embarrassed, guilty, hate, sad, scared,** and **stressed.**
3. Count the number of circled positivity items that you endorsed as 2 or higher.
4. Count the number of underlined negativity items that you endorsed as 1 or higher.
5. Calculate the ratio by dividing your positivity tally by your negativity tally. If your negativity count is zero for today, consider it instead to be a 1, to sidestep the can't-divide-by-zero problem. The resulting number represents your positivity ratio for today.

Keep in mind that this test merely provides a snapshot. Everybody's emotions change by the day, hour, and minute. Some scientists would tell you that your emotions change by the millisecond.[2] Given your ever-shifting emotional landscape, any single measure of your positivity ratio can capture only so much. Also, when it comes to emotions, no measurement tool is flawless. Whether scientists rely on surveys or sophisticated biological markers, all measures of emotions include some degree of random error and bias. As you can imagine, this poses some difficulties for the science of emotions. Yet instead of throwing up their hands in the face of such obstacles, scientists find ways to minimize the error and equalize the bias.[3]

Zoom Out: Weigh In Often

One solution to the measurement problem is to measure repeatedly. Even if you completed the Positivity Self Test as honestly as you could, your score for today should be viewed with skepticism. Was today representative? Probably not. Days vary. So the more days you can average together to create your estimate, the more trustworthy that estimate becomes. That is, you can often get a more accurate lay of the land from a bird's-eye view than by limiting your view to the single acre you can see from the ground. The ideal is to take stock of many days, not just one.

To get a more accurate estimate of your positivity ratio, I recommend that you live life as usual and complete a fresh copy of the Positivity Self Test at roughly the same time every evening for the next two weeks. By fresh, I mean unmarked. You don't need your responses from some prior day staring you down as you consider your current day's emotions. (There's a fresh copy of the Positivity Self Test in an appendix to this book to photocopy if you wish.) After two weeks, count up your positive emotions over the entire two-week period and do the same for your negative emotions, then calculate your ratio. An added benefit of calculating your ratio over longer time spans is that it's highly unlikely that you'll face the can't-divide-by-zero problem. While it's possible to go a day without any noticeable negativity, I doubt that streak will last for two weeks. Also, because it's based on more data, this two-week positivity ratio is more reliable; it provides a better estimate of what your current life feels like.

Number-Cruncher at Your Service

Though it may well be interesting and useful for you to understand the scoring method that yields your positivity ratio, making photocopies and hand-scoring may be just cumbersome enough to keep you from doing this on a regular basis. So why not assign these tasks to a computer? I created the website to accompany this book to be your own personal number-cruncher. You can use it to help you compute your positivity ratio with the added accuracy that comes with repeated measurement. So I welcome you to visit www.PositivityRatio.com.

Far beyond automatically scoring your responses, this website can also help you track changes in your positivity ratio week by week, month by month, and year by year. You'll want to know what difference it makes as you begin experimenting with new ways to raise your ratio. Using the website tools, you'll be able to track the impact of your efforts. Here's how the website works: you log in, using a self-chosen pseudonym and password. If you choose to contribute your scores to a growing database maintained by my research lab, you'll also be asked to provide a bit of background information about yourself.[4] If it's your first visit, then you'll simply complete the Positivity Self Test much like the one at the start of this chapter and log out. From log-in to log-out, your first visit should take no more than five minutes. After that, it can take as little as a minute a day. If you visit the site regularly to complete the Positivity Self Test, you may then use the charting tools to create displays of your own past positivity ratios as you continue to make new entries. You can flag your ongoing records with key dates that reflect the beginnings of new rituals intended to raise your ratio (e.g., "began meditation practice") as well as compute average positivity ratios over time spans of your own choosing (e.g., "during my baseline," "during vacation," or "from when I started keeping a gratitude journal to today").

Even if you're not sure yet whether you'll want to make use of all the website's features, I encourage you to take a moment later today to log in to the website and complete a Positivity Self Test. Then, tomorrow—whether or not you're able to find more time to read *Positivity*—do the same. Repeat this simple daily reflection for the next two weeks or so. Here's why: To tell whether any self-change effort is working, you'll need a benchmark against which you can compare yourself down the road. Just like stepping on the scale *before* you start your diet, this benchmark allows you to chart your progress. Keep in mind that just like your pre-diet weight, your baseline positivity ratio may well be sobering. Even so, you'll need a solid estimate of where your typical ratio falls as you live "life as usual." My sense is that you'll come to appreciate having started your self-study early, before you take action to raise your positivity ratio.

Zoom In: An Archaeological Dig into a Single Day

One way to increase the accuracy of emotion measures is to zoom out and measure repeatedly. Another way is to zoom in and measure smaller units of time. When you take the Positivity Self Test with reference to a whole day, even if you average across several days or weeks, you get a picture of your positivity ratio painted in rather broad brushstrokes. In this section I'll show you how to paint a picture with far finer detail. Taken each day, the Positivity Self Test gives you a bird's eye view of your positivity ratio. In contrast, when you use the same test in zoom-in mode, you get a rich description of your ratio from the vantage point of an archaeologist just stepping up from the dig site.

Why bother to zoom in? If you're like most people, your memory is far from photographic. When you sit down each evening to complete the Positivity Self Test, can you fully trust your ability to recall the emotional nuances of your day? Scientific studies suggest that you shouldn't. My own early experiments on people's memories for past emotional experiences suggest that your end-of-the-day reports are unduly colored by two things: first, by how you felt during the most intense moment of your day, and, second, by how you're feeling at day's end. I call this the "peak-and-end rule."[5] It's the reason the Positivity Self Test asks you to rate the "most" you felt of each emotion, rather than how much you felt "on average" or for "how much of the time." Studies of human memory tell me that your accuracy rises when you assess peaks.

Zooming in provides a more accurate assessment. But it's not for the fainthearted. It takes time, lots of time. More like an hour instead of a minute. That said, I suggest you consider undertaking this more intensive and accurate method of calculating your positivity ratio from time to time, perhaps once before you start making changes in your life, and then again several months later. Think of it like going to the doctor for a full physical exam instead of simply weighing yourself again on your own bathroom scale.

Like a doctor's visit, this more detailed measurement method gives you additional information about yourself. You can use it to gain insight into your personal negativity land mines and positivity wellsprings. Emotions are highly personalized. Although science has discovered that certain patterns of thought serve as universal levers for certain emotions, the circumstances that reveal those levers vary from person to person. The source of one person's dread is another person's challenge. The same event that arouses anger in some raises compassion in others.

I strongly suspect that even though you're different in many ways from every other person reading this book, you can find patterns across the events and circumstances that give rise to your own day-to-day experiences of gratuitous negativity and heartfelt positivity. Many life circumstances recur time and again. Some of those recurring circumstances are land mines that trigger habitual negative thoughts and, in turn, habitual negative emotions. Others are wellsprings that reliably lift your spirits and bring you to life.

So I invite you to study your days. Study your routines. Pay special attention to the circumstances that you find yourself in day in and day out, or with any degree of regularity. Honestly examine how those circumstances make you feel. What patterns do you see? Where does your gratuitous negativity accumulate? Where does your heartfelt positivity spring forth? Develop an eye for your own land mines and wellsprings.

A simple variation on the Positivity Self Test can help you do this. Used in conjunction with what's called the Day Reconstruction Method, you can calculate your positivity ratio in finer detail and also conduct an intensive study of your own sources of positivity and negativity. First developed by Princeton's Nobel Prize–winning psychologist Daniel Kahneman (my collaborator on the peak-and-end rule[6]), the Day Reconstruction Method has been featured in the prestigious pages of *Science* magazine.[7] I've adapted this emotion-spotting technique to fit your purposes here.

To get started, grab paper and a pencil. It would also be helpful to have about thirty copies of the Positivity Self Test on hand, photocopied from the appendix. If that's inconvenient, it's certainly possible to record your responses to the repeated self tests in your own notes, if you're organized. Alternatively, if you have easy access to an Internet connection, you can save trees and time by doing this entire process online, at www.PositivityRatio.com.

Once you're situated—with either paper and pencil or computer before you—your task is to remember yesterday. Not all days are the same. Some are better, some are worse, and others are pretty typical. Here you should consider only yesterday. I should add that in scientific uses of the Day Reconstruction Method, it's always a surprise test. That is, while respondents were going about their business the day before, they had no idea that the next day they'd be dissecting their "yesterday." That's critical to capturing how days are actually lived, rather than snapping idealized poses for the camera. I encourage you to try the Day Reconstruction Method following an ordinary day, making no special efforts to make yourself look good.

Because it's sometimes hard to remember all the details, it helps to do this process in steps. First, record when you woke up and when you went to sleep. Then reconstruct what your day was like, as if you were writing in a diary. Think about your whole day yesterday—from the moment you woke up until the time you went to bed—and divide your day into a series of episodes. Give each episode a number and a short descriptive label, like "eating breakfast with the kids" "commuting," "checking e-mail" or "meeting with my boss." Write down the approximate times at which each episode began and ended, without gaps or overlap in time.

In one way, episodes are like the scenes in a movie. One ends (and a new one begins) when you change locations, activities, or the people you're with. Divide your day into a *continuous* series of episodes, skipping over none. Your task in completing this test is to consider *all* of the episodes of your day yesterday. With typical episodes lasting between ten minutes and two hours, you may have as few as ten or as many as thirty listed within your day. To illustrate, so far this morning mine are something like this:

> 6:05–6:15 a.m.:   get up and dress
> 6:15–7:00 a.m.:   go for a jog
> 7:00–7:35 a.m.:   meditate
> 7:35–8:00 a.m.:   eat breakfast
> 8:00–9:40 a.m.:   write in home office
> 9:40–9:55 a.m.:   take a break, get snack
> 9:55–11:30 a.m.: continue to write

You're free to skip over minor scenes like using the bathroom, loading the dishwasher, and the like.

After you've identified all the episodes of your day yesterday, revisit each one to paint in the emotional details. Relive each in your mind for a moment. Once you've done so, complete a Positivity Self Test, rating each of the ten negative and ten positive emotional states for that particular period. To catalog the various circumstances of your day, it helps to record a few key facts about the episode, such as where you were, what you were doing, and whether you were alone or interacting with others.

Scoring Your Day Reconstruction

You score your Day Reconstruction much as you score the Positive Self Test. Tally the positive items and the negative items, and divide the former by the latter. This can quickly feel like a mountain of number-crunching if you've rated a lot of episodes. Here's when you might consider using the online tools available at www.PositivityRatio.com. You'll not only save yourself time, but also gain considerable flexibility in working with your day's data. With a mouse click you'll be able to tailor the scoring of your Day Reconstruction to fit your needs. If you're not able or inclined to go online, then go ahead and score it as described. I describe two different scoring methods below. Each tells you something different about where you stand with respect to positivity.

Here's how you compute your positivity ratio across the entire day:

1. As before, circle the positivity items and underline the negativity items.
2. Across *all* the episode reports you made, count the number of circled positivity items rated at 2 or higher.
3. Again, across *all* the episode reports, count the number of underlined negativity items rated at 1 or higher.
4. Divide your day's positive emotions by your day's negative emotions.[8] The resulting number gives you sharp resolution on your positivity ratio.

Here's how to compute your positivity ratios by episode to locate your negativity land mines and positivity wellsprings:

1. As before, circle the positive items and underline the negative items.
2. In each episode, count the number of circled positivity items rated at 2 or higher.

3. In each episode, count the number of underlined negativity items rated at 1 or higher.

4. Divide each episode's tally of positive emotions by that same episode's tally of negative emotions. When you face the can't-divide-by-zero problem, substitute ones for zeros. The resulting numbers are your positivity ratios by episode.

5. Using the short descriptive labels you gave to each episode, order your episodes from least to most positive.

If your "yesterday" was fairly typical for you, the ranking of episodes allows you to identify your negativity land mines as well as the activities of your day that buoy you up the most. There's certainly nothing magical about this method. Because you supply all the information about your day, it doesn't truly tell you anything you didn't already know. But it can draw your eye to the emotional details of your daily life, to the activities and circumstances that bring you down and lift you up. Once you've developed your eye for the emotional nuances of your day and come to appreciate the downstream consequences of them, you may not need to rely on this tool. You can instead mentally assess your emotions at key turning points in your day. *What was I feeling during breakfast? How was my commute today? What's it like when I chat with my colleagues or eat lunch at my desk?* In addition to putting your positivity ratio into sharp focus, repeated use of the Day Reconstruction Method may help you develop more awareness of the emotional texture of your days.

Putting Your Scores in Context

Whether taken on just one day or over a span of weeks or within the Day Reconstruction Method, the Positivity Self Test offers a yardstick by which you can capture your own ratio. Let's discuss your score.

If you scored below 3 to 1, you've got plenty of company! More than 80 percent of the people I've tested score below the 3-to-1 threshold, averaging around 2 to 1.[9] People who are depressed or otherwise suffering often score below 1 to 1.[10] Knowing that most people fall short of the prescribed 3-to-1 emotional guideline serves as a reminder of just how far we all need to go, and of how much untapped potential for flourishing lies dormant within all of us. If your current positivity ratio is lower than 3 to 1, reading this part of the book can help you locate opportunities for change in your daily life. These often small changes can broaden your mind, open your heart, and help you build your best future.

If your positivity ratio is seriously and persistently low, below 1 to 1, I urge you to seek assistance outside of reading this book. You may want to ask yourself whether you might be clinically depressed. If you want to learn more about the symptoms of and treatments for depression, the National Institute of Mental Health has an excellent and easy-to-read online brochure, currently available at www.nimh.nih.gov/health/publications/depression/nimhdepression.pd.

Depression is extraordinarily common, affecting one in five people.[11] If you suspect depression, please seek the input of an experienced mental health practitioner. If you don't connect well with the first practitioner you find, find another one. And another! Be persistent. You'll need a caring and knowledgeable support person as you address what may well be a genetic or physiological issue. In combination with more-conventional treatment, reading this book can help you identify the small changes you can make to give yourself temporary relief from depressed moods and eventually assist in paving your way back to more carefree and buoyant living.

If you scored at or above 3 to 1, you're one of the lucky few. It's likely that you are already living well and that positivity resonates in your bones. If so, reading the rest of this book may make you nod your head with recognition from time to time. It will also give you a language and a rationale for sharing your personal take on positivity with others. Perhaps one or more of the people you love does not enjoy the fruits of positivity as much as you do, and you've longed to share it with them, so that they too might flourish. Or perhaps your workplace is burdened by excessive negativity, and you wonder how you might make a difference. Insights from this book can help you start a dialogue with your co-workers about the value of positivity.

Moving a River

Although changing your entrenched emotional habits is possible, it's no easy feat. Think of it as moving a river: easier than moving a mountain, yet not something done on a whim, or without concerted effort over extended time. It requires nothing less than building a new foundation, a new riverbed, along which your desired emotions can flow. Indeed, the best new research suggests that forging lasting changes in your positivity ratio requires as much intention, effort, and lifestyle change as losing weight or lowering cholesterol levels.[12] This is why a simple platitude like "Don't worry, be happy" rings hollow. It's just a wish. It tells you nothing about how to move the riverbed.

Good intentions alone won't raise anyone's positivity ratio. It's not enough to tell yourself (or others), "Don't be so negative. Be positive." Flourishing is not a matter of sheer willpower. Your emotions are like a river. If you're like most people, your habitual river of emotions runs through a valley marked by a low positivity ratio. Perhaps you're now inspired to move that river to higher ground. What I invite you to do is to set your sights on the riverbed and examine the foundations that shape your emotions.

More than anything else, your habitual patterns of thought are what set the location and course of the riverbed. Yet even though your mental habits have likely been shaped and strengthened over a lifetime, your prognosis is good. Hundreds of scientific studies tell us that when people change the course of their thinking, they change the course of their emotions.[13] This holds true both in the moment, if you want to zap an unwanted worry, and over the long haul, if you want to recover from a full-blown anxiety disorder. And it holds equally true for negative and positive emotions—for your lows of sadness and your highs of joy. That's because the flow of your emotions follows how you interpret your current circumstances. Dire interpretations create dire emotions. Charitable and optimistic interpretations breed positivity.

You might be concerned that moving a river is futile. Won't nature win in the end? Won't the pull of history and genes bring the river back to its age-old location the minute you let your guard down? Hasn't science documented a set-point for happiness? If genes fully determine happiness, then trying to raise your positivity ratio would be as pointless as trying to be taller.[14] It would be *worse* than moving a mountain. Because if somehow you were able to move that mountain, you could rest easy feeling fairly certain it would not move back. But can you really trust a river to stay put in its new location?

Though it's true that science has shown that the genes you inherited from your family tree play a part in determining your habitual positivity ratio, science has also shown that they're literally only half of the story. The other half depends on a combination of your circumstances and how you choose to think and act each day.[15] And the most recent evidence from neuroscience provides even more reason for hope. This new work suggests that as you create new habits of thought, you fundamentally rewire your brain.[16] Such *neuroplasticity*, as it's called, means that moving the riverbed to higher ground is far from futile. Rewiring your brain reinforces and fortifies the new location you choose for your riverbed. This means that, quite literally, you get to choose. No matter where your river of emotions flows today, over time and with continued effort and attention, you can change its course and location.

Embark on Change

Because your positivity ratio may well be the key to whether or not you flourish in life, knowing how to raise it is essential. Science has shown that we can learn to shape and reshape our emotions, to increase our relative positivity. As we do so—and as our ratios cross the critical 3-to-1 threshold—we increase the ranks of those who are not merely happy and self-sufficient, but also creative, resilient, productive, and—perhaps most important of all—growing and becoming better each day. More of us can flourish. Indeed, greater numbers of us—as family members, neighbors, community members, and global citizens—need to flourish. We need more people in our homes, and across the globe, poised to make this world a more livable place for future generations and lift the many burdens from society. Flourishing people will make this positive difference. Gaining control of your positivity ratio is the place to start. It's a win-win proposition. If you feel good, you will do good.

As with many change efforts, there are multiple paths toward achieving your goals. Indeed, there are three ways to increase any ratio: increase the numerator, decrease the denominator, or both. The next chapters provide concrete examples of how to change these key numbers and become more fully alive.

The View from Here

If you took the Positivity Self Test, you now have an approximation of where you stand today. To get a more stable measure, take the test every evening for the next two weeks as you live your life as usual. Once you become familiar with the measure—and if you use the resources on www.PositivityRatio.com—it will take you less than a minute or two each day to weigh in, and just a few mouse clicks to compute your ratio. You now also know how you can dig deeper to extract a more intensive and accurate portrayal of your ratio using the Day Reconstruction Method.

If you're like most people, you probably learned that your positive ratio falls short of the 3-to-1 ratio that marks a flourishing life. Don't despair! Having read thus far, you already know a few things about positivity. You know what it is and what it leads to. You can now appreciate how a moment of positivity can open your mind and allow you to see the world with fresh eyes. Over time, the new "look" that positivity gives you adds up. It launches an upward spiral that sets you on a path of growth and positive change.

My goal in the first part of this book was to enlighten and inspire. My hope was that by sharing the latest scientific news about positivity, I might spark in you the urge to experiment with positivity on your own. But inspiration goes only so far. To act on your inspiration you need more, which is where this section comes in. It offers the guidance and tools you'll need to take action and make positive changes in your life.

You can reduce negativity, increase positivity, and raise your positivity ratio. Now, let's get started with the first of these projects.

CHAPTER 9

Decrease Negativity

*Life always gives us exactly the teacher we need at every moment.
This includes every mosquito, every misfortune, every red light,
every traffic jam, every obnoxious supervisor (or employee), every
illness, every loss, every moment of joy or depression, every
addiction, every piece of garbage, every breath.*

—CHARLOTTE JOKO BECK

This is a book on positivity. So why focus on negativity? Simply put, everything's relative. The discoveries revealed in Part I tell us that the value of your positivity depends vitally on how it stacks up against your negativity. Also, the well-documented scientific principle of *negativity bias* ensures that efforts to reduce negativity—targeting the denominator of your positivity ratio—hold great promise. This is because, as stated earlier, measure for measure, bad is stronger than good. More than you perhaps think, your ratio depends on your daily diet of negativity. Reducing negativity may be the fastest, most efficient way for you to increase your ratio. If your current ratio is seriously low, this is where you'll want to begin. This is also where you'll want to begin if your positivity seems fairly high already, but is matched by comparably high negativity.

Bear in mind that the goal is to reduce your negativity, not eliminate it. At times, negative emotions are appropriate and useful. It is proper and helpful, for instance, to mourn after a loss, to resonate on your anger to fight an injustice, or to be frightened by things that could cause harm to you or your children. Appropriate negativity keeps us grounded, real, and honest.

Your best goal is to reduce inappropriate or gratuitous negativity. Whereas some of your negativity is corrective and energizing, not all of it is. Gratuitous negativity is neither helpful nor healthy. Does it help to snap at the cashier after you've waited in line longer than you expected? Is it healthy to berate yourself for not getting the laundry done? What's to be gained when you dwell on an off-the-cuff comment a co-worker made? At times your entrenched emotional habits can intensify or prolong your bad feelings far beyond their usefulness. Your negativity becomes corrosive and smothering. Like an out-of-control weed, gratuitous negativity grows fast and crowds out positivity's more tender shoots.

In this chapter I highlight the grand legacy of clinical psychology, which has amassed and tested numerous techniques for reducing gratuitous negativity. I will also help you identify recurring events that infuse your daily life with needless negativity, ranging from an aversive commute or a toxic co-worker to sarcastic humor and gossip. Your media diet is also important. If you're a news junkie or a video game enthusiast, you risk elevating your negativity to unhealthy levels.

My message here is that gratuitous negativity can hold you hostage, as if you had cinder blocks tied to your ankles and a black hood pulled over your face. It can keep you so constrained and smothered that you are simply unable to flourish. But the good news is that you have what it takes to free yourself.

Dispute Negative Thinking

It's been a bad week. It's already Wednesday and I've logged hour upon hour sitting in front of my computer, and I haven't even been able to squeeze out four pages since Monday. How am I ever going to finish this chapter? With the writing time in May that I lost dealing with my husband's unexpected hospitalization, I'll never finish this book during the summer months as I'd planned. Then I'll be faced with trying to finish it during the fall semester. I already know that I'll have too many plates spinning then: I'll be teaching, starting two large new research projects, mentoring a double load of graduate students, and chairing committee after committee. I can never finish the book when I'm juggling all that. I have a friend who started writing her own book and is just now finishing it—twenty-three years later! Oh man, now I know how that happens. When my agent and editor find out how behind schedule I am, they'll regret agreeing to work with me. They'll discover that I was just full of hot air as I pitched this book to them, that I really don't have what it takes to inspire a wide audience with the latest science. My throat is getting tight just thinking about what a failure I've become. My stomach hurts. My fingers barely have the strength to type these words. I'm not getting anywhere today. Why don't I just quit?

Had days like this? Probably. Maybe you failed to meet a deadline or goal you set for yourself. Maybe it was a work goal, like mine. Or maybe it was a personal goal, like getting the grocery list together so that you could make your family a home-cooked meal for a change. Or maybe you stepped on the scale to discover that you'd gained five pounds. Whatever the initial unwanted and often unexpected event, negativity can quickly spin out of control, making you anxious or depressed, if not both.

Perhaps the biggest advance in twentieth-century psychological science was to unlock the ways in which predictable patterns of negative thinking breed negative emotions, so much so that they can even spiral down into pathological states like clinical depression, phobias, and obsessive-compulsive disorders.[1] Negative emotions—like fear and anger—can also spawn negative thinking.[2] This reciprocal dynamic is in fact why downward spirals are so slippery. Negative thoughts and negative emotions feed on each other. And as they do, they pull you down their abyss.

One scientifically tested way to stop this life-draining cycle is to dispute negative thinking. Dispute it the way a good lawyer would, by examining the facts. Let me go back to my own downward spiral. What set it off? What negative thoughts and beliefs got triggered? What did those thoughts and beliefs in turn make me feel? And how do those thoughts and beliefs compare to reality? What are the facts of my situation? When I take in those facts—truly take them in—how do I feel?

If I dig deeply enough, it's clear that what set me off was my slow progress yesterday: I produced only one and a half new pages. I even had a false start: I wrote two pages that I ended up tossing out when I discovered I'd written something almost identical back in chapter 2. Disappointed with the fruits of my writing, I overgeneralized: *I'll never finish this book.* . . . I completely discounted the positive progress I had made. It was as if pages of new writing didn't count at all. I also jumped to conclusions: I became certain I'd be trying (in vain) to finish the book during my busy fall semester and that I was destined to follow in the footsteps of my friend's twenty-three-year book project. Magnifying my setback all out of proportion, I became certain that my agent and editor would discover what a failure I am. The twisted logic in all this negative thinking twisted my stomach and made it hard for me to breathe. I became supremely unmotivated to write. Even my fingers felt deflated. I'd worked myself into an anxious, hopeless, and depressed mess.

But hold on. What happens when I check in with the facts of my situation? Why don't I review my writing log? Long ago I discovered that my thinking was sharpest and I was most productive in the morning. So I set aside my mornings to write. Data junkie that I am, after each writing session, I log how many hours I devoted to writing that morning, and how many pages I produced. In the forty-eight writing mornings I've devoted to this book so far, my average output has been 3.03 pages a day. On my most productive days, I write five pages. On my least productive days, I write one or two pages. When I started this book project, I calculated that three pages a day was all I needed to finish the book on schedule. This pace would also allow me to stay on top of my many other work-related projects, from designing new studies and mentoring graduate students to carrying out my teaching and administrative duties. So an average of three pages a day is all I need. And an average is just an average. Some days I'll produce more, some days less. I did, in fact, make progress yesterday. I wrote about moving the river.

And when I check the calendar to test the "conclusion" I reached that I'd still be working on the book this fall, and even over the next twenty-some years, I see at least twenty mornings I can clear for writing this summer. Doing the math, that comes to around sixty more pages. Given the plan for the book, I should be working on the last chapter as summer comes to a close. If I'm lucky, I'll have finished the book. But maybe I won't. Even so, it could hardly take twenty years to complete a fragment of a chapter. I can still meet my publisher's October 1 deadline.

When I take in these facts—really take them in—I breathe easier. The knot in my stomach disappears. I type at a quicker pace. Scanning my Word document, I see that I've already written three pages today, and I've still got more in me. I feel hopeful, energized. It's realistic to have some days that are less productive than others. My writing log tells me I can count on that. And I'll bet most every writer has to throw out some pages now and then. Also, given the family medical emergency I faced in May, it's realistic to have lost a long stretch of days that I'd earmarked for writing the book. My family needed me then more than the book did. I certainly wouldn't have changed my choices back in May, so there's no point in harboring regrets. And thank goodness that my original plan had me finishing the book before summer started. With several months of padding built into my writing schedule, I can deal with life's unexpected turns. I can revise my plans and find other ways to carry out my mission.

Disputing negative thinking nips negativity in the bud. When you dispute negative thoughts, you're left with a mild sense of disappointment, mixed with a healthy dose of hopefulness. When you fail to dispute them, you wallow in disappointment, which mushrooms into anxiety, hopelessness, shame, dread, and more. There's no room in this immobilizing heap of negativity for hope or any other good feeling. You're smothered.

Learning to dispute twisted forms of negative thinking is the heart of cognitive-behavioral therapy, or CBT. You don't need to have a diagnosable mental illness to benefit from this skill. You can use it to keep inevitable negativity at bay—in keeping with the facts. Several books, written by leading scientists and practitioners, can help you learn the skills of disputation as well as the other tools I'll discuss in this chapter and beyond. See the Recommended Resources section at the back of this book. Scientific studies show that these books truly do provide help. Reading them lastingly reduces people's depression.[3]

It's important to recognize that disputation is not wishful thinking. It doesn't mean that you simply paper over your negative thoughts with rosy ones. In fact, although disputation has positive consequences, it's not positive thinking at all. My friend Marty Seligman, author of a best-selling book on the subject, calls it "non-negative thinking."[4] By disputing your negative thoughts, you don't suppress them, push them out of mind, or whitewash them. Instead, as you check them against reality, you literally dissolve them. They melt away just as the Wicked Witch of the West did when Dorothy poured that fateful bucket of water on her in *The Wizard of Oz*. You don't need wishful thinking to defang gratuitous negativity. In nearly every case, reality is on your side.

Break the Grip of Rumination

Our minds are often high-traffic places. When something bad happens—say you've had an argument with your spouse—it's easy to go over it again and again in your mind. You think, *What did he mean when*

he called me selfish? . . . Am I really selfish? . . . If I can't make this marriage work, I'll be doomed to live alone. . . . I wonder if I'm not cut out to make it in relationships? . . . What if he's right? . . . Maybe he doesn't really love me anymore. . . . Am I really so unlovable? . . .

Scientists call this style of thinking rumination. It happens when you go over and over your negative thoughts and feelings. You examine them from every angle. You question them. Though you may well intend to "think this thing through," you don't really get anywhere. Instead, your thinking gets stuck in a rut of endless questions, and you quickly become overwhelmed and demoralized. You're not certain you'll ever find the answers you seek.

This way of thinking fans the flames of negativity. That's because when you ruminate you see everything through the distorted lens of negativity. And negativity doesn't play fair. It doesn't allow you to think straight or see the big picture. Studies show that when people experience negative emotions, they selectively call to mind negative thoughts. That's simply the way our brains work: we create a chain of thoughts that are linked by their negative tone. So, when you ruminate, you dredge up thoughts that only add fuel to the fire of your negativity. And because negative emotions and narrowed, negative thinking feed on each other, they drag you down.

Ruminating on endless questions and concerns is another way to send your positivity ratio into a tailspin. It multiplies your negative emotions exponentially. And it seems to work this way for all negative emotions. You start out a little bit worried, ruminate, and your worry expands toward a full-blown anxiety attack. Take a little bit of sadness, add rumination, and you bring on the symptoms of depression. Likewise for anger. Experience a setback, rant and rave internally, and you may well lash out in violence or become a verbal loose cannon. With the starter dough of honest negativity, rumination creates an expanding rat's nest of gratuitous negativity that usurps your mental space.

Rumination hardly leaves you in a position to dispute negative thinking. After all, checking in with the reality of your circumstances requires clear eyes. Before you can think straight about the situation you're facing, you need to put the brakes on the downward spiral you're in. You need to break the grip of rumination. Fortunately, there are scientifically tested ways to do so. These, too, are part of the grand legacy of cognitive-behavioral therapy, this time with an emphasis on the behavioral side.[5]

As with many things, the first step is awareness. You need to be able to spot the damaging cycle of rumination when it's happening. You need to recognize that your endless mulling isn't doing you any good. Only then can you choose to do something altogether different.

What seems to help most is any form of healthy distraction. Do something that literally takes your mind off of your troubles. Go for a jog. Swim in the ocean. Fix your bike. Lift weights at the gym. Meditate or do yoga. Whatever it is, find an activity that totally absorbs you. Maybe you could call your friend and ask about his latest trip. Or you could read those articles you've been meaning to read for your next project at work. Or program your new cell phone.

What you're looking to do is lift your mood. Sure, it helps if you can find an activity you enjoy, something that not only lifts your mood out of the gutter, but also brings you joy, fascination, or pride. But distractions can also be neutral. So long as they keep you from ruminating—from thinking too much—they'll fit the bill. Fairly neutral activities can break the cycle of rumination and allow you to step out of your downward spiral. Then, once you're off the slippery downward slope of negativity, you'll have eyes clear enough to dispute negative thinking and address whatever problem you face.

You may have noticed that I said *healthy* distractions. Not all distractions are good for you. Many people try to numb their excessive ruminations with alcohol or drugs. In fact, people who have a high tendency to ruminate are at high risk for alcohol abuse.[6] Food can be another unhealthy distraction. Some people use food to escape painful self-awareness, which can lead to bingeing and other problematic forms of emotional eating.[7] And, as I'll discuss later in this chapter, bingeing on media can pose its own problems. Many TV programs, for instance, although absorbing, also shower you with violent content. Doused in negativity this way, you're often worse off emotionally when you lift your eyes from the screen. The same can be true for loading up your iPod with sad songs. Recognizing how you may be using alcohol, food, or the media to escape from painful thoughts can help you choose healthier forms of distraction.

Come to recognize when your thinking is going nowhere. Create a stable of activities you can turn to that can break the grip of rumination and lift your emotions.

Become More Mindful

Your habitual thoughts are the riverbed, your emotions the river. Negative thoughts inevitably arise. Yet all too often negativity gushes, seemingly out of your control. Negative thoughts can spring forth in long chains of association, populating your mind with unwanted negative emotions. It can be tempting to dam up the spring—to suppress your negativity. But science shows that attempts to block out negative thoughts and emotions backfire. Instead of reducing unwanted negativity, suppression multiplies your misery, mentally, physically, and socially.[8] Perhaps counterintuitively, being open to negativity is healthier than being closed off from it. Another scientifically tested way to curb negativity's momentum is practicing mindfulness.

In Buddhism, meditation practices specifically crafted to develop the skill of mindfulness have been refined over centuries. If you're like many people, you view Buddhism as a religion or a spiritual practice emanating from Eastern cultures. Yet Western scientists, myself included, have come to see it as much more. With its detailed accounts of how the human mind works, and how we can willfully train our minds to be healthier and happier, Buddhism is also a bona fide psychology.[9]

Jon Kabat-Zinn was the first Western scientist, in the early 1980s, to cull the psychology of mindfulness from age-old Buddhist practices and teach them to his Boston-area medical patients. He called this work Mindfulness-Based Stress Reduction, or MBSR, and gave his patients a straightforward definition of mindfulness. As he put it,

"Mindfulness means paying attention in a particular way: on purpose, in the present moment, and nonjudgmentally."[10] Becoming more mindful, then, entails attending to your own inner experience with full awareness and without judgment. Mentally, you take a step back from the stream of your thoughts and sensations, to gain a wider perspective on your thinking. With practice, you learn to observe the contents of your mind calmly, in a nonreactive way. You learn to accept a thought as just a thought. It's simply an occurrence in your mind that arises, takes shape, and passes, much as a particular pattern among the clouds forms in the sky, then soon dissipates. In a state of mindfulness, it becomes possible to accept one's thoughts—even negative thoughts—without acting on them or reacting to them emotionally.

The power of mindfulness is that it can literally sever the link between negative thoughts and negative emotions. When you come to accept a negative thought as just a thought—that in time will pass—you've disarmed it. With fuller awareness of how negative thoughts and negative emotions feed on each other, you can choose not to go there. You can both accept a negative thought and choose not to magnify it.

Mindfulness is a skill. It doesn't come naturally. Like learning to play the piano or hit a good backhand in tennis, it requires instruction and practice. That's the perspective in both Buddhist psychology and Kabat-Zinn's model. Formal training in mindfulness has now accrued an impressive record of results. Scores of scientific studies confirm the physical and mental health benefits of beginning a practice of mindful awareness. Those who have taken Kabat-Zinn's course, for instance, have been shown to experience less stress, less pain, reduced anxiety, clearer skin, and better immune functioning.[11] Inspired by Kabat-Zinn's work, other scientists have incorporated mindful awareness into treatments that have been shown to prevent depression relapse,[12] reduce self-injury,[13] alleviate obsessive-compulsive disorder,[14] and better manage the stress of chronic disability, either your own or that of a loved one.[15] Science has also documented that mindfulness training leaves a lasting mark on the brain. It alters the basic metabolism in brain circuits known to underlie emotional responding, reducing activity in circuits linked with negativity,[16] and increasing activity in circuits linked with positivity.[17] This means that you can willfully change the way your brain works—you can harness neuroplasticity to reinforce the move you make in your own mental riverbed.[18]

Perhaps the best way to develop the skill of mindfulness is to take a class or a workshop. An experienced teacher can help you up the steepest parts of the learning curve and inspire you to keep at it. Then you can practice on your own, setting aside regular time in your day to meditate or otherwise practice mindful awareness. Remember, mindfulness does not require meditation. It's simply a way of paying attention.

Of course, taking a class or workshop isn't strictly necessary. You can also start by reading this book or one of the many other books written to introduce mindfulness skills to interested readers. I can tell you from personal experience that reading books like these, and beginning your own meditation practice, can get you moving in the right direction. Back in the late 1990s, that's what I did. I read one of Kabat-Zinn's books, listened to a few of his guided meditations, and taught myself to meditate. Again, data junkie that I am, I tracked the effects of my beginning meditation practice on my day-to-day emotions and mindsets. The results were clear: I was less anxious and better able to focus, whether I was at work considering my research ideas or teaching plans, or at home connecting to my husband or preparing for the birth of our firstborn. I even credit my budding skill in mindfulness with helping me endure the pains of labor and childbirth without medication.[19]

Yet despite my seeming success in learning mindfulness on my own through books and intermittent practice, I can attest that formal instruction makes an enormous difference. Seven years after I began my informal dabbling in meditation, I landed in that seven-day silent retreat for scientists studying meditation. This was my first formal instruction with in-person experts in the practice of mindfulness. We were blessed to have some of the most renowned and cherished Western teachers: Jon Kabat-Zinn, Joseph Goldstein, Sharon Salzberg, and Guy Armstrong. My practice deepened more than I knew was possible after that awe-filled week. Although I'd made forward progress by learning mindfulness on my own, I'd have developed this skill faster and with greater benefit had I taken formal training earlier. With classes and workshops in mindfulness meditation springing up in cities all over the world—in hospitals, in workplace wellness programs, and in yoga studios—there's every reason to enroll in one to jump-start your ability to become more mindfully aware. You have nothing to lose but a lot of gratuitous negativity.

Defuse Your Negativity Land Mines

Chapter 8 showed how you can use the Day Reconstruction Method to locate some of your negativity land mines. You can also spot these by reflecting on your typical daily routine and asking yourself which circumstances usher in the most negativity. Is it your commute? Mealtime? Interactions with certain family members or co-workers? Once you've rounded up the usual suspects, ask yourself, Is this negativity necessary? Is it gratuitous? Is it both?

Carefully examine the circumstances. But be warned, you'll need clear eyes to do this. If the episode in question has safely passed, there's a good chance you've since removed the negativity lenses that perhaps colored your judgment during that particular incident. Nonetheless, before you do your postmortem, check in with how you feel right now. Feeling either neutral or positive is okay. Scientific studies show that we do our most accurate self-assessments in such states.[20] If you notice some negativity in yourself right now, take a breather. Try using another of the negativity-dissolving tools in chapter 11 first. Return to your self-study when you're feeling better.

Here's how to tell the difference between necessary and gratuitous negativity. Necessary negativity faces the facts and moves you forward. You may well need to cry when you've lost something that's dear to you. Crying could very well be what it takes to help you move on. And speaking up at work or at home to raise concerns about what's right or fair is rarely easy. Doing so may arouse anger, anxiety, and more. But perhaps you were able to set your work team on a better course or clear the air of unspoken tension in your marriage. Likewise, feeling guilty about a misdeed can be a learning experience. Some sources of negativity are simply inevitable in the commerce of daily life. They are called forth by the facts of the circumstances and are commensurate with those facts. This sort of negativity helps you stay healthy, productive, and grounded in reality.

In contrast, gratuitous negativity doesn't lead you anywhere good. You'll come to recognize it by its sheer size relative to the circumstances at hand. It's excessive, redundant, ugly—blown up all out of proportion. Perhaps it reflected a self-centered maneuver on your part, a thoughtless verbal aggression, or the drumbeat of self-flagellation. It becomes negativity for negativity's sake. And it lingers on far beyond its usefulness.

When you spot gratuitous negativity, ask yourself whether that activity or circumstance is likely to recur. Is it common for you? If so, consider whether you need to repeat it. Maybe it's altogether avoidable. More than a decade ago, on leaving the movie theater after seeing a critically acclaimed yet immensely violent film, my husband and I felt as if we'd just been through the negativity wringer. We agreed that we'd just witnessed far more gruesomeness than we needed. When given a choice now to go see something we know will be over-the-top violent, either of us might say, "What for? I don't want to go there." So we pick a different kind of movie or do something else. Sometimes with a little self-knowledge you can avoid those situations that spark gratuitous negativity altogether. It's like choosing to rinse the food off your dishes instead of letting it dry into that crusty mess that you know full well will create a nasty kitchen chore later.

Of course, you can't choose to avoid all situations that provoke negativity. Your daily commute may well be as inevitable as doing the laundry or a trip to the dentist. If you can't avoid a situation that brings you needless negativity, you have at least three options for curbing it: you can modify the situation, you can attend to different aspects of the situation, or you can change its meaning.[21]

Suppose you recognize that your commute is a particular drag on your positivity ratio. Though you may well dream of telecommuting or moving to a downtown condo a few steps from your office door, assume that at least for the next year or so, your long drive is unavoidable. How might you modify the situation? For instance, what do you want to learn more about? Physics? History? Poetry? Fiction? Whatever it is, you can dig up endless audiobooks to transform your drive into an engaging learning experience. Or maybe you could find someone with whom to share your ride and your audiobooks. You could have your own book club right there, riding in the commuter lane. Or you could take a train or bus instead and curl up with a book the old-fashioned way—or the new—it's up to you.

Suppose you find that the time you spend eating breakfast and lunch every weekday brims with anxiety. You're always rushing to eat and mentally juggling your ever-expanding to-do list for the rest of the day. Here's where you might simply deploy your attention differently. Attend to the moment, the meal. Drop your thoughts of "what's next" in favor of "what's now." Eating can itself be a huge source of pleasure and gratitude if we only pay attention. Devote mealtime to the sensations of eating, and you not only defuse needless negativity, but also unlock hidden sources of positivity. Notice the pleasing tastes and textures of your food choices. Consider where your food came from. Think of the farmers, grocers, and cooks involved along the way. Their gifts nourish you. In time, by eating mindfully, you may even lose weight as you become more aware of the subtle signs that your body's had enough. Above all, don't multitask. You can set aside time before or after your meal to add to your to-do list—externalize it on paper or into your handheld, and it won't infect your mindscape while eating.

If you need to, you can change the meaning of the situation that triggers your excessive negativity. The cognitive tools in the CBT tool-box do just that. They enable you to replace one meaning with another. I could take writing one and a half pages and throwing out two pages to mean that I'm a failure, or I could take it to mean that I'm a writer. You could take going to the dentist as a pain-fest, or as a challenge to experience discomfort without further magnifying it. Or you could choose to accept it as a necessary means of protecting your health.

Reinterpretations like these defang needless negativity. Once you become attuned to the recurrent sources of gratuitous negativity in your day, you'll know when you most need to forge new positive meanings. Experiment with casting these new meanings up into your new riverbed. Observe how it makes you feel, how it can calm you and energize you to move forward.

Although each person needs to discover on their own the recurrent circumstances in life that carry needless negativity, I find that a few negativity land mines are worth singling out for deeper discussion. The next three sections take on our media habits, social banter, and toxic relationships.

Assess Your Media Diet

If it bleeds, it leads. In one way or another, we've all heard this rule of thumb for news broadcasting. Negativity leads the way because marketers long ago discovered just what scientists have: that negativity grabs your attention, draws you in, and keeps you watching. Certainly, we all need to keep informed about what's happening in our community, nation, and world. And some of what's happening is inevitably bad: forest fires, shootings, war. But when journalists and other media-shapers bring together all these riveting stories, the picture that emerges is unbalanced. In fact, surveys show that the more people watch television, the more violent they judge the world to be. You might think that those who watch a lot of TV are simply better informed about the evils of the world. They're not. They grossly overestimate rates of violence. People who watch less TV are more accurate judges of the degree of risk we all might encounter each day.[22]

Violence is similarly used to captivate and entertain us, in movies, television, video games, and more. Audiences clearly enjoy being pushed to the edge of what they can comfortably take. Violent entertainment is a booming part of the world economy. Yet the downstream psychological costs of viewing violent media have been well studied. Science shows that as you consume violent media, you increase the odds of becoming violent yourself, in large and small ways. You are more likely to hurt others, be suspicious of others, and find violence to be an acceptable solution to interpersonal problems. Media violence zaps your empathy and your kindness.[23]

Yet the negativity spawned by media is often far more subtle than violence. Consider, for instance, the implicit messages about thinness, sexuality, beauty, and race that pervade the visual media. Even more than family and friends, or schools and the workplace, our media teaches us what's to be expected and what's "normal." It's not hard for viewers—especially young viewers—to feel that they don't measure up. This can set the stage for an enduring sense of shame that infects interactions with peers and otherwise reduces everyday enjoyments.[24]

As a culture, we're coming to care a lot about the foods we eat. If we don't want to ingest unnecessary toxins, we buy organic produce. If we want to avoid unhealthy fats, we read ingredient labels. Yet we ingest toxic messages without a thought. As you study the recurrent activities in your life that inflate your levels of gratuitous negativity, pay close attention to how you feel ingesting media, both during and after. Was all the negativity you felt necessary? Was some of it gratuitous? How could you alter your media diet to cut out the saturated fats—the needless negativity? One solution I've found is to get my news online. This enables me to scan headlines and be choosier about what I "eat." Your media diet is double-edged: it informs and entertains you, but often at a price of lowering your positivity ratio.

Find Substitutes for Gossip and Sarcasm

Most days, you swap stories with your colleagues or shoot the breeze with your friends and family. Here, just like a Hollywood TV producer, you seek an audience and make choices about the messages you convey. If you're like many people, you've learned over time that a little verbal violence is titillating. It gets you noticed. This may be what draws you to gossip about the foibles of others or to become cynically sarcastic toward your conversation partners. But these ways of amusing yourself are double-edged; they come at a price to you and others.

If gossip or sarcastic humor is habitual for you, consider whether you are needlessly shackling your own positivity ratio and also bringing those around you down. If this is you, challenge yourself to find substitutes. When you talk about others, highlight their positive qualities and good fortunes, not their weaknesses and mishaps. When you want to poke fun, poke fun lightly. Hurl puns, not barbs. Avoid hidden forms of verbal aggression that cause needless guilt, humiliation, irritation, or self-consciousness to you or your conversation partners. As we know, occasions for necessary negativity abound, so there's little need to manufacture negativity with your daily banter. Doing so needlessly cripples your positivity ratio and crushes your odds of flourishing.

Dealing with Negative People

Suppose it's not you, but someone else. Someone who reliably shows up center stage in your needlessly negative episodes each day. Maybe it's the person sitting next to you at work who complains about everything. Or your boss, who's prone to angry outbursts. Or perhaps your spouse is really good at raining on your parade. Time and again, I'm asked this question: "How do I deal with the negative people in my life?"

Here I think the best advice is to act on one of the three basic ways to curb needless negativity in any circumstance: modify the social situation, attend to it differently, or change its meaning. Although it may well be possible to limit your exposure to this negative person, doing so should perhaps be your last recourse. The three other paths—described as "social aikido" below—may well teach you the most about yourself and your inherent capacity to change.

Aikido is a Japanese martial art described by its founder as the "art of peace."[25] The guiding principle of aikido is to neutralize aggression without causing harm to yourself or your attacker, which is the spirit underlying each of the following three techniques for dealing with difficult people. Think of these techniques as ways to neutralize negativity by extending compassion, love, and openness to those who may well be suffering and lashing out.

Technique 1. Modify the situation. Consider how you might alter the typical situations in which you and this person interact. Start by asking yourself some tough questions. I urge you to mull these questions over earnestly. Push yourself to be truly open about this self-inquiry and see what surfaces: Is there any way that I inadvertently feed this person's negativity? Might I somehow bait them with my own reactions or words? Am I to any degree closed down when we interact? What assumptions do I make about this person?

We all prejudge others now and then. So it becomes useful to really push yourself to discover what you think you "know already" about this person. Once you've located your hidden assumptions, explore how those assumptions might affect your behavior toward that person. In particular, might your assumptions make you less open, less curious, or less warm? People will often use negativity as a bid to get your attention, however childish that approach may seem. So try experimenting with how you act when you're together. What happens when you give your attention and openness first and freely? Express more warmth. Ask more questions. Show particular interest when the messages are lighter and perhaps less when they needlessly turn dark.

Another way to change the situation is to be proactive in setting your collective agenda. Choose joint activities that inspire you. And consider whether you might reserve the tasks that irritate you—for example, paying the bills or cleaning up—for when you're each alone and less likely to fan the collective negativity flames.

A final way to modify the situation, once negativity surfaces, is to inject compassion, hope, or even humor. Curb your tendency to respond "in kind" to gratuitous negativity with yet another helping of it. You don't need to escalate the problem. Instead, offer positive reframes of the negative messages delivered. Convert their "half empty" to "half full." Point out something that you both might see as funny. Scientific studies have shown that relationships in which one partner somehow manages to break the cycle of negative reciprocity—by responding to negativity in a neutral or positive way—fare far better than those in which partners mirror each other's ill will.[26]

Technique 2. Attend differently. Another strategy is to consider how you might attend to different aspects of this person. Sure, there are things about him that you dislike, but what are his positive qualities? What do you appreciate about him? What does he bring to the table? Perhaps your co-worker is better than anyone else on your team at analyzing budgets and trimming the fat, allowing your team to be fiscally more efficient. Or maybe your boss's frequent bursts of anger are matched by his stand-out passion for making a positive difference in the world. Consider the times when your spouse has stood by you, loyal and faithful. Consider how you might give voice to what you appreciate. Scientific studies have documented that, in relationships, the areas where you choose to cast your attention and devote your words grow in strength and significance over time.[27]

Technique 3. Change meanings. Yet another opportunity to experiment is with the meanings you give to these situations. Instead of seeing this person as bringing you down, revisit the quote by Zen teacher Charlotte Joko Beck that opened this chapter. Could this person—or this situation—be a teacher in disguise? They may well be, if you reframe your time with her as a challenge—a challenge to be more mindful, less judgmental, or more compassionate. After all, you get to choose whether to react to the negativity this person spews. Her negativity need not be yours. Working on your own reactions in a mindful way may even remove some of the fuel that keeps this person's negativity flaming. But even if it doesn't, you still come out ahead. You'll have further developed your skill in mindfulness.

I had a great lesson in this when I attended that seven-day silent meditation retreat for scientists. More than once, our teachers urged attendees to minimize disruptions by arriving at the meditation hall on time and staying until the formal group practice was over. Even so, the guy next to me arrived ten or more minutes into every meditation and left whenever he felt like it, disrupting my delicious silence. Midweek, one of the teachers addressed this exact form of irritation directly. He urged us first to mindfully acknowledge the anger we felt: "This is anger. It comes with an urge to rant about how you should be treated differently. It makes you want to lash out." Then he suggested we silently thank the latecomer for giving us the opportunity to practice nonjudgment and nonreactivity in the context of anger. Our gratitude, he suggested, would build our compassion and restore our serenity. I was amazed at how effective this simple reframe could be. It defused irritation every time. Afterward, when my neighbor rustled in late, disrupting my meditation, I'd acknowledge what had just happened and silently express my gratitude. This reframe never failed to bring a smile to my face—however slight—which enabled me to return to where I was. I invite you to try it for yourself. This is social aikido at its best—negativity disarmed with no harm done to you or anyone else.

The View from Here

We've now taken a close look at the amount of negativity—both necessary and gratuitous—in your daily life, and I've introduced several tools you can use to dismantle needless negativity. Chapter 11 offers more. Study upon study documents that these tools work. They've been shown repeatedly to make a positive difference in people's lives. I can say with confidence that learning how to use them is well worth your time. Experiment with disputing your negative thoughts and using healthy distractions to break the grip of rumination. Experiment with mindful awareness. Use the tools available at www.PositivityRatio.com to more readily uncover your negativity land mines. We all have immense room for improvement in our positivity ratios. Taking some of the weight out of your denominator is a great place to start.

Yet it's not the whole story. We're always going to have at least some negativity. That's life. To provide a healthy counterweight to it, you also need to learn how to lift your positivity. Now that you know how to untie those cinder blocks and cast aside that black hood, let's see what it takes to fully blossom.

CHAPTER 10

Increase Positivity

*One evening an old Cherokee told his grandson about a battle
that goes on inside people. He said, "My son, the battle is between
two wolves inside us all. One is Evil. It is anger, envy, jealousy,
sorrow, regret, greed, arrogance, self-pity, guilt, resentment,
inferiority, lies, false pride, superiority, and ego.*

*"The other is Good. It is joy, peace, love, hope, serenity,
humility, kindness, benevolence, empathy, generosity, truth,
compassion, and faith."*

*The grandson thought about it for a minute and then asked his
grandfather, "Which wolf wins?"*

The old Cherokee simply replied, "The one you feed."

—ANONYMOUS

Ridding your days of gratuitous negativity is a great place to start.
But let's now focus on the numerator within your positivity
ratio. Increasing the numerator—your heartfelt positivity—is
your key to unleashing flourishing possibilities in your life. The
emerging science suggests that once your ratio rises above 3 to 1 you'll
be happier. But that's not the half of it. You'll also be more creative and
more resilient. You'll be learning and growing, becoming better each

day. Once your ratio enters this buoyant, flourishing territory, you'll be prepared to make the positive contributions that this world sorely needs.

Sincerity Matters

Heartfelt. Take a moment to appreciate this word. To truly feel positivity in your heart requires that you slow down. The pace of modern life is often so relentless that it keeps you focused outward, away from your inner core. Over time, this stance numbs your heart. To increase your positivity, you'll need to "un-numb" your heart. Let it feel. Let it be open. Slow yourself down enough so that you can see and hear and sense with your heart, not just with your eyes, ears, and mind. Let yourself breathe in and fully absorb the goodness that surrounds you. Connect to that goodness. Revel in it. Together with a sincere attitude, this slower pace unlocks your heartfelt positivity.

Why does this matter? Because positivity that is *not* felt—that does not register in your heart or in your body—is empty. It does you no good. Actually, it can be worse than no good. It can be downright harmful. We saw that back in chapter 2. Fake smiles, just like sneers of anger, predict heart wall collapse.[1] Positive words not matched with positive feelings wash the body in stress hormones.[2] Insincere positivity is not positivity at all. It's negativity in disguise. To truly benefit from the gestures of positivity—whether a smile, a touch, or an embrace—you need to slow down and drink in what that gesture means. Make it heartfelt.

Enter Positive Psychology

Before the twenty-first century, science had scarcely concerned itself with increasing heartfelt positivity. True, a handful of scientists—

myself included—toiled away to discover the causes and consequences of positive emotions. But we worked mostly in isolation, and only a few practitioners were motivated to apply the scientific findings we uncovered.

That scene has changed dramatically. At the beginning of this century, Martin Seligman, then-president of the American Psychological Association, made it his mission to found the new scientific movement of "positive psychology." Seligman argued that psychology had unwittingly adopted a disease model, concerning itself primarily with alleviating human suffering. Indeed, he'd devoted most of his career to understanding depression and developing interventions to curtail it. Although no doubt a worthwhile enterprise, psychology's intense focus on reducing negativity and its attendant damage eclipsed virtually all else. Precious little scientific research, Seligman pointed out, was devoted to discovering how to call forth what makes life worth living.

If the spectrum of life possibilities ranges from –10 to +10, psychology had, until then, made extraordinary advances in the ability to move people from, say, –8 to zero. But we knew little about how to raise people above zero, to +6 or +10. Seligman invited psychologists to imagine the contributions they could make if they shifted their focus beyond alleviating human suffering to include cultivating human flourishing.[3]

The idea spread like wildfire. People were hungry for it, scientists and practitioners alike. My expertise in positive emotions put me at the forefront of positive psychology. At one of the first meetings held to galvanize this new movement, located in the stunning beauty of Akumal, Mexico, I helped articulate the mission and scope of the new positive psychology.[4] Only a decade old, positive psychology has already produced a wealth of information about how to unlock positivity. This chapter spotlights many of those contributions.

Find Positive Meaning

A common thread running through many approaches featured in this chapter is that your habitual patterns of thought are pivotal. Your thinking reveals how you interpret your current circumstances—the meaning you find within them. A key way, then, to increase your positivity and move your positivity ratio to higher ground is to find positive meaning more frequently within your day-to-day life circumstances.

Finding positive meaning is always possible. Does the local forecast predict a partly cloudy sky, or a partly sunny sky? Is the cup or cupboard half empty or half full? Most of the circumstances you face in life are not 100 percent bad. So the chance to find the good, and honestly accentuate the positive meaning in your current circumstances, is always present, even if it's simply to realize that "this too shall pass." When you reframe unpleasant and even dire circumstances in a positive way, you boost the odds that positive emotions—like hope—will flow forth.

Granted, such "silver lining" positivity is often subtle—so much so that it doesn't fully neutralize the aversive situation. But keep in mind that eliminating negativity is not your goal. Even when positivity doesn't eliminate negativity, it still unleashes positive dynamics. We saw that in the study I conducted after 9/11, which I described in chapter 6. After this national tragedy, positivity provided a lifeline that enabled some U.S. citizens to put the brakes on depression's downward spiral and bounce back to become even stronger than before. Likewise, scientists who have studied the emotional upheaval of bereavement have found that people who experience at least some heartfelt positivity intermixed with their grief recover far faster.[5] Some bereaved people cultivate their positivity by reflecting on the good qualities of their lost loved one. Others do it by cherishing the care they're receiving from loved ones still present. Still others reignite their positivity by resuming their daily activities and making a difference for others. No matter how they do it, positivity opens up space in them, space enough to develop their plans and goals for the future. Plans and goals are the fruit of positivity's broadened minds. And sure enough, together with positivity, having plans and goals is what helps bereaved people bounce back.[6]

Meanings are interpretations, the sense you make of your current circumstances. Whether you acknowledge it or not, you forge meanings all day long. Although you might call these small, if you cast them in a positive manner, you pave the way for streams of positive emotions to follow.

What about big meaning? How about the meaning of life itself? What sense do you make of your life as a whole? What story do you tell yourself about why your life has gone the way it has? Does that story energize you, or does it hold you down? Can you say with confidence what your ultimate mission is for your life? If so, does that mission serve as your touchstone, a compass that helps you get back on track when you've wavered off course?[7]

Although the riverbed of your mental habits is shaped more by the accumulation of the small interpretations you make as your days unfold, articulating your biggest interpretation—the meaning of your life as a whole—supplies a blueprint for the smaller meanings you forge moment by moment.

Savor Goodness

Silver-lining positivity results from finding the good within the bad, from turning something negative into a positive. But another strategy for increasing your positivity is to find the good within the good, by turning something positive into something even more positive. You might call this gold-plated positivity.

When something good is about to happen to you, what are you saying to yourself? When you're surrounded by good fortune, what are you thinking? Or when something wonderful is shrinking from view in your rearview mirror, what's running through your mind? People vary in their responses. Some people let their doubts and suspicions lead the way: "It won't really happen to me," "This can't be happening!" or "I knew it wouldn't last." Others don't give it much thought one way or the other. Goodness seems to sneak up on them suddenly and disappear just as quickly. Yet some people find a way to savor goodness.

Whether it's in their future, present, or past, they think about it in such a way that stretches it out and pumps it up. Before some good event happens, these folks might tell themselves, *It's going to be fabulous when . . .* During such an event they may think, *I just want to drink it all in!* And after such an event, they might replay it in their mind's eye, reliving all the good feelings it gave them. People who savor like this extract more positivity from life.[8]

Whether people naturally savor is often a matter of self-esteem, about whether they feel they "deserve" good things to happen to them or not.[9] Even so, savoring is a mental habit you can develop. My Open Heart Study, described in chapter 5, confirmed that the ability to savor is a resource you can build. Beyond merely accepting goodness, you can learn to relish it, deeply appreciating each facet of its pleasantness. If savoring is new to you, learning to do it well can multiply your positivity threefold as you extract more heartfelt goodness before, during, and after pleasant events. To savor simply means considering good events in such a way that you willfully generate, intensify, and prolong your heartfelt enjoyment of them.

Learning to savor entails slowing down and attending mindfully, like taking the time to appreciate all the good aspects of preparing a meal, from the feel of the vibrant fresh vegetables and the aroma of the mix of herbs you've added, to the taste of it all as you adjust the seasonings. And then later you get to savor some more as you fully absorb the experience of sharing your creation with friends or family.

Keep in mind, though, that savoring is not analysis. Boosting positivity requires a light mental touch. Take in the experience as a whole, appreciate the feeling it gives you. Don't dissect it or otherwise pull it apart. Recall that experiments have shown that overanalysis deflates positivity.[10]

Savoring can also mean modifying your circumstances. John, a student in my Positive Psychology seminar, experimented with adding savoring to his life. It was his first semester away at college, and the people he loved most—his family and his girlfriend—were no longer present in his daily life. They were on the phone instead. Never before had talking on the phone mattered so much to him. Yet he came to realize that he'd developed bad phone habits as a teenager. He'd talk on the phone while surfing the web or without adequate privacy. Inspired by the scientific work on savoring, John suspected that something was missing for him. His relationships were important to him, yet he didn't treat his phone calls as important. So he decided to change. Whenever he made or received a phone call from his girlfriend or one of his parents, he'd turn off his laptop and find a private room with a comfortable chair. Now he was able to pay more attention to what they said to him and how he felt. He was also able to share more freely with them. His positivity rose, his experiences of hope and love especially. By modifying the circumstances in which he talked on the phone with the important people in his life, John was able to savor his moments with them. He was surprised by how good it made him feel, how connected. He had learned how to cherish.[11]

Savoring need not remain a private activity. Scientists have shown that one of the simplest ways to multiply the positivity you extract from good fortune is to make a habit of sharing your good news with your spouse, partner, or even with a close friend. Let them in on it. Celebrate together. As you might suspect, it matters how this person responds. Do they rain on your parade, either with their telling silence or by remarking the equivalent of "They give that award to everyone, didn't you know that?" Or do they toast your success, bask in your glory, and otherwise encourage you to fully absorb and celebrate your good fortune? If they actively support you, the positivity yield from that single good event grows significantly. And—as a bonus—your relationship blooms. You become closer and more happily entwined.[12] This gives you even more cause for savoring, which can bring even further positivity. You've entered upward-spiral territory. All this just from sharing your good news.

Count Your Blessings

By moving the riverbed of your habitual thoughts you can reframe something bad as something good and make good things even better. You can even do the same with seemingly ordinary things. You can take something flat, dull, and commonplace, and make it sparkle.[13]

You can make this mental shift by developing the habit of counting your blessings. Recast aspects of your daily life that before seemed hidden from view or altogether mundane as veritable gifts to be cherished. Every day, for instance, on your way to catch the train to work, you pass the same neighborhood shops. Perhaps you never really took notice of the cut flowers standing in large buckets along the sidewalk in front of the produce stand. But one day you do. You realize that flowers bring people bouquets of joy, and that each person who'll put some of these flowers in a vase at home later today will be blessed with a bit of this joy. But at this moment the abundant joy is all yours, as you take in the vivid colors and heady aromas of armful upon armful of fresh-cut flowers. Your eyes widen. You feel alive. Your pace quickens. You find yourself feeling grateful that your path takes you by this storefront every weekday. You find yourself looking forward to seeing each day's new harvest. You feel blessed when you pass this shop day in and day out.

The yield of transforming seemingly ordinary events into blessings may be even greater in your personal relationships. Kindness is common in relationships, so common that it sometimes fades into the background. Yet when you recognize and truly appreciate someone else's kindness toward you, you feel grateful. Their thoughtfulness touches your heart. When you express your gratitude in words or actions, you not only boost your own positivity but theirs as well. And in the process you reinforce their kindness and strengthen your bond to each other.[14]

Years ago, Oprah popularized the idea of keeping a gratitude journal. She encouraged people to write down five things they love each day. She claimed that this simple exercise would change your entire outlook on life. Surveying the new science that has emerged from positive psychology, I'd say Oprah was pretty much on target. Scientists have randomly assigned people to regularly record things that made them feel grateful. Others received different journaling assignments, or no assignment at all. Study participants who regularly drew their attention to aspects of their lives that made them feel blessed increased their positivity.[15] Some caveats emerged, however, such as that it may be better to count your blessings only a few days out of the week than every day. Doing it every day may make it too monotonous, which can zap heartfelt positivity.[16]

Kindness Counts

Kindness has at least two sides. When you count your blessings, you often appreciate how others have been kind to you and have elicited your gratitude. Recognizing the other side of kindness—your side—is another simple and cost-free way to boost your positivity. When my collaborators and I have asked people to become more aware of their kindness toward others, keeping a daily tally of each and every act of kindness, their positivity rises considerably.[17] This "counting kindnesses" intervention seems to work because people who flourish are more attuned to kindness, more focused on others, more alert to how they might make a positive difference. Kindness and positivity feed on each other. Simply recognizing your own acts of kindness initiates this upward spiral.

Developing an eye and appreciation for your kindness is simply a mental shift. You notice it more. You can get an even larger boost in your positivity by stepping up your kind actions. By doing it more. Experiments have shown that intentionally boosting your kindness can increase your positivity.[18] But again, there's a caveat about timing. It helps to perform several large acts of kindness on a single day each week, rather than spread them out across the week. Rather than feeling routine or commonplace, you want to keep your new acts of kindness feeling fresh and extraordinary. Creating a regular "kindness day" seems to do just that. The idea is to maintain your typical expressions of kindness on typical days, but choose a particular day to step up to a much higher level. This may be why devoting a day or an afternoon to volunteer work, either once a week or once a month, can yield so much positivity.[19] It may also be why scientific studies show that helping others predicts living longer.[20]

Follow Your Passions

Live with passion. Give yourself permission to play. Find the activities that uniquely allow you to enter into flow. Flow states are those peak moments in which you become fully absorbed in an activity, when the challenges that the activity poses are high and well-matched by your ever-increasing skills. Your every action, movement, and thought flows naturally from the last. You're fully engaged.[21] Some people enter into flow with their hobbies. For my husband, it's surf fishing. He can stand in the ocean waves for hour upon hour, reading the water and casting out, ever hopeful that he'll stay there forever. It's hardly about landing dinner. (Whenever I ask whether he's got dinner on the line, he reminds me that it's called "fishing," not "catching.") For me, it's cooking. I enjoy reading cookbooks and planning and preparing elaborate meals. As my cooking skills increase, I keep on the lookout for new challenges, such as cooking for thirty at one of our regular neighborhood meals.

More often than not, though, people experience flow at work.[22] I certainly do. I feel that I have the best job in the world. Designing studies, analyzing data, making discoveries, mentoring emerging scientists, finding just the right ways to communicate what I've learned—these are all activities that can fully engross me and make me lose all track of time. Given the outrageous proportion of our lives that we devote to work, you should settle for nothing less than something that carries potential to boost your positivity daily.

Dream About Your Future

Another simple way to boost your positivity is to dream more frequently about your future. Conjure up the best possible outcomes for yourself. Visualize your future successes in great detail. People who are assigned at random to carry out such an exercise show reliable increases in their positivity relative to those who carry out more mundane self-reflections.[23] Although it's not yet clear how visualization works, one suggestion is that it gives you insight into how your everyday goals and motives fit into your dreams about your future. This may well help you extract more goodness out of your daily activities. Strikingly, visualization has been shown to activate the same brain areas as actually carrying out those same visualized actions.[24] That's why visualization has been such a powerful tool for winning athletes. Mental practice can perhaps be just as effective as physical practice. At the very least, it's a positive and energizing complement.[25] Visualization may work especially well if you have long-range projects, such as getting an education, writing a book, or building community.

Apply Your Strengths

People who have the opportunity every day to do what they do best—to act on their strengths—are far more likely to flourish.[26] Strengths are highly individualized, varying from person to person. Some strengths define the contributions you're most poised to make at work. Others are psychological and, when taken in combination, define the unique impact and contributions you might make in life as a whole. Research has shown that learning about your strengths can give you a high.

One of the largest early efforts in positive psychology—spearheaded by Seligman himself—has been to develop a survey that reliably classifies people on the basis of twenty-four character strengths, ranging from curiosity and integrity, to kindness, fairness, humility, and hopefulness. Together with Christopher Peterson, my colleague at the University of Michigan, Seligman surveyed diverse world cultures to create a comprehensive index of character strengths and virtues called the VIA Signature Strengths Questionnaire. Another very compelling way to learn about your strengths is to consult people who know you well and ask them to describe times they've witnessed you at your very best. This Reflected Best Self Exercise was developed by my colleagues at the business school at the University of Michigan.[27] It has since gained wide acclaim, having been featured in the *Harvard Business Review* as an effective and energizing tool for personal development.[28] See chapter 11 to learn how to use either or both of these methods to discover your own signature strengths.

However you learn about your strengths—whether through a survey or through the eyes of others—the key to extracting more than a temporary high out of your new insights is to reshape your work or daily life in such a way that you're able to apply your strengths more often. Whereas re-crafting your job or daily life is a more demanding task than simply keeping a gratitude journal or visualizing your best possible self, it promises deep and recurrent fulfillment. Simply exercising a strength and making a contribution is profoundly gratifying, a source of heartfelt personal meaning. Controlled experiments have compared the effects of either simply learning about your signature strengths or learning about them and also making efforts to apply those strengths. From this work, scientists have discovered that the boost in positivity that comes from learning your strengths is significant but temporary. By contrast, the boost in positivity that comes from finding new ways to apply your strengths is significant and lasting.[29]

Connect with Others

Flourishing is not a solo endeavor. It's scientifically correct to say that nobody reaches his or her full potential in isolation. Every person who flourishes has warm and trusting relationships with other people, whether it's with a spouse or romantic partner, close friends, family, or all of the above. And compared with those who languish, people who flourish spend more time each day with the people they're close to, and less time alone. Indeed, the tie between flourishing and enjoying good social relations is so strong and reliable that scientists have called it a necessary condition for flourishing.[30]

This may in part reflect that simply being with others—whether you know them well or not—is an extraordinarily reliable way to increase your positivity. Scientists have documented this basic fact extensively. Some have tracked people's day-to-day activities and emotions. Others have taken a more controlled approach, by assigning people at random to either be together with someone else or not. No matter how you look at it, the results are clear: people gain more positivity by being with others than by being alone.

So connect with others, every day and no matter what. And even if you're not naturally a very outgoing person, act like you are. Scientific experiments document that if you simply pretend to be extraverted when you're with others—that is, if you act bold, talkative, energetic, active, assertive, and adventurous—no matter what your natural inclinations are, you'll extract more positivity from those social exchanges.[31] My own Open Heart Study suggests that you don't particularly need to be or act outgoing; cultivating loving concern for others seems to be enough. People who made regular efforts to cultivate such tenderness and compassion pulled more positivity out of their ordinary exchanges with others than did those who lived life as usual. I encourage you to experiment with putting on extraversion or loving concern for others. See what new sources of positivity spring forth. My prediction is that when you're with others you'll smile more, laugh more, enjoy greater positivity, and all the while build deeper and more satisfying connections that enrich your life and enable you to flourish.

Connect with Nature

Natural environments may be as important to flourishing as social environments. So another very simple way to increase your positivity is to go outside. More precisely, go outside in good springtime weather. This advice is based on the work of a former student of mine, Matt Keller (now an assistant professor at the University of Colorado at Boulder).

Matt was keenly interested in the effects of weather on positivity. Having lived his entire life in sunny Texas, he suddenly found himself transplanted in Ann Arbor, Michigan, with its "lake effect" cloud cover. The clouds hang so low in Ann Arbor that when I lived there I often felt that they accumulated on my head! Intrigued by the links he noted between the weather in Ann Arbor and his own moods, Matt reviewed the scientific research on the subject. He was shocked to learn that the mood-boosting quality of good weather was judged to be an old wives' tale, completely unsupported by empirical evidence.[32] Matt simply didn't believe it.

He had a hunch that the surprising lack of scientific evidence might be due to people's limited time spent outdoors. A sad fact of modern life is that we're almost completely insulated from direct exposure to the weather, spending an average of 93 percent of our time indoors.[33] Noting this, Matt predicted that good weather would raise people's positivity only if they spent a reasonable amount of time outdoors.

My laboratory routinely collects data on study participants' moods, as well as on their broadened thinking, or open-mindedness. One spring Matt added a simple question to our standard battery: "How much time did you spent outside so far today?" He later downloaded precise measurements on the local weather from the National Climatic Data Center. Two clear findings emerged. People who spent twenty or more minutes outside when the weather was nice showed the predicted boost in positivity. Yet for people who spent little time outside, weather and positivity were largely unrelated. We also learned that people who spent at least twenty minutes outside when the weather was nice had more expansive and open thinking. Even their working memory span was larger. They could literally hold more thoughts in mind. This discovery stunned us because working memory span has long been viewed as a proxy measure of intelligence. If so, simply going outside can make you smarter!

The following spring, we tested Matt's prediction experimentally, assigning study participants at random to spend time outside or not, and then measuring positivity and broadened thinking. We got the same results. This told us that we hadn't discovered something that simply held for "outdoorsy" people. Everyone who spent time outside when the weather was good showed a boost in positivity and more expansive thinking. Later studies, done year-round, revealed that these were seasonal effects, evident in the spring and early summer only.[34]

Matt's discovery resonates well with the scientific research on the benefits of nature experiences. Being immersed in nature carries both *fascination*, in that it draws your attention involuntarily, and *vastness*, in that it provides sufficient scope and richness to fully occupy your attention. These two qualities of experiencing nature may well produce positivity and openness. They're also what seem to make your time in nature so healing and restorative. Remember the finding that the length of your hospital stay depends on whether the view from your hospital window reveals nature's greenery or not? Similar studies show that people can put themselves on healing trajectories by spending time outdoors connecting to nature.[35] Simply put, being outdoors allows you to see farther, and seeing farther may be all it takes to expand your thinking and give you more to feel good about.

Open Your Mind

Positivity opens your mind naturally, like the day lily that opens with the sunlight. The beauty of this arrangement is that positivity and openness feed on each other, each triggering and reinforcing the other. This bidirectional link means that another lever you can grasp to increase positivity is to be open. Be open and positivity will follow.

I felt this upward spiral viscerally as I practiced mindfulness hour upon hour during that seven-day retreat. Positive emotions flooded me—awe, gratitude, joy, and deep and abiding serenity. Wave upon wave of positivity kept me open to learning and practicing more. I became deeply curious. I knew the evidence about how mindfulness reduced the pains of negativity, but how exactly did mindfulness unleash the gush of positivity that I was now experiencing? How did mindfulness relate to my own life's work? What was its relationship to my broaden-and-build theory?

My teachers at the retreat underscored time and again that mindfulness was a skill that one learned and practiced by focusing on the present moment and being experientially open. Being mindful provided a skillful means of coping with the challenges of day-to-day living. What struck me then was that mindfulness training teaches people to do something that comes naturally and automatically with positive emotions. It teaches people to open their minds. When you practice mindfulness, instead of cultivating positivity directly, you make a beeline to openness. Yet because openness and positivity are fused—each causing and amplifying the other—your newly cultivated openness throws open the doors to positivity, creating the rush of the upward spiral.

You, like every other person, have already experienced open and mindful attention from time to time. Positivity is your birthright. You inherited it from a long and successful line of human ancestors. By nature's design, positivity opens your mind. Nature has ensured that you'll have at least a taste of mindful awareness in your life, a taste of the openness that sets you on trajectories of growth and builds your resources. You get those broaden-and-build moments automatically and effortlessly every time you experience heartfelt positivity. And if you want more of those broaden-and-build moments, you can be open. Practice mindful awareness of your surroundings. By doing so, you deliberately open your mind. It's a skillful means of arriving at the same open mindscape that positivity produces automatically. Yet, thanks to the architecture of our human emotional systems, once you deliberately cultivate openness, positivity follows automatically, along with its broaden-and-build entourage.[36]

Supporting these ideas, one study randomly assigned groups of people to begin a practice of mindfulness meditation or not. Both groups underwent laboratory testing before and after the target group learned to meditate. Among other tests, they wore a cap that distributed twenty-seven tiny sensors across their scalp to monitor their brain activity. Both immediately after the training period and four months later, meditators showed increases in left-side brain activation, a pattern repeatedly linked to greater positivity.[37] Another study found that, compared with beginning meditators, advanced meditators reported more self-awareness and acceptance in addition to more positivity.[38] Sure enough, openness and positivity go hand in hand. Data from studies like these suggest that efforts to be open, practiced through mindfulness meditation, will indeed raise your positivity.

So openness breeds positivity. And meditation is a skillful way to increase openness. But it's not the only way. Another route is to reduce certain habits of mind that tend to constrain and compartmentalize experience. Recently, scientists have argued that you and every other human faces a "pleasure paradox." That is, when you think too much about a positive experience, you actually dampen that experience and reduce the positivity you derive from it.[39] We crave information without realizing that this information can be a positivity killer. Therefore, explaining goodness paradoxically erases it. One lesson here is that you're best off accepting random acts of kindness as random. Be open to goodness however it arrives: practice acceptance, not analysis, and your positivity will blossom.

A while back, my husband kidded me about my old cell phone. It had a small banner of text on its main screen that I could modify. For years it simply read, BARB'S PHONE. "Can't you think of anything more original than that?" he teased. I gave it a moment's thought and changed the banner to BE POSITIVE. But even as I did so, the message seemed contrived and unsatisfying. I knew full well that despite the wealth of benefits that flow from positivity, people can't simply will themselves to be positive. We can't strong-arm our emotions. In other words, even I couldn't enact the advice within the BE POSITIVE message. Reflecting more deeply on the dance between positivity and openness, I later changed the banner again. It now reads BE OPEN. I've been amazed at how pivotal this simple reminder can be.

Open Your Heart

Whereas the practice of mindfulness meditation opens your mind, other age-old meditation practices seem to more directly unlock your heart. Practicing these other forms of meditation helps you experience your connections with others, bringing forth the deep and heartfelt positivity of community.

I described in chapter 5 what I've come to call my Open Heart Study. Whereas most Western science on meditation has centered on mindfulness meditation, I chose to investigate the effects of a cousin technique, loving-kindness meditation.[40] I was initially attracted to loving-kindness meditation because it more directly aims to evoke positive emotions, especially within the context of our relationships. Along the way, we uncovered a lot about the emotional repercussions of initiating a practice of loving-kindness meditation. Here I describe how to begin experimenting with it yourself.

Loving-kindness meditation is a technique used to increase feelings of warmth and caring for self and others. Like mindfulness, loving-kindness evolved from ancient Buddhist mind-training practices. Each practice involves quiet contemplation in a seated posture, often with eyes closed and an initial focus on the breath, but in loving-kindness meditation you aim to train your emotions toward warm, tender, and compassionate feelings in an openhearted way. You direct these warm and tender feelings first to yourself, and then to an ever-widening circle of others.

Practicing loving-kindness is not a magic bullet to the heart that unfailingly makes your positivity soar. Still, the positivity generated by this form of meditation practice accounts for a wide sweep of benefits in people's lives—from improved abilities to savor and be mindful, to having an easier time accepting themselves, finding positive meaning, and trusting others. Practitioners even suffer fewer aches, pains, colds, and flus. Practicing loving-kindness helps people move the riverbed for their day-to-day emotions to higher ground. Ultimately, they become less depressed and more satisfied with life as a whole. If you're inspired to experiment with loving-kindness in your own life, try the meditation described in chapter 11 or seek out a class or a teacher. A number of useful books can also help you get started (see Recommended Resources).

The View from Here

Positive psychology is a young field, but despite its youth, it has already developed some wisdom. Born into the clan of science, positive psychology has a skeptical bent. It feeds on data, seeking out general-izations you can trust. So you can relax, knowing that the wisdom it offers is tried and tested. Mere fads have been discarded. Throughout this chapter I've limited the discussion to approaches that have been tested scientifically and shown to increase people's positivity. See whether and to what extent they lift your positivity ratio, allowing you space to grow and flourish.

Perhaps you've noticed by now that some of the approaches are quite simple. Open your eyes to kindness and gratitude. Savor good-ness when you see it. Visualize your best possible future. Be more so-cial. Go outside. These are the small changes you can make to elevate your positivity any time you want. Together these approaches will un-lock more of the six most common positive emotions within you—love, joy, gratitude, serenity, interest, and hope. As they do so, they will open your mindset and put you on a course of resilience and growth.

Other approaches require more effort. Redesign your job or your daily life to better utilize your strengths. Learn to meditate, with mindfulness training, loving-kindness, or both. Make finding positive meaning your default mental habit. Although these self-change efforts are larger, their positivity payoffs have already been shown to be great. Investing your efforts in these approaches is well worth your time.

Positive psychology has literally just begun. The approaches fea-tured in this chapter are the cream of its first crop. In the next chapter I distill these approaches into tools you can use any time you want to cultivate positivity. I'll also share some new ideas fresh from the draw-ing board, in line to be tested. Only time will tell what future harvests in positive psychology will yield. The true test for you, though, is how using these tools makes you feel as you try them out yourself.

CHAPTER 11

A New Toolkit

When they tell you to grow up, they mean stop growing.
—Tom Robbins

The multitude of studies that I and other scientists have conducted on positivity is destined to remain merely interesting dinner conversation until you deepen your self-study. You need to pivot away from what's worked for others and toward what works for you. Have your own "Eureka!" moments. Discover for yourself what rouses genuine and heartfelt positivity.

This shift is important because scientists have found repeatedly that emotions are highly individualized. They reflect the self-styled sense we each make out of our current circumstances. What makes you grateful might be all but invisible to others. Everybody's different when it comes to the exact events and circumstances that trigger their emotions. This means that your own path to flourishing will be unique.

As you begin your self-study, keep your yardstick handy. That is, keep taking the Positivity Self Test each day, either in your journal or online at www.PositivityRatio.com. It takes just a minute or so. Then see how you measure up once you begin experimenting with change. Compare your ratio against where it was before.

I suspect that even without charting data, you'll be able to feel a new sense of energy and vitality. Allow these good feelings to draw you back to doing the right things. Notice and appreciate the broader outlook on life they give you. Celebrate this "big picture" thinking. Know that this openness is all you need to keep the juices of positivity flowing.

Working from the preceding two chapters, I've assembled a tool-kit to decrease negativity and increase positivity, consisting of a dozen tools to help you raise your ratio. Each is backed by science. Each has been shown to be effective for some. Try them out and see what works best for you.

Tool 1. Be Open

The goal here is to experiment with mindful awareness while carrying out your day. Make your motto "be open." Temporarily rid your mind of expectations and judgments. All too often these cloud your ability to be open. Instead, give yourself permission and time to experience the richness of the present moment. No matter what you encounter, no matter what happens, experiment with both awareness and acceptance.

One way is to tune in to and appreciate your direct sensory experiences. On your morning walk, rather than being lost in your ever-expanding mental to-do list, practice being open to the colors of the leaves and blooms, the call of the nearby birds, the smell of the wet grass, the feel of the cool morning air against your skin, or even the pressure of the earth beneath your feet. Being open means cultivating both curiosity about and acceptance of whatever you're currently experiencing. Attend to what's happening without trying or wishing for change. There's no need to view any of the thoughts, feelings, or sensations that come to mind as disruptions that must be suppressed. Instead, acknowledge them, appreciate them, and allow them to pass. Tell yourself, "It is what it is," and simply observe. Mindful awareness casts a wider, more accepting stance toward the present moment than is typical. Watch what feelings emerge as you experiment with openness.

Tool 2. Create High-Quality Connections

Truly connecting with others can be a breath of fresh air. Any social interaction—whether with family, co-workers, or the person ahead of you in line at the post office—is a chance to create a high-quality connection. According to Jane Dutton, cofounder of the Center for Positive Organizational Scholarship at the University of Michigan's Ross School of Business, your moments of connection with others form a dynamic, living tissue that can be either life-giving or life-depleting. High-quality connections are life-giving.[1] You recognize them instantly by several telltale signs: they foster mutual appreciation and encourage truly being or doing things together; they recharge your energy and your vitality; they bring real physiological changes. You can literally feel high-quality connections resonate within your body.

Dutton's research points to four ways to build high-quality connections. The first is respectful engagement. Be present, attentive, and affirming. The second is to support what the other person is doing. Do what you can to help her succeed. The third is trust. Believe you can depend on this person to meet your expectations, and let it show. The fourth way is play. Allow time simply to goof off, with no particular outcomes in mind. Engaging with others in one or more of these ways transforms ordinary or corrosive interchanges with others into endless sources of genuine positivity.

The challenge I put to you is to cultivate high-quality connections where none previously existed. Do it all day long with everyone you encounter. Notice how different you feel compared with when you're gossiping with or oblivious to others. Notice how energized and buoyant you become. Notice, too, how the other person reacts. Do your eyes meet more often? When your conversation comes to a close, do either of you carry on with a smile on your face or a spring in your step? Think of the gift you're giving, both to yourself and others.

Tool 3. Cultivate Kindness

This exercise draws from research done by Sonja Lyubomirsky, author of *The How of Happiness*. Give yourself the goal of performing five new acts of kindness on a single day. Aim for actions that really make a difference and come at some cost to you, such as donating blood, helping your neighbor with her yard work, or figuring out a better way that your ailing father might manage his chronic pain. Be both creative and thoughtful. Assess what those around you might need most. Although some of the kind acts you choose may take some advance planning, make a point to carry them all out on a single day. At the end of the day, take stock. Notice the good feelings that come with increasing your kindness: the positive connection to the person you helped, the fitting sense of pride you get from making a contribution. For lasting impact, make your kindness day a recurring ritual. Be creative each week. Find new ways to make a positive difference in the lives of others. Try it for a few months and see the difference it makes.

Tool 4. Develop Distractions

Distractions are important tools for breaking the grip of rumination and curbing needless negativity. The goal is simple—to get your mind off your troubles. The most effective distractions demand your full attention. You get lost in the activity, fully absorbed by it, so that when you emerge you've cleansed yourself of the blues and are ready to approach your problems with a clear mind.

I suggest you make two lists. Label one HEALTHY DISTRACTIONS and the other UNHEALTHY DISTRACTIONS. Ask yourself, "What can I do to get my mind off my troubles?" Then brainstorm. Identify things you already do, as well as new activities you'd like to try on for size. Be sure to come up with things you can do in good and bad weather, whether you're at work, at home, or on the road. In good weather perhaps you'd work in the yard, go for a bike ride, or play soccer with the neighborhood kids. In bad weather maybe you'd go to the gym, learn a new knitting technique, or play chess with your son. At work, maybe you'd dive into research, clean your desk, or catch up on past e-mails. On the road you might read a novel, take on a Sudoku puzzle, or run through some yoga poses in your hotel room. The aim is to come up with activities you can turn to at virtually any time you need to break the downward pull of rumination.

Next, write down the unhealthy distractions that tempt you. Maybe you're too quick to pour yourself a drink, open the fridge, or visit the bakery when your downward spiral tugs. Or maybe you're drawn to numb yourself by consuming media. If so, ask whether the media you choose furthers your negativity. For each unhealthy distraction that tempts you, come up with a healthy alternative: a drink or a snack that doesn't take a toll; a movie, computer game, or song list that's more uplifting.

Suppose you wanted to engage in each activity right now. Would you need anything to get started? Yarn? A good book? A Sudoku website? Keep your distraction resources handy. Needless negativity can strike at any moment. To fight it, you need to be ready to distract yourself at a moment's notice. Most of all, give yourself permission to be distracted. It only takes a few minutes to break the cycle of a downward spiral. Yet the benefits of the turnaround are priceless.

Tool 5. Dispute Negative Thinking

This exercise is adapted from the Penn Resiliency Program, a depression-prevention effort rooted in cognitive-behavioral therapy that teaches non-negative thinking.[2] For this, you'll need a set of index cards. On each one, write one of your typical negative thoughts, such as, *Overslept again! How will I ever get everything done?* or *Why hasn't she called by now? Doesn't she care about me?* What's important here is to write down negative thoughts that are realistic and truly yours. Capture your inner critic, that voice in your head that's skeptical of you, of others, and of everything around you—the voice of ill will.

Once you have written out your set of usual suspects, shuffle the cards and pick one at random. Read it out loud. Then—as fast and as thoroughly as you can—dispute it! Do it out loud and with some conviction. What are the facts here? When you're satisfied that you've shot down your menacing negativity with your rapid-fire facts, move on to the next card. Repeat. As you work your way through your negativity deck, let your conviction grow as you become a seasoned disputer. Whenever you find gratuitous negativity lurking in your mind, externalize it by adding it to your deck of cards. Challenge yourself to meet it out in the open—out loud—with your rapid-fire facts.

Negative thoughts roll out automatically, against your best intentions. Your goal with this exercise is to become just as quick with disputation as you are with negative thoughts. Nip them in the bud with your fast facts, before they have a chance to blanket your day with doom and gloom. Try this exercise and see if facts alone can disarm the negativity spawned by automatic negative thinking.

Tool 6. Find Nearby Nature

When the weather is good, you need to be ready. Locate a dozen places you can get to in a matter of minutes that will connect you to green or blue, to trees, water, or sky. These have been shown to boost positivity. Perhaps a few natural spots bloom just steps from your door. If so, explore them thoroughly. Make them your own. Go to your library or local bookstore and pick up a guide to the walking trails and gardens in your area. Although a public fountain or square will do in a pinch, seek out more-natural sanctuaries: forests and rivers, meadows and oceans, the more expansive the better. Make these places regular destinations, whether to exercise, socialize, or just be one with nature.

Tool 7. Learn and Apply Your Strengths

One way to learn your strengths is to take a free, online survey that Martin Seligman and Chris Peterson developed with support from the Values in Action Institute.[3] Allow yourself plenty of time to take this survey: it contains 240 items to measure twenty-four character strengths. You can find it by visiting Seligman's website at the University of Pennsylvania's Positive Psychology Center, or point your browser to www.AuthenticHappiness.com. After completing the survey, you'll receive a report that ranks the twenty-four strengths by the degree to which they characterize you. The report will also feature your top five strengths and encourage you to reflect on which ones truly resonate for you, which strengths, when you act on them, make you come alive. This self-reflection is critical. It's how you locate your "signature" strengths among your top five.

A second, more personal way of discovering your strengths is through the Reflected Best Self Exercise, developed by the Center for Positive Organizational Scholarship at the University of Michigan's Ross School of Business.[4] This involves contacting between ten and twenty trusted people in your life, ranging from colleagues and customers to friends and family members. You ask each to give you three detailed stories about the ways you add value and make important contributions. Once all the feedback has arrived, you analyze it, looking for commonalities and themes. Your task is to pull those themes together in a Reflected Best-Self Portrait, a short essay that captures the wisdom within the narrative data you've gathered and studied.

Odds are you'll be deeply moved by this exercise. Your story requests will have unlocked a veritable river of appreciation from the significant people in your life. Despite your extended contact with these people, their stories of why and how much they appreciate you have likely gone unspoken. Sad to say, it's not normal for us to speak frankly and openly about the ways we love and appreciate one another. Yet gaining access to these reflections ignites positivity. You'll feel grateful to the people who sent you stories, more connected to them. You can take pride in the ways you've made a difference. And you'll be energized to move closer to your best self more often. Your Reflected Best-Self Portrait can serve as a guidepost when you flounder or lose your way. Reading it when you're down can help you get back on track.

Once you've learned your strengths, the hard part follows: redesign your job and life so you can use them every day. Which aspects of your job or daily activities draw on your strengths? Which aspects squelch them? How might you devote more of your energy toward doing what you do best? What changes do you need to make to truly use your strengths each day?

Tool 8. Meditate Mindfully

Deepen your practice of mindful awareness with daily meditation. Read through this section once or twice, then set the book down and try it now. Set an alarm to go off in five or ten minutes so you can experiment without worrying about time. As you get more comfortable, challenge yourself to practice for longer. About twenty-five minutes is ideal, but carve out whatever is possible on any given day.

Find a quiet place where you can sit comfortably without being interrupted. If you're in a chair, place your feet flat on the floor, scoot back in the seat so that your lower back is well supported, and straighten your spine upward. Rest your hands lightly on your lap, palms up.[5] Or find any other position that makes you feel both alert and relaxed. Let your eyelids drift closed. If that feels awkward, gaze lightly at a spot on the floor in front of you, or at some common object, like a lit candle.

Take a few deep breaths. Notice how it feels. Where do you feel your breath? Is it at your nostrils? In your rib cage? In your belly? What's the progression of sensation for each in-breath and each out-breath? Now just breathe normally. No need to make your breath deep or patterned in any way. Just let it be. Continue to observe your breath. What does each in-breath feel like? What does each out-breath feel like? Witness each in-breath and out-breath with reverence. Each is you—alive—here and now.

The goal in attending to your breath in this way is to practice being present, right here and right now. Sounds simple enough. Yet the moment you start experimenting with being present, you discover how hard it truly is. Invariably, your mind wanders. Thoughts come up and entice you along grand mental adventures. You might find yourself reliving something that bothered you earlier today or earlier this week, or planning next week's work presentation or family menu. In either case, one thought leads to the next and soon enough you're planning a detailed rebuttal or grocery list. You've become lost in your thoughts—fully absorbed by your mental time travel and utterly unaware of your current surroundings.

Wherever your mental adventures land you, it's okay. Don't beat yourself up for it. It's virtually inevitable that you will lose track of the now. Expect it. Instead of berating yourself with gratuitous negativity, simply notice that your attention has strayed and return to your breath. See how long you can stay in the present—in your own, personalized version of now. Experiment with becoming the observer. Become aware of your mind in action. Thoughts will arise. It's only natural that they do.

See if you can quietly observe your thoughts arising. Gently identify them. Using the lightest touch possible, connect a neutral description to each arising thought or feeling. Something like, *Here's a thought coming now,* or *This is what anger feels like.* See if you can observe the allure of your thoughts and feelings. See if you can notice yourself being pulled to follow them. See, too, if you can choose to stay in the present. If you can, you'll also become aware of your thoughts and feelings as they fade away.

There's no need to suppress your thoughts. Indeed, a long line of scientific evidence suggests that doing so backfires.[6] Actively trying to stop thinking just breeds more thinking. Your mind's going to do what your mind's going to do. Accept that. Be kind to yourself when you notice it. Recognize that this is where you are and simply begin again.

You'll start over countless times. Never stop starting. Each moment brings a chance for a new beginning. Beginning again in the present moment is what mindfulness is about. It's about observing your mind in action and practicing being where you are now. Know, too, that attending to your breath is simply a vehicle for strengthening your ability to remain in the present moment. The payoff is not in how many breaths you can count while you're sitting, but rather in how well you can stay present and aware during the rest of your life.

Tool 9. Meditate on Loving-kindness

You can also use your daily meditation time to cultivate loving-kindness. Read through this section once or twice, then put the book down and set an alarm to go off in ten minutes. As you get more comfortable, allow yourself to experiment for longer, aiming for twenty-five minutes when possible.

Loving-kindness meditation is a bit like guided imagery, although the practice targets emotions more than visual images per se. Start by focusing on your breath and the region of your heart. Once grounded in the feeling of your own heart in this quiet moment, reflect on a person for whom you already feel warm, tender, and compassionate feelings. This could be your child or spouse, or even a pet. Your goal is to rouse warm and tender feelings naturally, by visualizing how being with this loved one makes you feel. Once these tender feelings of love and compassion have taken hold, creating genuine positivity in you, gently let go of the image of that particular loved one and simply hold the feeling.

Now extend that warm feeling to yourself. Cherish yourself as deeply and as purely as you would cherish your own newborn child. For many—especially for westerners—this is a large hurdle. We're not accustomed to directing our love inward. It takes patience and practice to make it genuine. At first you might spend the entire time directing love to yourself.

Next, radiate your warm, tender, and compassionate feelings to others, first to a person you know well, then gradually calling to mind all your friends and family, and then all people with whom you have a connection—even a remote connection, like the service person you reached on your last call for tech support. Ultimately, extend your feelings of love and kindness to all people and creatures of the earth. To do this you might visualize your city, your region of the country, your continent, and finally the whole earth.

Traditional loving-kindness meditation comes with a set of statements that you repeat silently to yourself. The words themselves are not as critical as the sentiments they evoke. I encourage you to rephrase the statements in ways that stir your heart most. The traditional statements go something like this: *May this one* [or I, we, he, she, or they] *be safe. May they be happy. May they be healthy. May they live with ease.* Repeat these phrases slowly and silently to yourself. Let them cultivate genuine warmth and tenderness as you move your attention from yourself to an ever-widening circle of others. As you end your meditation, remind yourself that you can generate these good feelings for yourself any time you wish.

Tool 10. Ritualize Gratitude

Being grateful simply requires that you notice the gifts that surround you. If you're drawn to record your thoughts in writing, consider buying a handsome blank book to be your gratitude journal. In it, describe the things for which you're grateful each day. Beyond simply listing good things in your life, one effective strategy is to describe why each good thing happened, in a few sentences. Doing so draws your eye to the precursors of good events.[7]

If, like me, you're not the journaling type, you can still create potent gratitude rituals within your daily routine. Consider, for instance, reviving the time-honored ritual of saying grace before meals: either in your head or out loud, take a moment to offer your sincere thanks for the food that's before you. You choose whom to thank, whether it be God, the earth, farmers, food handlers, chefs, or all of the above. Feeding yourself will not feel so ordinary if you do. Or try a ritual that I use. For decades I've been fascinated with endings. I'm intrigued by how these turning points create and carry heartfelt meaning.[8] Good endings include an appreciative summary—an honest acknowledgment of the goodness that transpired prior to leave-taking. When I face an ending—little or big—I take stock of what good has happened in that location. If I'm leaving a person or group, this ritual often inspires me to express my appreciation aloud. If I'm simply leaving a place—even if it's a hotel room on a work-related trip—I'll silently thank that place for supporting me and whatever insights or experiences that occurred there. You'd be surprised how many times each day you face endings. If departures become your cue to give thanks, this ritual will leave you afloat in gratitude each day.

Tool 11. Savor Positivity

To experiment with savoring, you'll need two things: first, a source of genuine love, joy, pride, or any other flavor of positivity in your life; second, a willingness to think differently about it. It doesn't matter if your source of heartfelt positivity happened in the past, is happening now, or has not yet come to be. I recommend practicing with all three time frames. See which suits you best. The key is to think about the event in a way that stokes your positivity flames right now. Truly cherish the event, and its benefits to you will grow.

Unearth a past moment of positivity, whether from yesterday, last week, or last year. Allow yourself time to roll your mental images around in your mind. Look at them from all angles. Pump them up and then drink in their sweetness now, cherishing them once again. Now consider whether you can consolidate those memories further. Did you take any photos? If so, perhaps you could organize them and select a few to frame or share. Do you, like me, have a love of words? Then perhaps you could write a poem or story about the most radiant moment. Or simply strike up a conversation with someone who'd also appreciate these cherished moments.

Once you recognize how valuable good feelings are to your mindset and your future, savoring becomes easier. You'll soon find that you can stretch and amplify your moments of heartfelt positivity simply by the way you attend to them. As a good moment unfolds, take mental pictures—or actual pictures—that allow you to accentuate what touches your heart the most. Narrate your experience with a gentle inner voice that truly appreciates what's unfolding before you. Notice the small details. Once you sharpen your skills for savoring the past and the present, use those newly honed skills to anticipate future good times. Cherish them in advance. As ever, keep a light touch. Simply tune yourself to be ready for goodness however it shows up. Believe that it will arrive, while also embracing the fact that the details will always surprise you. You'll come to enjoy good events in advance and be poised to savor them when they show up.

Tool 12. Visualize Your Future

Try this journaling exercise that I've adapted from work by scientist Laura King and performance coach Jim Loehr.[9] Imagine yourself ten years from now, after everything has gone as well as it possibly could. You have worked hard and succeeded at accomplishing all of the life goals you set for yourself. Visualize where and how you'd be if all your current dreams came true. Imagine that you've reached your own best potential. Carry on with this journaling assignment for several writing sessions, perhaps every day for a week. Fill in all the details you can imagine. Describe your surroundings and your feelings.

After about a week, review what you've written. Draw out from your dreams a life mission. What purpose do you want to drive you—each and every day? Why do you get up in the morning, feed yourself, and bother to stay healthy? In other words, what's the meaning of your existence?

Let yourself soak in these tough questions, and journal some more. Take time to let your deepest hopes and dreams rise to the surface. Give those visions words. Get your ideas out on paper, then distill them to their essence by crafting a mission statement, short enough to memorize and serve as your touchstone. When you think you've got it right, put it to the eulogy test. If you were to carry out this mission, would your time on earth be well spent? Would others resonate with appreciation and admiration? Now create a ten-year plan to help you meet your mission. Distill it to bullet points, so that your dreams can guide you through your decisions now.

Personalize Your Self-study

Deepen your self-study further by making it even more personal, more about you. In chapter 8, I described how to use the Day Reconstruction Method to locate wellsprings of positivity. If your "yesterday" was typical, you discovered which parts of your daily routine fuel you the most. Study those circumstances. What about them allowed your positivity to blossom? Were you with others? Were you completely uninterrupted? Did you have a purpose? A passion? To what were you attending? Identify the conditions that supported your positivity. See if you can import those conditions into more parts of your day. Can you rearrange your routines to better capitalize on positivity?

If you're like most people, though, your excavation of "yesterday" holds precious few clues about your full potential. To uncover your full capacity for positivity, cast your eye further back, beyond yesterday. Consider your life as a whole. As you do so, think about each of the ten different positive emotions featured in this book—joy, gratitude, serenity, interest, hope, pride, amusement, inspiration, awe, and, last but not least, love. If you think I've overlooked an emotion that's vital to your life, by all means think about that one too. Think about the times when you felt each of these emotions clearly or deeply. What were the triggers of these nourishing states for you? When was the last time you felt each of these mind-opening states? Where were you? What were you doing? What was happening?

Hunt and Gather

To really benefit from this deeper layer of self-study, my suggestion is that you get concrete. Pull together objects and mementos that create for you a heartfelt connection with each of the ten forms of positivity. Assemble these into a portfolio, a physical collection that you build as a shrine to each shade of positivity. Make each emotion into a project. Take this on as if it were an assignment you were doing for a class. Invest your time and savor the task for a full week. A week on joy, a week on gratitude, and so on, until you reach a week on love.

You may be thinking that this seems like a childish assignment. If so, this might be a good time to revisit the quote that opened this chapter and consider what children know that you've somehow forgotten. Or maybe it just seems like a lot of work—a frivolous or wasteful use of your valuable time.

Although at this very moment you may be comfortable and carefree, it's inevitable that you'll be facing tough times again—perhaps sooner than you think. And those tough times, whether they come as losses, offenses, or looming threats, are a breeding ground for negativity. And negativity, as we've seen, screams so much louder than positivity. It can pull you on a downward spiral so fast that it diminishes both you and your future prospects. To make a course correction toward positivity, you may well need more than a handful of dim recollections about what sparked positivity for you in the past. That's when physically getting your hands on one of your own unique positivity portfolios can make the difference. Reexamine its contents. Remind yourself of the good in your life. This simple break can often breathe life into you again and inspire you to find your way back to the nourishing upward spiral of positivity.

Each portfolio might contain photos, letters, quotes, or objects that carry deep personal meaning for you. In pulling these mementos together, your goal is not to scrutinize your joy or your gratitude and so on. Keep your mind expansive. Use only the light touch of recognition as you identify new mementos to add, not the heavy hand of intellectual dissection. Your goal is to create a new fusion of personal artifacts, personalized triggers that revive your heart with positivity each time you engage with them.

You might store your portfolio in a simple file folder or box. If you've got artistic leanings, you might create a small scrapbook or a curio box. If you've got computer skills, you might create a web page or an electronic folder of digital photos to download to your handheld. If you want to create something immensely portable and ever-present, you might first create a physical portfolio and then commit the entire contents of it to memory.

Whatever the format, your portfolios will come to reflect the inner workings of your heart, your own positive emotions. Nutritionists ask their clients to pay attention to how certain foods make them feel. I ask you to pay attention to how certain activities, circumstances, and lines of thinking make you feel. Become familiar with what uplifts and enlivens you. As you do so, you gain both insight and control over your everyday experiences.

Don't rush through this process. Savor it and enjoy. Take a full week to resonate on each emotion and build a portfolio for that feeling that truly moves you. People find that building the portfolio can itself be a deeply rewarding and uplifting experience. Don't miss out!

The idea of building these portfolios came to me from James Pawelski, director of education and senior scholar at the world's foremost Positive Psychology Center, at the University of Pennsylvania.[10] As a budding positive psychologist, James was invited to interview for a job as an assistant professor at Vanderbilt University. He was both excited and nervous. To build his confidence for that interview, he created what I would call a pride portfolio. He included in it connections he had made with the founding fathers of positive psychology, scholars he deeply respected and admired—an encouraging e-mail message from Mike Csikszentmihalyi, a snapshot of himself with Marty Seligman. He also added other mementos that made him feel secure and socially valued. Once he'd fully prepared for the interview, he spent the final thirty minutes revisiting his portfolio and connecting with it emotionally. It reminded him that, although young, he was both respected and capable. He entered the interview feeling calm and confident. Because his own portfolio worked so well for him, years later, as director of education working side by side with Marty Seligman, James shaped these ideas into a research project that he regularly assigns to students enrolled in the University of Pennsylvania's Master of Applied Positive Psychology program, the world's first degree program in positive psychology. I regularly serve as a guest faculty member in that master's program, and some of James's students have shared with me their experiences in making and using their own positivity portfolios. I'm now collaborating with him and others to test the effectiveness of these portfolios in a wide range of circumstances.

I've made my own portfolios too. The first one was for love. It holds pictures of my two young sons and my devoted husband. Together with these is a quote by the early-twentieth-century French writer Marcel Proust: "Let us be grateful to people who make us happy, they are the charming gardeners who make our souls blossom." I've also added a snapshot of what we call our "love chair"—an overstuffed chair-and-a-half in our living room where we cuddle quietly and share time together. Of course, it's not the chair that matters. But having the picture of the chair reminds me to go there with my family members more often, to make and savor more cozy moments. Finally, perhaps again reflecting my inner scientist, my love portfolio has a picture of a pair of chimpanzees grooming each other. This helps me remember that the urge to love is ancient, universal, and unstoppable. Revisiting my love portfolio reminds me to take breaks more often, to call home if I'm on campus or traveling, or otherwise connect with my boys and my husband more deeply, to hug and hold them close. The love I share with them never fails to open my heart, re-energize me, and teach me how to live more fully.

Build Your Own

To structure this process, I'll guide you through each of the ten positive emotions. For each, I'll pose a set of questions to get you started. Write notes to yourself as you answer these. What memories and images come to mind? After you've pulled together some ideas, go on your treasure hunt. Find just the right photos, words, and objects to create each portfolio. Perhaps a song or video clip would evoke the right feeling, or a scent, taste, or tactile sensation. Assemble your portfolios with care and creativity. Each is a gift to yourself.

To envision and then build your **joy portfolio**, consider:

1. When have you felt safe, relaxed, and joyful, utterly glad about what was happening in that moment?
2. When have things truly gone your way, perhaps even better than you expected?
3. When have you felt a spring in your step, an unstoppable smile, or a warm glow?
4. When have you felt playful, as if you wanted to jump in and get involved?

To begin building your **gratitude portfolio**, think about:

1. When have you felt grateful or thankful, deeply appreciative of someone or something?
2. What gifts do you treasure most? When has someone gone out of their way to do something good for you?
3. When have you simply basked in how lucky you are?
4. When do you feel the urge to repay a kindness? What inspires you to get creative about giving back?

To pull together your **serenity portfolio**, consider:

1. When have you felt fully at peace and serene, truly content with where you are?

2. When has your life felt so comfortable and so very right?
3. When does your body feel completely relaxed, with all your physical tensions melted away?
4. When do you feel like simply sitting back and soaking it all in, savoring the goodness you feel, thinking of new ways to get this feeling in your life more often?

To envision and build your **interest portfolio**, consider:
1. When have you felt fully alert and curious, deeply interested in the mysteries or possibilities unfolding before you?
2. When have you felt both safe and yet also captivated by something new and unknown?
3. When have you felt intensely open and alive, as though your own inner horizons were expanding before your eyes?
4. When have you felt an intense pull to explore and learn more, to fully immerse yourself in your new discoveries and take in a feast of new ideas?

To begin your **hope portfolio**, think about:
1. When have you felt hopeful and optimistic, encouraged by the possibilities of a good outcome?
2. When faced with uncertainty, when have you feared the worst but still somehow believed that things could change for the good?
3. When have you physically yearned for something better to happen?
4. When have you tapped into your inventiveness to work toward a better future?

To start on your **pride portfolio**, consider:
1. When have you felt most proud of yourself, fully confident in your abilities, and self-assured?
2. When have you done something praiseworthy? Achieved something through your own concerted efforts?
3. What makes you hold your head high and stand up tall? What makes you want to share your good news with others?

4. What draws you to dream big, into visions of what you might accomplish in the future?

When you're ready to envision and build your **amusement portfolio**, reflect on:
1. What makes you feel silly and fun-loving? What amuses you?
2. Remember nonserious social incongruity? When have you and others uncovered or kicked up some unforeseen bit of humor?
3. What makes you laugh? When have you and others infected one another with irrepressible laughter?
4. When do you have the urge to share your joviality with others, to goof off and perhaps in the process build a friendship?

When you're ready to start your **inspiration portfolio**, consider:
1. When have you felt truly inspired, uplifted, or elevated by goodness?
2. When have you come across true human excellence or virtue? When have you seen someone perform or act better than you ever imagined was possible?
3. When have you felt drawn to simply witness the excellence that was unfolding before your eyes? When has your jaw silently dropped when seeing the best in humankind?
4. When have you felt an urge to do your best, so that you too might reach your higher ground?

When you're ready to envision your **awe portfolio**, reflect on:
1. When have you felt intense wonder or amazement, truly in awe of your surroundings?
2. When have you felt overwhelmed by greatness, or by beauty on a grand scale?
3. When have you been stopped in your tracks, transfixed by grandeur?
4. When have you felt part of something much larger than yourself?

When you're ready to dive into creating your **love portfolio**, consider:

1. When do you most readily feel the warmth of love well up between you and another? When do you feel close, safe, and secure within your relationship, trusting?
2. When does a relationship of yours spark one of the many other forms of positivity—joy, gratitude, serenity, interest, hope, pride, amusement, inspiration, or awe?
3. When do you find yourself leaning in toward your beloved, affirming his or her uniqueness?
4. When do you have the urge just to be with and enjoy the companionship of your beloved, to cherish him or to bask in his reflected glory?

How to Use Your Portfolios

I encourage you to view your positivity portfolios as living documents. Let them evolve. Update them. Bear in mind that they need to stay fresh to lift your positivity. Remember the hedonic treadmill? That's the phrase scientists coined to describe the quick evaporation of people's emotional highs and lows. If you make just one portfolio, keep it in full view on your desktop, never adding to it or changing it in any way, I can almost guarantee that it will soon lose its charge. Looking at it will become completely commonplace. It will fade into the background like wallpaper.

The beauty of having ten ever-growing portfolios is that you stand a chance to outpace the treadmill—to keep positivity alive and kicking. Perhaps counterintuitively, I suggest that you keep all but one of your portfolios filed away, hidden from view. Carry only one with you to serve as your shield against the downward spirals of life, your toehold on the upward spirals that are possible for us all. And when you first notice that the lift you get from this portfolio is weakening, think about how you might recharge it with new items, and then give it a rest. Give it a sabbatical while you make use of another portfolio. Rotated in this way, none of them will be overtaxed and worn thin.

Another key to keeping the shine on your positivity portfolios is to engage with them mindfully, with the single purpose of awakening your heart to the positivity you seek. Don't just look at the contents of your portfolio; take time to engage with each item deeply. Remember how you felt when you first encountered each item. Breathe in that memory. Let it permeate you as fully as possible. Let it resonate. Then look around you to discover what else might unlock this kind of heartfelt positivity in you. Science has shown that mindful engagement with treasured objects keeps your positivity yield high.

As you engage with the contents of your portfolios, remember to keep a light touch. Positive emotions are both powerful and fragile. You can't force them, or force them to endure, by sheer willpower. So don't try to strong-arm them. The best triggers of positivity are often subtle and unforeseen—unexpected smiles, beauty, or generosity. The best strategy, then, may well be simply to remain open, so you can soak up these subtleties as they occur. If you choose to see them, you'll soon find that they surround you. Having found them, savor them. Keep in mind that scientific studies have shown that positive emotions need not be intense or protracted to be powerful.

Always keep one close at hand, in your briefcase, backpack, or handheld. That way, you can turn to it when you need it most. Maybe you'll soon be stuck in the waiting room while a loved one has surgery.[11] Maybe you're about to give an important presentation to an unfamiliar audience. Maybe you've simply had a jam-packed, stressful day at work and need to switch gears before you greet your family at home. Notice how engaging with one of your portfolios helps you to breathe easier, how it opens your heart and broadens your mind. I suspect that you'll soon be thinking more expansively and compassionately.

Ten Tips for Creating and Using Positivity Portfolios

1. Be sincere. Let your positivity be heartfelt, not forced.
2. Create depth within your positivity portfolio. Include multiple artifacts.
3. Make several portfolios. Don't rely on any single positive emotion.
4. Let your portfolios evolve over time. Keep adding to them.
5. Always keep one of your portfolios at hand.
6. Pull out your portfolio when you feel the tug of a downward spiral.
7. Engage with your portfolio mindfully, with an open heart.
8. Keep a light mental touch. Don't analyze.
9. Rotate to another portfolio when one loses its charge.
10. Ask, "What could I do right now to cultivate this feeling?"

The View from Here

The time you invest in self-study and tracking your emotions is well spent. Each time you pick up a tool to undo negativity's pull, you initiate a rebound and take a step on your pathway toward flourishing. You meet the world with clear eyes that can newly appreciate the abundant goodness that surrounds you. You trigger your own upward spiral. In time, grounding yourself with your unique sources of positivity becomes habitual, a ritual for trying times or any other time you simply feel stuck or lifeless. Once you cross the threshold into flourishing—in a sustained way—you may no longer need to use these tools and portfolios consciously. At that stage, each day becomes a treasure hunt for hidden sources of positivity—a treasure hunt that you're winning.

As you experiment with positivity, please keep in touch. Share your challenges and successes. Even if you don't create your own database on www.PositivityRatio.com, you can visit the website simply to send me a message. Inspiring personal accounts will be posted on a special page so that you can connect with others who are also plumbing their own wellsprings of positivity.

With the river of your emotions running through higher ground, you can't help but flourish. If you can keep your positivity ratio above the critical 3-to-1 threshold—honestly, with genuine, heartfelt positivity that fully accepts life's inevitable sources of negativity—you'll soon become your best. And at your best, before long you'll become a positive influence on the world around you.

CHAPTER 12

Future Forecast: Flourishing

*I don't want to get to the end of my life and find that
I lived just the length of it. I want to have lived the
width of it as well.*

—DIANE ACKERMAN

So now you know the news about positivity. Before you picked up this book, you knew that positive emotions felt good. You knew instinctively that you'd rather feel joy than sorrow, or hope than despair. You already appreciated positivity at this surface level.

My aim in this book has been to deepen your appreciation, to give it scientific legs, to let you see below the surface and into the future, to open your eyes to the vital role that positivity plays in the unfolding saga of your own life story. Just as night-vision goggles amplify starlight, enabling you to see in darkness, my hope is that the scientific insights about positivity offered here give you a revelatory set of lenses—lenses that amplify and multiply the goodness in your life, enabling you to flourish.

You know now that the good feeling you get with positivity is just the start of something much more profound. And this new knowledge just might change your life if you let it. In this closing chapter, I'll reprise and weave together the six most important scientific facts about positivity. I offer these to you based on my twenty years of studying the subject. Although Facts 2, 3, 4, and 5 represent my own discoveries, I take only partial credit for shaping Facts 1 and 6. Each fact nonetheless plays a vital role. My aim is to show you how these facts can come alive and dance with one another in the complex symphony of life.

Fact 1. Positivity Feels Good

Though this first and most obvious fact may not seem profound, it is. Positive emotions sparkle with a pleasing inner experience, an enjoyable glow, for a reason. Remembering the glitter of past moments of positivity, you welcome new ones with delight—so much so that you seek them out. At a deep, inborn level, you *want* to feel positivity. Yet all that glitters is not gold. Counterfeits and distant cousins abound. The counterfeits are modern exploitations of the ancient wisdom of positive emotions: recreational drugs, gambling, and other addictions. The cousins are bodily pleasures, like eating and sexual stimulation. My strong scientific hunch is that my discoveries, distilled as Facts 2 through 5 following, apply only to positive emotions.

Fact 2. Positivity Broadens Minds

The second fact is that positivity opens your mind and expands your range of vision. Although this broadened mindscape is temporary, it creates much-needed mental space. You escape the tightness of negativity and gain elbow room for greater flexibility and seeing the big picture. You feel a growing sense of oneness. This fundamental yet unheralded fact about positivity is the first core truth in my broaden-and-build theory.

Fact 3. Positivity Builds Resources

The third fact about positivity is that it transforms you for the better. However subtle and fleeting, your moments of positivity accumulate and compound over time to build lasting resources for life. You become stronger, wiser, more resilient, and more socially integrated. Positivity spells growth. It sets you on a trajectory toward becoming a better person. This second and final core truth in my broaden-and-build theory is perhaps my most unique scientific contribution.

Fact 4. Positivity Fuels Resilience

The fourth fact about positivity is that it's the secret active ingredient that makes you resilient. When hard times threaten to suck you down negativity's downward spiral, positivity applies the brakes and allows you to bounce back. At the physical level, positivity is your reset button. So although positivity may seem weak and puny in the looming shadow of negativity, it holds its own. Even in dark times, positivity continues to broaden your mind and build your resources.

Fact 5. Positivity Ratios Above 3 to 1
Forecast Flourishing

The fifth fact about positivity is that its relative frequency in your life is subject to a tipping point. If you're like most people, your positivity outnumbers your negativity by about 2 to 1. At this ratio, life is rather ordinary. You get by, but you're hardly growing. This is languishing. As you raise your ratio above 3 to 1, a transformation occurs. You feel more alive, creative, and resilient. You have a palpable sense of personal growth and of making a positive difference. This is flourishing. It feels and *is* totally different from languishing. You've stepped up to a whole new level of life.

Fact 6. People Can Raise Their Positivity Ratios

The sixth fact about positivity gives me a profound sense of hope. It's why I wrote this book. It's that, through their own efforts, people can raise their positivity ratios and tip themselves from languishing to flourishing. You have more control over your ratio than you realize.

Allowing the Facts to Dance

Simply lining up Facts 1 through 6 leaves the picture incomplete. To see the full beauty of positivity, we need to step back and let the facts mingle. Let them strike up conversations and connect with one another. Let them take a spin on the dance floor. As they do so, they inspire and build off one another's energy in the ancestral dance of reciprocal causality.

Watch what happens, for instance, as each fact in turn joins arms with Fact 1, Positivity Feels Good. See the pace quicken. The dynamic really takes off. This is because Fact 1 is perhaps the most crucial design feature built into the positivity system by Darwinian natural selection. Why? Because "feeling good" provides both incentive and reward for flourishing. It drives the system and provides the fuel.

Consider this: Who teaches kids how to play? Nobody! It's in their genes. Kids play because it feels good to play. And in playing, kids try out and learn new ideas, make new friends, and strengthen their bodies. Play spells learning and growth because positive emotions broaden and build. But kids don't need to know the underlying scientific theory. They simply need to keep doing the things that generate those good feelings. Likewise, I can say with confidence that you were designed, by natural selection, to flourish. You simply need to do the things that generate heartfelt positivity in you.

Yet perhaps, like many adults, you've long since lost the strong play ethic you had as a kid. Somehow our culture led you to believe that other things were more important than feeling good, like working hard or making money. If so, remember that feeling good is vital if you want to be fully alive. Let the sparkle of positivity draw you in.

Now let's watch again as Fact 2—Positivity Broadens Minds—works the party. Everywhere it goes, eyes widen and new ideas pop. Sure, some of those ideas turn out to be silly and completely fruitless. But others are more intriguing. They end up being consequential down the road. They bear fruit.

Fact 2 is like a random act generator: A broadened mind allows you to break out of old habits and well-worn ruts, to do something different—anything different. Randomness like this is essential to building resources (Fact 3), rebounding from adversity (Fact 4), and flourishing (Fact 5). Indeed, random variation plays a vital and necessary role within life itself, as shaped by Darwinian natural selection. Technically, reproduction is never perfect. That is, organisms don't clone themselves when they reproduce. Random genetic variations sneak in that make each offspring slightly different, both from their parents and from other offspring. In terms of helping offspring survive, those genetic differences might be helpful, harmful, or completely inconsequential. The helpful ones get passed on, becoming more common in later generations. Simply put, without random genetic variation, life—including yours—would not have evolved. Random genetic variations can even lead to new forms of life altogether. Perhaps similarly, the randomness inherent in the "do anything" spirit of positivity will lead you to a new form of life. Fact 2 might just help you break out of the monotonous rut of languishing and step up into the vibrancy of flourishing.

Fact 3, Positivity Builds Resources, brings its own touch to each dance. It moves slowly, but builds momentum with time. It draws your attention to the future, the long-range future. It promises that you'll be better off this time next year—maybe even next season. And when it spins with Fact 2 (Positivity Broadens Minds), randomness and usefulness join hands and set off positivity's upward spiral.

The elegant upward spiral dance between Facts 2 and 3 creates the dynamic energy that ushers in Fact 4, Positivity Fuels Resilience. If you look closely, you'll see that positivity's upward spiral is no mirror opposite to negativity's downward spiral. By nature's design, it's more social, more open and permeable. And thank goodness it is because with it you can rebound from hardships, heal within community, and grow stronger.

And here comes Fact 5, Positivity Ratios above 3 to 1 Forecast Flourishing. In one grand gesture, it unlevels the dance floor and surprises everybody. A tipping point rises up and separates the crowd of dancers into two crowds. On one side, the point of positivity is lost altogether. Not much is happening. Dancing eventually stops. But on the other side, things are really hopping. All the Facts are shining and doing their stuff. They're breaking out, blooming, spiraling, rebounding, and going back for more, all with great beauty and grace. Truly a sight to behold. It's clear which side of Fact 5's tipping point you want to join.

So you thank your lucky stars when you see Fact 6, People Can Raise Their Positivity Ratios. Fact 6 smiles warmly with open arms, welcoming you and everyone else to join the party. After learning a few ground rules about sincerity and keeping a light touch, you grab a partner and step onto the dance floor. You make things happen. As I've said, it's win-win: you do good for the world as a result of feeling good yourself.

Karma Unpacked?

Do you have enough positivity to pull off the age-old recipe for a flourishing life? If you find yourself short, you can surely gather up more. After all, simply by virtue of being human, you have within you the seeds of flourishing. You can generate positivity anytime, anywhere. You reap what you sow, that's the biblical scripture. Eastern traditions refer to this same idea about cause and effect as *karma*.

As a scientist, I'm hardly in a position to advance religious doctrine. Even so, the complex evolved systems of negativity and positivity may well be the core of karma. Viewed in this way, there needn't be any score-keeping deity up in the sky drawing up a list of who's naughty and nice. Positive consequences emerge from positive emotions simply as the unfolding of a natural process. If you plant seeds of positivity, you flourish. If not, at best you languish. Yet perhaps a science metaphor would sit better for you than a spiritual one. If so, try this one on for size: if you want a barometer that can forecast your prospects for flourishing—for being happier and making a contribution—simply check your own positivity ratio.

The View from Here:
Choose the Upward Spiral

A few years ago I came across a greeting card that read, "Life gives us negativity on its own. It's our job to create positivity." I like this phrasing because it reminds us that positivity is a choice—a choice we all need to make again and again, day after day. Before you close this book for the last time, I'd like to remind you that your emotions are as far from random as they are from being fixed by your genes. They stem to a large degree from your daily activities and your entrenched mental habits. Perhaps more than you ever thought possible, you get to choose them. Sure enough, negativity that's necessary will always know where to find you. But you can choose to minimize the gratuitous kind. And the more you value positivity, the more often its upward spiral will lift you to new heights.

Your nutritionist asks you to track your food intake and activity levels each day. Your financial adviser asks you to track how cash flows both in and out of your wallet and bank account. Likewise, I ask that you monitor your momentary emotions, both negative and positive. Awareness will reveal hidden opportunities to raise your ratio. Just like watching calories or cash can in time help you meet your fitness or financial goals, monitoring your positivity ratio today can help you flourish next season.

So tune in to kindness—your own and that of others. Seek out and savor all manner of goodness, beauty, and excellence. Treasure these moments and you'll unlock recurrent waves of gratitude, awe, inspiration, and more. Become like a plant and turn toward the light, in all its spiritual, earthly, and human forms. Feed on it. The more you train your eye, mind, and heart to the positivity in your life, the more of it you'll find. Remember that the intensity of your positivity matters far less than its relative frequency. This means that even mild positivity, experienced often, can lead you to your higher ground. Gratuitous negativity, which once grew out of control, will no longer control your destiny. By cultivating positive actions and positive thinking, you seed more positivity in your life. The more positivity you seed and harvest, the better become your prospects for flourishing.

And as you reach this noble goal of flourishing, you help create a world that is truly worth leaving to our children. I find that we often look too far ahead to find our happiness. We try to be wealthy or famous instead of trying to be loving or fascinated. By making more moments glisten with positivity, you make the choice of a lifetime: you choose the upward spiral that leads to your best future—and to our best world.

Appendix

POSITIVITY SELF TEST

How have you felt over the past twenty-four hours? Look back over the past day and, using the 0–4 scale below, indicate the *greatest amount* that you've experienced each of the following feelings.

> **0** = not at all
> **1** = a little bit
> **2** = moderately
> **3** = quite a bit
> **4** = extremely

1. What is the most **amused, fun-loving,** or **silly** you felt? ____

2. What is the most **angry, irritated,** or **annoyed** you felt? ____

3. What is the most **ashamed, humiliated,** or **disgraced** you felt? ____

4. What is the most **awe, wonder,** or **amazement** you felt? ____

5. What is the most **contemptuous, scornful,** or **disdainful** you felt? ____

6. What is the most **disgust, distaste,** or **revulsion** you felt? ____

7. What is the most **embarrassed, self-conscious,** or **blushing** you felt? ____

8. What is the most **grateful, appreciative,** or **thankful** you felt? _____

9. What is the most **guilty, repentant,** or **blame-worthy** you felt? _____

10. What is the most **hate, distrust,** or **suspicion** you felt? _____

11. What is the most **hopeful, optimistic,** or **encouraged** you felt? _____

12. What is the most **inspired, uplifted,** or **elevated** you felt? _____

13. What is the most **interested, alert,** or **curious** you felt? _____

14. What is the most **joyful, glad,** or **happy** you felt? _____

15. What is the most **love, closeness,** or **trust** you felt? _____

16. What is the most **proud, confident,** or **self-assured** you felt? _____

17. What is the most **sad, downhearted,** or **unhappy** you felt? _____

18. What is the most **scared, fearful,** or **afraid** you felt? _____

19. What is the most **serene, content,** or **peaceful** you felt? _____

20. What is the most **stressed, nervous,** or **over-whelmed** you felt? _____

Take this Positivity Self Test and more at www.PositivityRatio.com.

Notes

CHAPTER 2. POSITIVITY: MEANS, NOT ENDS

1. Frijda, N. H. (1986), *The Emotions* (Cambridge, England: Cambridge University Press); Lazarus, R. S. (1991), *Emotion and Adaptation* (New York: Oxford University Press).

2. Levenson, R. W. (1994), "Human emotions: A functional view," in P. Ekman and R. Davidson, eds., *The Nature of Emotion: Fundamental Questions* (New York: Oxford University Press, 123–26).

3. Sapolsky, R. (1994), *Why Zebras Don't Get Ulcers: A Guide to Stress, Stress-related Diseases, and Coping,* 2nd edition (New York: Freeman).

4. Frijda, 1986.

5. Lazarus, 1991.

6. Levenson, R. W., P. Ekman, and W. V. Friesen (1990), "Voluntary facial action generates emotion-specific autonomic nervous system activity," *Psychophysiology* 27: 363–84.

7. Fredrickson, B. L. (1998), "What good are positive emotions," *Review of General Psychology* 2: 300–19; see also Fredrickson, B. L. (2001), "The role of positive emotions in positive psychology: The broaden-and-build theory," *American Psychologist* 56: 218–26.

8. Dolhinow, P. J. (1987), "At play in the fields," in T. Topoff, ed., *The Natural History Reader in Animal Behavior* (New York: Columbia University Press), 229–37.

9. Mateo, J. M., and W. G. Holmes (1999), "Plasticity of alarm-call response development in Belding's ground squirrels (*Spermophilus beldingi,* Sciuridae)," *Ethology* 105: 193–206. Also from personal communication with Warren Holmes.

10. Fazio, R. H., J. R. Eiser, and N. J. Shook (2004), "Attitude formation through exploration: Valence asymmetries," *Journal of Personality and Social Psychology* 87: 293–311.

11. Adam's story is a fictionalized composite based on scientific facts discovered by Judith Moskowitz, Susan Folkman, and their colleagues. The

scientific details are presented in Moskowitz, J. T. (2003), "Positive affect predicts lower risk of AIDS mortality," *Psychosomatic Medicine* 65: 620–26, and in Folkman, S., J. T. Moskowitz, et al. (1997), "Positive meaningful events and coping in the context of HIV/AIDS," in B. H. Gottlieb, ed., *Coping with Chronic Stress* (New York: Plenum Press), 293–314.

12. Danner, D. D., D. A. Snowdon, and W. V. Friesen (2001), "Positive emotions in early life and longevity: Findings from the nun study," *Journal of Personality and Social Psychology* 80: 804–13; see also Levy, B. R., M. D. Slade, et al. (2002), "Longevity increased by positive self-perceptions of aging," *Journal of Personality and Social Psychology* 83: 261–70; and Ostir, G. V., K. S. Markides, et al. (2000), "Emotional well-being predicts subsequent functional independence and survival," *Journal of the American Geriatrics Society* 48: 473–78.

13. Lyubomirsky, S., L. King, and E. Diener (2005), "The benefits of frequent positive affect: Does happiness lead to success?" *Psychological Bulletin* 131: 803–55.

14. Biernat, M., T. K. Vescio, et al. (1996), "Values and prejudice: Toward understanding the impact of American values on outgroup attitudes," in C. Seligman, J. M. Olson, and M. P. Zanna, eds., *The Psychology of Values: The Ontario Symposium,* vol. 8 (Hillsdale, NJ: Lawrence Erlbaum), 153–89.

15. I found this to be the case in one of my latest field experiments, conducted in collaboration with Michael Cohn, Kimberly Coffey, Jolynn Pek, and Sandra Finkel (see chapter 5); see also Easterlin, B. L., and E. Cardena (1998), "Cognitive and emotional differences between short and long term Vipassana meditation," *Imagination, Cognition & Personality* 18: 69–81.

16. Carstensen, L. L., and J. A. Mikels (2005), "At the intersection of emotion and cognition: Aging and the positivity effect," *Current Directions in Psychological Science* 14, no. 3: 117–21.

17. Jen's story is a fictionalized composite based on scientific facts described in Moskowitz, J. T., and E. S. Epel (2006), "Benefit finding and diurnal cortisol slope in maternal caregivers: A moderating role for positive emotions," *Journal of Positive Psychology* 1: 83–91.

18. Williams, R. (1998), *Anger Kills: Seventeen Strategies for Controlling the Hostility That Can Harm Your Health* (New York: Harper Torch).

19. Victor's story is a fictionalized composite based on scientific facts presented in Rosenberg, E. L., P. Ekman, et al. (2001), "Linkages between facial expressions of anger and transient myocardial ischemia in men with coronary artery disease," *Emotion* 1: 107–15.

20. To read what other scientists working in positive psychology think of the yellow smiley face, see "Some Dark Thoughts on Happiness," *New York Magazine,* July 2006.

CHAPTER 3. WHAT *IS* POSITIVITY?

1. Cabanac, M. (1971), "Physiological role of pleasure," *Science* 173 (September 17): 1103–7.

2. For example, there is fascinating new work on the little-studied emotion of elevation. See Haidt, J. (2003), "Elevation and the positive psychology of morality," in C. L. M. Keyes and J. Haidt, eds., *Flourishing: Positive Psychology and the Life Well-Lived* (Washington, DC: American Psychological Association).

3. Tugade, M. M., B. L. Fredrickson, and L. Feldman Barrett (2004), "Psychological resilience and positive emotional granularity: Examining the benefits of positive emotions on coping and health," *Journal of Personality* 72: 1161–90.

4. Lyubomirsky, S., L. Sousa, and R. Dickerhoof (2006), "The costs and benefits of writing, talking, and thinking about life's triumphs and defeats," *Journal of Personality and Social Psychology* 90: 692–708; Wilson, T. D., D. B. Centerbar, et al. (2005), "The pleasures of uncertainty: Prolonging positive moods in ways people do not anticipate," *Journal of Personality and Social Psychology* 88: 5–21.

5. These depictions of joy draw on Lazarus, R. S. (1991), *Emotion and Adaptation* (New York: Oxford University Press); Ellsworth, P. C., and C. A. Smith (1988), "Shades of joy: Patterns of appraisal differentiating pleasant emotions," *Cognition and Emotion* 2: 301–31; Izard, C. E. (1977), *Human Emotions* (New York: Plenum Press); and Gross, M. M., E. A. Crane, and B. L. Fredrickson (2008), *Methodology for assessing bodily expression of emotion* (manuscript under review).

6. These depictions of gratitude draw from Fredrickson, B. L. (2004), "Gratitude, like other positive emotions, broadens and builds," in R. A. Emmons and M. E. McCullough, eds., *The Psychology of Gratitude*

(New York: Oxford University Press) 145–66; Algoe, S. B., J. Haidt, and S. L. Gable (2008), "Beyond reciprocity: Gratitude and relationships in everyday life," *Emotion* 8: 425–29.

7. This portrayal of interest builds on the following works: Csikszentmihalyi, M. (1990), *Flow: The Psychology of Optimal Experience* (New York: HarperPerennial); Izard (1977); Tompkins, S. S. (1962), *Affect, Imagery, Consciousness,* vol. 1, *The Positive Effects* (New York: Springer); Kaplan, S. (1992), "Environmental preference in a knowledge-seeking, knowledge-using organism," in J. H. Barkow, L. Cosmides, and J. Tooby, eds., *The Adapted Mind: Evolutionary Psychology and the Generation of Culture* (New York: Oxford University Press), 581–98.

8. Lazarus, 1991.

9. My depiction of hope also draws on Tong, E. M. W., B. L. Fredrickson, and W. Chang (2008), *Re-examining the nature of hope: The roles of agency and pathways thinking* (manuscript under review); Snyder, C. R. (2002), "Hope theory: Rainbows in the mind," *Psychological Review* 13: 249–75; Pettit, P. (2004), "Hope and its place in mind," *Annals of the American Academy of Political & Social Science* 592: 152–65.

10. Tiger, L. (1995, original edition 1979), *Optimism: The Biology of Hope* (Kodansha Globe).

11. This depiction of pride draws on the following works: Tracy, J. L., and R. W. Robins (2004), "Show your pride: Evidence for a discrete emotion expression," *Psychological Science* 15: 194–97; Tracy, J. L., and R. W. Robins, (2007), "The psychological structure of pride: A tale of two facets," *Journal of Personality and Social Psychology* 92: 506–25; Williams, L. A., and D. DeSteno (in press), "Pride and perseverance: The motivational role of pride," *Journal of Personality and Social Psychology*"; Lewis, M. (2000), "Self-conscious emotions: Embarrassment, pride, shame, and guilt," in M. Lewis and J. M. Haviland-Jones, eds., *Handbook of Emotions,* 2nd edition (New York: Guilford Press), 623–36; Fredrickson, B. L., and C. Branigan (2001), "Positive emotions," in T. J. Mayne and G. A. Bonnano, eds., *Emotion: Current Issues and Future Developments* (New York: Guilford Press), 123–51.

12. Answer: Someone who lies awake at night wondering if dog exists.

13. My portrayal of amusement draws heavily on Gervais, M., and D. Sloan

Wilson (2005), "The evolution and functions of laughter and humor: A synthetic approach," *Quarterly Review of Biology* 80: 395–430.

14. David Foster Wallace, "Federer as Religious Experience," *New York Times,* August 20, 2006.

15. My portrayal of inspiration draws from Thrash, T. M., and A. J. Elliot (2004), "Inspiration: Core characteristics, component processes, antecedents, and function," *Journal of Personality and Social Psychology* 87: 957–73; Haidt, 2003; Cohn, M. A., "Rescuing our heroes: Positive perspectives on upward comparisons in relationships, education, and work," in A. P. Linley and S. Joseph, eds., *Positive Psychology in Practice* (Hoboken: John Wiley & Sons).

16. This imagery comes from the opening paragraphs of Jane Goodall's awe-filled memoir *Reason for Hope: A Spiritual Journey* (London: Warner Books, 1999).

17. Keltner, D., and J. Haidt (2003), "Approaching awe, a moral, spiritual, and aesthetic emotion," *Cognition and Emotion* 17: 297–314.

18. My multifaceted view of love draws heavily on Izard, 1977; see also Shaver, P. R., H. J. Morgan, and S. Wu (1996), "Is love a 'basic' emotion?" *Personal Relationships* 3: 81–96; Gonzaga, G. C., D. Keltner, et al. (2001), "Love and the commitment problem in romantic relations and friendship," *Journal of Personality and Social Psychology* 81: 247–62; Gonzaga, G. C., R. A. Turner, et al. (2006), "Romantic love and sexual desire in close relationships," *Emotion* 6: 163–79; Schultheiss, O. C., M. M. Wirth, and S. J. Stanton, "Effects of affiliation and power motivation on salivary progesterone and testosterone," *Hormones and Behavior* 46: 592–99.

19. Scherer, K. R., A. Schorr, and T. Johnstone, eds. (2001), *Appraisal Processes in Emotion: Theory, Methods, Research* (Oxford, England: Oxford University Press).

20. Wilson, T. D., D. B. Centerbar, et al. (2005), "The pleasures of uncertainty: Prolonging positive moods in ways people do not anticipate," *Journal of Personality and Social Psychology* 88: 5–21.

21. Available from Star Thrower Distributions, www.starthrower.com.

22. Cooperrider, D. L., and D. Whitney (2005), *Appreciative Inquiry: A Positive Revolution in Change* (San Francisco: Berrett-Koehler). See

also, Kelm, J. B. (2005), *Appreciative Living: The Principles of Appreciative Inquiry in Personal Life* (Wake Forest, NC: Venet Publishers).

CHAPTER 4. BROADEN YOUR MIND

1. Cooperrider, D. L., and D. Whitney (2005), *Appreciative Inquiry: A Positive Revolution in Change* (San Francisco: Berrett-Koehler).

2. Fredrickson, B. L., and C. Branigan (2005), "Positive emotions broaden the scope of attention and thought-action repertoires," *Cognition and Emotion* 19: 313–32.

3. We evoked these specific feeling states by showing participants short film clips, known from past testing to produce the intended feelings. We amused one group of people with footage of penguins at play, while we made others feel serene with soothing nature scenes. To make others angry, we showed them innocent people being treated unfairly. To make another group fearful, we showed a jarring mountain-climbing accident. When we didn't want to evoke any feeling at all, we occupied people with an abstract display of colored lines piling up on a black background—the screen saver from one of my old computers.

4. Fredrickson and Branigan, 2005.

5. The technique is called facial electromyography. We also measure the electrical activity within the corrugator supercilii, the muscle responsible for furrowing your brow. Researchers have linked this muscle to negativity. Tassinary, L. G., and J. T. Cacioppo (1992), "Unobservable facial actions and emotion," *Psychological Science* 3: 28–33.

6. Johnson, K. J., C. E. Waugh, and B. L. Fredrickson (2008), *Smile to see the forest: Expressed positive emotions broaden attentional scopes and increase attentional flexibility* (manuscript under review). Marketers tap into this to some degree, although I think they have the logic twisted. As they try to persuade us to buy their products, they bombard us continually with smiling faces. Although it may well be true that smiles forecast greater openness, it's not "their" smile that matters—it's your smile. Only to the extent that their smile evokes your smile will you become more open to their message. By now, at least in American culture, we're so overly inundated with smiling faces—often hideously over-the-top smiling faces—that many of us are completely numbed to

them. This may well be an adaptive response to media messengers that don't necessarily have your best interests in mind.

7. Waldlinger, H. A., and D. M. Isaacowitz (2006), "Positive mood broadens visual attention to positive stimuli," *Movitation and Emotion* 30: 89–101. For more information about eye-tracking research, visit Dr. Isaacowitz's laboratory website at Brandeis University, http://people.brandeis.edu/~dmi/.

8. Here, positive emotions were injected by giving a randomly selected subset of volunteers a small gift just before they viewed the pictures. The gift was a small bag of chocolates offered as a token of appreciation for their participation. This classic method of bestowing positivity was first used by Alice Isen, whose work I describe later in this chapter. In case you're wondering whether we should be attributing any effects of the candy to a sugar high instead of to positivity, the researchers wrap the candy tightly in an attractive cellophane bag and ask participants not to eat the candy until the end of the study. They all comply. At the end of the study, volunteers in the other experimental groups get a bag of candy too. We can be certain, then, that any sugar highs occur after the data are safely collected.

9. Rowe, G., J. B. Hirsh, and A. K. Anderson (2007), "Positive affect increases the breadth of attentional selection," *Proceedings of the National Academy of Sciences of the United States of America* 104: 383–88.

10. This study used music to induce emotions. Happy, upbeat music was known to induce positivity. Sad music was played to induce negativity. And to keep people neutral, no music was played.

11. The correct answer here is *power*. This classic test of verbal creativity is called the Remote Associates Test, developed by Mednick, M. T., S. A. Mednick, and E. V. Mednick (1964), *Journal of Abnormal Psychology* 69: 84–88.

12. For more on the brain correlates of positivity, see Ashby, F. G., A. M. Isen, and A. U. Turken (1999), "A neuropsychological theory of positive affect and its influence on cognition," *Psychological Review* 106, no. 3: 529–50.

13. Bryan, T., and J. Bryan (1991), "Positive mood and math performance," *Journal of Learning Disabilities* 24: 490–94.

14. Isen, A. M., A. S. Rosenzweig, and M. J. Young (1991), "The influence of positive affect on clinical problem solving," *Medical Decision Making* 11: 221–27.

15. Staw, B. M., and S. G. Barsade (1993), "Affect and managerial performance: A test of the sadder-but-wiser vs. happier-and-smarter hypothesis," *Administrative Science Quarterly* 38: 304–31.

16. Sy, T., S. Cote, and R. Saavedra (2005), "The contagious leader: Impact of the leader's mood on the mood of group members, group affective tone, and group process," *Journal of Applied Psychology* 90: 295–305.

17. Kopelman, S., A. S. Rosette, and L. Thompson (2006), "The three faces of Eve: Strategic displays of positive, negative, and neutral emotions in negotiations," *Organizational Behavior and Human Decision Processes* 99: 81–101.

18. Fredrickson, B. L., and T. Joiner (2002), "Positive emotions trigger upward spirals toward emotional well-being," *Psychological Science* 13: 172–75.

19. Burns, A. B., J. S. Brown, et al. (2008), "Upward spirals of positive emotion and coping: Replication, extension, and initial exploration of neurochemical substrates," *Personality and Individual Differences* 44: 360–70.

20. Aron, A., E. N. Aron, and D. Smollan (1992), "Inclusion of other in the self scale and the structure of interpersonal closeness," *Journal of Personality and Social Psychology* 63: 596–612.

21. How did we keep people from simply remembering which pair of circles they chose the first time (e.g., "the second set on the second row") and selecting that same pair the second time, just to be consistent? We didn't let them. To mix things up a bit, the second time we presented our participants with overlapping circles, we showed them twice as many pairs: the original seven pairs, plus additional pairs midway between each of the original choices. Because the scale looked different, people couldn't simply rely on memory to complete it; they'd have to consider their reactions anew. Even so, because the two scales were related, we could still directly compare the choice a participant made before we injected emotion to the choice he or she made after.

22. To do this, Ahalya and Keiko located film clips that would reliably

produce positivity, negativity, and neutrality in their respective cultures.

23. One group saw a comedian, another group saw a suspenseful scene from a horror movie, and a third group saw an instructional video on how to make a box in a woodshop. These clips elicited joy, fear, and neutrality, respectively.

24. Meissner, C., and J. Brigham (2001), "Thirty years of investigating the own-race bias in memory for faces," *Psychology, Public Policy, and Law* 7: 3–35.

25. You might be wondering how scientists know this. The method is clever. By turning an image upside down, you disturb the spatial configuration of the features, although the features are still discernible. To the extent that people rely on the overall configuration of people's faces to recognize them, inverting the faces should disrupt face recognition. It does so, but only for own-race faces. Just like common objects, faces of another race are recognized just as well whether they are presented right side up or upside down. Rhodes, G., S. Brake, et al. (1989), "Expertise and configural coding in face recognition," *British Journal of Psychology* 80: 313–31.

26. Ito, T., and G. R. Urland (2003), "Race and gender on the brain: Electrocortical measures of attention to the race and gender of multiply categorizable individuals," *Journal of Personality and Social Psychology* 85: 616–26.

27. Johnson, K. J., and B. L. Fredrickson (2005), "Positive emotions eliminate the own-race bias in face perception," *Psychological Science* 16: 875–81.

28. Dovidio, J. F., S. L. Gaertner, et al. (1995), "Group representations and intergroup bias: Positive affect, similarity, and group size," *Personality and Social Psychology Bulletin* 21: 856–65.

29. Yes, in the 1970s, pay phones were everywhere and dimes were still valuable.

30. Isen, A. M., and P. F. Levin (1972), "Effect of feeling good on helping: Cookies and kindness," *Journal of Personality and Social Psychology* 21: 384–88; Isen, A. M., M. Clark, and M. F. Schwartz (1976), "Duration of the effect of good mood on helping: 'Footprints on the sands of time'" *Journal of Personality and Social Psychology* 34: 385–93. For a

more extensive review, see Isen, A. M. (1987), "Positive affect, cognitive processes, and social behavior," *Advances in Experimental Social Psychology* 20: 203–53.

31. Cialdini, R. B., S. L. Brown, et al. (1997), "Reinterpreting the empathy-altruism relationship: When one into one equals oneness," *Journal of Personality and Social Psychology* 73: 481–94.

32. Hatfield, E., J. T. Cacioppo, and R. L. Rapson (1994), *Emotional Contagion* (New York: Cambridge University Press).

33. This grew out of an unprecedented collaboration between Asian Buddhist scholars and Western scientists. To learn more, visit www .InvestigatingTheMind.org.

CHAPTER 5. BUILD YOUR BEST FUTURE

1. Crowley, C., and H. S. Lodge (2004), *Younger Next Year: A Guide to Living Like 50 Until You're 80 and Beyond* (New York: Workman).

2. Loehr, J., and T. Schwartz (2003), *The Power of Full Engagement: Managing Energy, Not Time, Is the Key to High Performance and Personal Renewal* (New York: Free Press).

3. Kempermann, G., H. G. Kuhn, and F. H. Gage (1997), "More hippocampal neurons in adult mice living in an enriched environment," *Nature* 86: 493–95.

4. Cotman, C. W., N. C. Berchtold, and L. Christie (2007), "Exercise builds brain health: Key roles of growth factor cascades and inflammation," *Trends in Neurosciences* 30: 464–72.

5. Crowley and Lodge, 2004; see also Davidson, R. J., D. Jackson, and N. H. Kalin (2000), "Emotion, plasticity, context, and regulation: Perspectives from affective neuroscience," *Psychological Bulletin* 126: 890–909.

6. As part of their compensation for completing the surveys, this comparison group was offered the same meditation workshop free of charge about six months later. Technically, this is called a "waitlist control group." One of the benefits of this type of comparison group is that all study participants wanted to join the meditation workshop, which means we can assume that the two groups had comparable curiosity about meditation and comparable desires for change in their lives.

7. Kahneman, D., A. B. Krueger, et al. (2004), "A survey method for characterizing daily life experience: The Day Reconstruction Method," *Science* 306: 1776–80.

8. An outstanding team of graduate students worked with me on this project. Their quantitative expertise and insights added many dimensions, far beyond what I'd envisioned when I dreamed up this experiment years ago. I'd like to offer special thanks here to Michael Cohn, Kimberly Coffey, and Jolynn Pek for joining me on this journey to test the build hypothesis. Fredrickson, B. L., M. A. Cohn, et al. (in press), "Open hearts build lives: Positive emotions, induced through loving-kindness meditation, build consequential personal resources," *Journal of Personality and Social Psychology.*

9. In this study, we had not yet measured inspiration.

10. Brickman, P., and D. T. Cambell (1971), "Hedonic relativism and planning the good society," in M. H. Appley, ed., *Adaptation Level Theory: A Symposium* (New York: Academic Press), 287–302; see also Brickman, P., D. Coates, and R. Janoff-Bulman (1978), "Lottery winners and accident victims: Is happiness relative?" *Journal of Personality and Social Psychology* 36: 917–27; Diener, E., R. E. Lucas, and C. N. Scollon (2006), "Beyond the hedonic treadmill: Revising the adaptation theory of well-being," *American Psychologist* 61: 305–14.

11. Keep in mind that we didn't tell our participants in advance that we were planning to ask them detailed questions about their day. We wanted an ordinary day, not the kind of day you might have if you knew your actions and feelings would later be combed through like an archaeological dig site. For the sake of time, we asked people to describe the first ten episodes of their day, or to take us through the episode that involved "having lunch," whichever came first. We also thought it would be most interesting to see how people balanced work and home life, so we tapped them on a workday. The day we chose was about two weeks after the last workshop session.

12. Fredrickson, B. L., M. M. Tugade, et al. (2003), "What good are positive emotions in crises?: A prospective study of resilience and emotions following the terrorist attacks on the United States on September 11, 2001," *Journal of Personality and Social Psychology* 84: 365–76; Fredrickson et al. (in press); Fredrickson and Joiner, 2002.

13. Gervais, M., D. S. Wilson (2005). "The evolution and functions of laughter and humor: A synthetic approach." *Quarterly Review of Biology,* 80, 395–430.

14. Gable, S., H. Reis, et al. (2004), "What do you do when things go right? The intrapersonal and interpersonal benefits of sharing positive events," *Journal of Personality and Social Psychology* 87, 2: 228–45.

15. These last two findings come from soon-to-be published research by Sara Algoe, a postdoctoral fellow working in my research laboratory.

16. Aron, A, C. C. Norman, et al. (2000), "Couples' shared participation in novel and arousing activities and experienced relationship quality," *Journal of Personality and Social Psychology* 78: 273–84.

17. Gottman, J. M. (1994), *What Predicts Divorce: The Relationship Between Marital Processes and Marital Outcomes* (Hillsdale, NJ: Lawrence Erlbaum).

18. Pressman, S. D., and S. Cohen (2005), "Does positive affect influence health?" *Psychological Bulletin* 131: 925–71.

19. Steptoe, A., J. Wardle, and M. Marmot (2005), "Positive affect and health-related neuroendocrine, cardiovascular, and inflammatory responses," *Proceedings of the National Academy of Sciences* 102: 6508–12.

20. Berk, L. S., S. A. Tan, et al. (1989), "Neuroendocrine and stress hormone changes during mirthful laughter," *American Journal of the Medical Sciences* 298: 390–96; Brown, W. A., A. D. Sirota, et al. (1993), "Endocrine correlates of sadness and elation," *Psychosomatic Medicine* 55: 458–67.

21. This comes from recent work with the hormone progesterone that I've done in collaboration with Stephanie Brown, Oliver Schultheiss, Michelle Wirth, and Emily Heaphy; see also Light, K. C., K. M. Grewen, and J. A. Amico (2005), "More frequent partner hugs and higher oxytocin levels are linked to lower blood pressure and heart rate in premenopausal women," *Biological Psychology* 69: 5–21.

22. Ashby, F. G., A. M. Isen, and A. U. Turken (1999), "A neuropsychological theory of positive affect and its influence on cognition," *Psychological Review* 106, no. 3, 529–50; Burns, A. B., J. S. Brown, et al. (2008), "Upward spirals of positive emotion and coping: Replication, extension, and initial exploration of neurochemical substrates," *Personality and Individual Differences* 44: 360–70.

23. Wager, T. D., D. J. Scott, and J. Zubieta (2007), "Placebo effects on

human μ-opioid activity during pain," *Proceeding of the National Academy of Sciences of the United States of America* 104: 11056–61.

24. Davidson, R. J., J. Kabat-Zinn, et al. (2003), "Alterations in brain and immune function produced by mindfulness meditation," *Psychosomatic Medicine* 65: 564–70.

25. Steptoe et al., 2005.

26. Fredrickson, B. L., R. A. Mancuso, et al. (2000). "The undoing effect of positive emotions," *Motivation and Emotion* 24: 237–58; Light et al., 2005.

27. Gil, K. M., J. W. Carson, et al. (2004), "Daily mood and stress predict pain, health care use, and work activity in African American adults with sickle cell disease," *Health Psychology* 23: 267–74.

28. Cohen, S., W. J. Doyle, et al. (2003), "Emotional style and susceptibility to the common cold," *Psychosomatic Medicine* 65: 652–57.

29. Bardwell, W. A., C. C. Berry, et al. (1999), "Psychological correlates of sleep apnea," *Journal of Psychosomatic Research* 47: 583–96.

30. Richman, L. S., L. Kubzansky, et al. (2005), "Positive emotion and health: Going beyond the negative," *Health Psychology* 24: 422–29.

31. Ibid.

32. Ostir, G. V., K. S. Markides, et al. (2001), "The associations between emotional well-being and the incidence of stroke in older adults," *Psychosomatic Medicine* 63: 210–15.

33. Light et al., 2005.

34. Lund, I., L. C. Yu, et al. (2002), "Repeated massage-like stimulation induces long-term effects on nociception: Contribution on oxytocinergic mechanisms," *European Journal of Neuroscience* 16: 330–38.

35. Holt-Lunstad, J., W. A. Birmingham, and K. C. Light (in press), "The influence of a 'warm touch' support enhancement intervention among married couples on ambulatory blood pressure, oxytocin, alpha amylase and cortisol," *Psychosomatic Medicine.*

CHAPTER 6. BOUNCE BACK FROM LIFE'S CHALLENGES

1. This Victor Frankl quotation is also the motto of one of my favorite literary magazines, *The Sun,* edited since 1974 by Sy Safransky. Each month, *The Sun* prints a page of "Sunbeams," an eclectic selection of thought-provoking quotations. I first discovered many of my own favorites among Sy's "Sunbeams."

2. Before conducting any research that directly involves human participants, the research protocol must be evaluated and approved by an independent committee (an institutional review board, or IRB). This ensures that the welfare and rights of participants are appropriately guarded in an ethical way. When researchers wish to collect data following an unforeseen disaster or tragedy, committee approval is still a necessary first step. With the normal review procedure taking weeks or months, I was immensely grateful to secure approval within days.

3. Block, J., and A. M. Kremen (1996), "IQ and ego-resiliency: Conceptual and empirical connections and separateness," *Journal of Personality and Social Psychology* 70: 349–61.

4. Fredrickson, B. L., M. M. Tugade, et al. (2003), "What good are positive emotions in crises?: A prospective study of resilience and emotions following the terrorist attacks on the United States on September 11, 2001," *Journal of Personality and Social Psychology* 84: 365–76.

5. Ong, A. D., C. S. Bergeman, et al. (2006), "Psychological resilience, positive emotions, and successful adaptation to stress in later life," *Journal of Personality and Social Psychology* 91: 730–49.

6. Fredrickson, B. L., R. A. Mancuso, et al. (2000), "The undoing effect of positive emotions," *Motivation and Emotion* 24: 237–58; see also Fredrickson, B. L., and R. W. Levenson (1998), "Positive emotions speed recovery from the cardiovascular sequelae of negative emotions," *Cognition and Emotion* 12: 191–220.

7. You may have noticed that none of the participants gave their speeches after all. This is an aspect of the study that was deceptive. This minor deception was deemed reasonable by my university's ethics committee when balanced against the value of information likely to be gained from the study overall.

8. McEwen, B. S. (1998), "Protective and damaging effects of stress mediators," *New England Journal of Medicine* 338: 171–79.

9. Tugade, M. M., and B. L. Fredrickson (2004), "Resilient individuals use positive emotions to bounce back from negative emotional experiences," *Journal of Personality and Social Psychology* 86: 320–33.

10. A little background on how fMRI works might be helpful here. It turns out that brain neurons do not store energy. To fire, they need to draw energy quickly—in the form of oxygen—from the bloodstream. Cir-

culating blood carrying more or less oxygen carries correspondingly more or less magnetic signal. Moment-by-moment changes in this magnetic signal are detected by fMRI. So, if a person's head is in the fMRI scanner, neuroscientists can track changes in blood oxygen levels in the brain and infer which neurons are most active during particular phases of experimental tasks. Using this and a variety of sensitive statistical techniques, Christian and his team of collaborators were poised to discover how the brains of people scoring high and low on Block and Kremen's fourteen-item resilience survey might differ.

11. For half of the participants, the "threat" cue was the circle, and the "safety" cue was the triangle. For the other participants, the cues were reversed. This counterbalancing procedure ensures that the experimental results don't reflect reactions to circles and triangles, but rather the psychological events they signal.

12. Waugh, C. E., T. D. Wager, et al. in press, "The neural correlates of trait resilience when anticipating and recovering from threat," *Social Cognitive and Affective Neuroscience.*

13. Tugade and Fredrickson, 2004; Waugh et al., in press; Waugh, C. E., B. L. Fredrickson, and S. F. Taylor (2008), "Adapting to life's slings and arrows: Individual differences in resilience when recovering from an anticipated threat," *Journal of Research in Personality* 42: 1031–46.

14. To some degree, resilience does appear to be controlled by our genes. Caspi, A., K. Sugden, et al. (2003), "Influence of life stress on depression: Moderation by a polymorphism in the 5-HTT gene," *Science* 301, no. 5631: 386–89.

15. Cohn, M. A., B. L. Fredrickson, et al. (2008), *Happiness unpacked: Positive emotions increase life satisfaction by building resilience* (manuscript under review).

16. Tugade and Fredrickson, 2004.

17. If you want to learn more, you can visit www.HealingConsulting.com.

18. Ulrich, R. S. (1984), "View through a window may influence recovery from surgery," *Science* 224: 420–21; see also Franklin, H. (2001), "Beyond toxicity: Human health and the natural environment," *American Journal of Preventive Medicine* 20: 234–39; Kaplan, S. (1995), "The restorative effects of nature: Toward an integrative framework," *Journal of Environmental Psychology* 15: 169–82.

19. I borrow this phrase from Anne Maston, who in 2001 described resilience as "ordinary magic" that arises from the unencumbered operations of basic human systems, such as positivity. Work by George Bonanno is relevant in that he also challenges the view that resilience is rare. Maston, A. S. (2001), "Ordinary magic: Resilience processes in development," *American Psychologist* 56: 227–38; Bonanno, G. (2004), "Loss, trauma, and human resilience: Have we underestimated the human capacity to thrive after extremely aversive events?" *American Psychologist* 59: 20–28.

CHAPTER 7. THE POSITIVITY RATIO

1. Dutton, J. E. (2003), *Energize Your Workplace: How to Create and Sustain High-Quality Connections at Work* (San Francisco: Jossey-Bass); I feature her work in chapter 11.

2. This paper has since been published: Losada, M., and E. Heaphy (2004), "The role of positivity and connectivity in the performance of business teams: A nonlinear dynamics model," *American Behavioral Scientist* 47: 740–65.

3. Fredrickson, B. L., and M. F. Losada (2005), "Positive affect and the complex dynamics of human flourishing," *American Psychologist* 60: 678–86.

4. As is typical among scientists, I refer to Marcial by his last name when describing his scientific contributions.

5. Losada's coders identified statements as "positive" if speakers showed support, encouragement, or appreciation, and as "negative" if they showed disapproval, sarcasm, or cynicism. They identified statements as "self-focused" if they referred to the person speaking, the group present, or the company, and as "other-focused" if they referred to a person or group neither present nor part of the company. And they identified statements as "inquiry" if speakers offered questions aimed at exploring an idea, and as "advocacy" if speakers simply offered arguments in favor of their own points of view.

6. Losada noted, for example, that the change over time in a team's likelihood of asking questions (inquiry-advocacy) turned out to reflect their degree of outward focus (self-other). And the change over time in a team's positivity (positivity-negativity) reflected both their de-

gree of outward focus (self-other) *and* their rate of asking questions (inquiry-advocacy). Finally, he saw that the change over time in a team's outward focus (self-other) reflected all three variables (positivity-negativity, self-other, and inquiry-advocacy) together with the team's prototypical degree of attunement with one another (connectivity). In combination, these three mathematical relationships described the team behavior that Losada saw unfolding in his data. Using statistics, he confirmed that his new mathematical model provided a good fit for his actual data. For the mathematical details, see Losada, M. (1999), "The complex dynamics of high performance business teams," *Mathematical and Computer Modelling* 30: 179–92.

7. First, the team itself was clearly a *system.* That is, the statements each team member made played a role in shaping the behavior of other team members as well as the ultimate team outcome. In other words, people's statements were not made in a vacuum. Rather, to some degree, each statement altered the likelihood of subsequent statements being made. Second, the team system was without question *dynamic;* that is, the team's behavior changed over time as the various components in the system—here the statements made—mutually influenced each other. For example, just as a team's positivity could trigger outward focus, so too could its outward focus trigger positivity. Stated another way, positivity and outward focus fed on each other, each reinforcing and catalyzing the other. Scientists say that dynamic systems like this have *reciprocal causality.* This phrase indicates that the causal arrow between two concepts runs in both directions at the same time. By now you might recognize this sort of dynamic as echoing the upward spirals triggered by positivity that I described earlier (e.g., chapter 4). If so, perhaps you're getting a taste of the excitement I felt about the possible fit between Losada's lifelong work and my own. Third, Losada knew that the best way to model reciprocal causality mathematically was to use *nonlinear* equations, such as the ones he'd formulated. It's fair to describe most of psychological science to date—including my own—as resting on the assumption of linearity. That is, when we cast our hypotheses, we expect changes in one entity—say positivity—to be linked with *proportional* changes in another entity—say breadth of mind. Departing from this age-old assumption, nonlinearity both

honors bidirectional effects and describes systems in which outputs are not always proportional to inputs. To read more about nonlinear dynamic systems, I recommend Nowak, A., and R. R. Vallacher (1998), *Dynamical Social Psychology* (New York: Guilford Press).

8. Lorenz, E. N. (1993), *The Essence of Chaos* (Seattle: University of Washington Press).

9. As it happens, this butterfly shape is the signature of what's known as the Lorenz system. First introduced by Edward Lorenz in 1963 to represent the complex dynamics underlying weather forecasting, the Lorenz system is seen by many as the opening shot of the complexity revolution. It has since been found to apply more generally across many areas of science. For a scholarly introduction to this area of science, see the 2004 textbook by M. W. Hirsch, S. Smale, and R. L. Devaney, *Differential Equations, Dynamical Systems, and an Introduction to Chaos* (Amsterdam: Elsevier/Academic Press). For a more informal introduction, see the 1987 best-seller by James Gleick, *Chaos: Making a New Science* (New York: Penguin). For Lorenz's own view, see Lorenz, 1993.

10. Losada in fact prefers to call chaotic attractors "complexors" (for COMPLEX ORder) to avoid the common misunderstanding that chaotic systems are unpredictable and random.

11. It has been established that when r, the control parameter in the Lorenz system, reaches 24.7368, the butterfly first emerges: Sparrow, C. (1982), *The Lorenz Equations: Bifurcations, Chaos and Strange Attractors* (New York: Springer-Verlag).

12. For the equation linking connectivity to the positivity ratio, see Fredrickson and Losada, 2005, p. 682.

13. In fairness to Marcial Losada, I should say that if he had written this sentence himself, he'd have referred to positivity ratios at or above 2.9013 to 1.

14. This measurement tool was developed by Corey Keyes of Emory University. See Keyes, C. L. M. (2002), "The mental health continuum: From languishing to flourishing in life," *Journal of Health and Social Behavior* 43: 207–22. To learn more, visit www.sociology.emory.edu/ckeyes/.

15. This is true in my own studies (Fredrickson and Losada, 2005), as well as in nationally representative samples. See Keyes, 2002.

16. Baumeister, R. F., E. Bratslavsky, et al. (2001), "Bad is stronger than good," *Review of General Psychology* 5: 323–70. Cacioppo, J. T., W. L. Gardner, and G. G. Berntson (1999), "The affect system has parallel and integrative processing components: Form follows function," *Journal of Personality and Social Psychology* 76: 839–55.

17. Cacioppo et al., 1999; Diener, E., and C. Diener (1996), "Most people are happy," *Psychological Science* 7: 181–85.

18. Using the traditional statistics of my field, I can also compare the positivity ratios of people who flourish against those of people who languish. Bear in mind that these statistics assume a linear, proportional relationship between flourishing and positivity ratios. Even so, it can be reassuring to know that—across the two different data sets—the differences between the positivity ratios of those who flourish and those who languish are beyond what you'd expect by chance alone. See Fredrickson and Losada, 2005.

19. For a scholarly overview, see Gottman, J. M. (1994), *What Predicts Divorce? The Relationship Between Marital Processes and Marital Outcomes* (Hillsdale, NJ: Erlbaum). For a more accessible introduction, see Gottman, J. M., and N. Silver (1999). *The Seven Principles for Making Marriage Work* (New York: Three Rivers Press).

20. Gottman, J. M., R. W. Levenson, et al. (2003), "Correlates of gay and lesbian couples' relationship satisfaction and relationship dissolution," *Journal of Homosexuality* 45: 23–43.

21. In their own work, Schwartz and colleagues represent that balance of positivity to negativity in proportional terms, by the ratio of positivity over the sum of positivity plus negativity. I used simple algebra to convert their figures to the P/N positivity ratio that I favor.

22. This quote comes from *DSM-IV*, the fourth edition of the *Diagnostic and Statistical Manual of Mental Disorders*, the universally consulted bible of mental illness, published in 1994 by the American Psychiatric Association in Washington, D.C.

23. Schwartz, R. M., C. F. Reynolds, et al. (2002), "Optimal and normal affect balance in psychotherapy of major depression: Evaluation of the

balanced states of mind model," *Behavioural and Cognitive Psychotherapy* 30: 439–50.

24. Waugh, C. E., and B. L. Fredrickson (2006), "Nice to know you: Positive emotions, self-other overlap, and complex understanding in the formation of a new relationship," *Journal of Positive Psychology* 1: 93–106.

25. Here again is where correspondence between Losada's model and the famous Lorenz model—each with its signature butterfly-shaped attractor—makes a difference. Past physicists and mathematicians have in fact discovered an upper limit to *r*, the control parameter within the Lorenz equations, in predicting chaotic attractors. Beyond this upper limit, the butterfly starts to falter, its complex dynamics beginning to disintegrate. Using the established link between *P/N* and the Lorenzian *r*, Losada pinpointed *P/N* = 11.6346 as the upper bound of flourishing. To illustrate this upper limit, Losoda and I featured a plot of a 100-to-1 positivity ratio in our *American Psychologist* article. At this ratio, the rich and complex dynamics of the butterfly are gone altogether. In their place a twisted and rigid limit cycle appears. Eerily, the plot resembles the exaggerated smile painted onto a clown's face. I call this the "Pollyanna plot." Fredrickson and Losada, 2005.

26. Gottman, 1994.

27. Wilson, E. O. (1998), *Consilience: The Unity of Knowledge* (New York: Knopf).

CHAPTER 8: WHERE ARE YOU NOW?

1. I developed these items based on earlier work by Carroll Izard, esp. *Human Emotions* (New York: Plenum Press, 1977).

2. Ekman, P. (1992), "An argument for basic emotions," *Cognition and Emotion* 6: 169–200.

3. I've prepared guidelines for my fellow scientists to use when attempting to measure emotions. These are described in Larsen, R. J., and B. L. Fredrickson (1999), "Measurement issues in emotion research," in D. Kahneman, E. Diener, and N. Schwarz, eds., *Well-being: Foundations of Hedonic Psychology* (New York: Russell Sage), 40–60.

4. Contributing to the database is not a precondition for using the website, but the requested background information helps researchers interpret the data. For example, if a particular experience is common only

among women, we would be cautious in generalizing to men. You will be given the opportunity to indicate your sex, ethnic background, age, marital status, etc. Supply this information only if you are comfortable doing so. Keep in mind that we will never ask for (or obtain) your name or address, and that we safeguard your information using industry-standard measures of security.

5. Fredrickson, B. L., and D. Kahneman (1993), "Duration neglect in retrospective evaluations of affective episodes," *Journal of Personality and Social Psychology* 65: 45–55.

6. Ibid.; see also Kahneman, D., B. L. Fredrickson, et al. (1993), "When more pain is preferred to less: Adding a better end," *Psychological Science* 4: 401–5.

7. See Kahneman, D., A. B. Krueger, et al. (2004), "A survey method for characterizing daily life experience: The Day Reconstruction Method," *Science* 306: 1776–80.

8. Here again you'll likely avoid the "can't-divide-by-zero" problem that may well plague any given episode.

9. These percentages are based on several hundred participants. See Fredrickson, B. L., and M. F. Losada (2005), "Positive affect and the complex dynamics of human flourishing," *American Psychologist* 60: 678–86.

10. Schwartz, R. M., C. F. Reynolds, et al. (2002), "Optimal and normal affect balance in psychotherapy of major depression: Evaluation of the balanced states of mind model," *Behavioural and Cognitive Psychotherapy* 30: 439–50; Gottman, J. M. (1994), *What Predicts Divorce: The Relationship Between Marital Processes and Marital Outcomes* (Hillsdale, NJ: Lawrence Erlbaum); Losada, M. (1999), "The complex dynamics of high performance business teams," *Mathematical and Computer Modelling* 30: 179–92.

11. Kessler, R. C., P. Berglund, et al. (2005), "Lifetime prevalence and age-of-onset distributions of DSM-IV disorders in the National Comorbidity Survey Replication," *Archives of General Psychiatry* 62: 593–602.

12. Lyubomirsky, S., K. M. Sheldon, and D. Schkade (2005), "Pursuing happiness: The architecture of sustainable change," *Review of General Psychology* 9: 111–31.

13. This core truth first emerged in appraisal theories of emotion, e.g.,

Scherer, K. R., A. Schorr, and T. Johnstone, eds. (2001), *Appraisal Processes in Emotion: Theory, Methods, Research* (Oxford, England: Oxford University Press) and has been honed and refined in cognitive-behavioral therapies that are very effective treatments for affective disorders and more (see Burns, 1999, under Recommended Resources).

14. This comparison has become famous in psychology and was first introduced by Lykken, D. J., and A. Tellegen (1996), "Happiness is a stochastic phenomenon," *Psychological Science* 7: 186–89.

15. Lyubomirsky, Sheldon, and Schkade, 2005; see also Lyubomirsky's book under Recommended Resources.

16. Begley, S. (2007), *Train Your Mind, Change Your Brain: How a New Science Reveals Our Extraordinary Potential to Transform Ourselves* (New York: Ballantine Books). Doidge, N. (2007), *The Brain That Changes Itself: Stories of Personal Triumph from the Frontiers of Brain Science* (New York: Penguin Books).

CHAPTER 9. DECREASE NEGATIVITY

1. A pioneer in this area of clinical science is Aaron T. Beck, who is often credited with launching cognitive behavioral therapy, or CBT, beginning in the 1960s. You can learn more at his website, www .beckinstitute.org.

2. Specific emotions create tendencies to interpret the world in certain ways and, in doing so, perpetuate the initial emotion. This is well described in Lerner, J. S., and D. Keltner (2001), "Fear, anger, and risk," *Journal of Personality and Social Psychology* 81: 146–59.

3. Jamison, C., and F. Scogin (1995), "The outcome of cognitive bibliotherapy with depressed adults," *Journal of Consulting and Clinical Psychology*, 63, 644–50.

4. This comes from Seligman's book, *Learned Optimism;* see Recommended Resources.

5. Lewinsohn, P. M., and J. Libet (1972), "Pleasant events, activity schedules, and depressions," *Journal of Abnormal Psychology* 79: 291–95; Nolen-Hoeksema, S., and J. Morrow, "Effects of rumination and distraction on naturally occurring depressed mood," *Cognition and Emotion* 7: 561–70.

6. Nolen-Hoeksema, S., and Z. A. Harrell (2002), "Rumination, depression, and alcohol use: Tests of gender differences," *Journal of Cognitive Psychotherapy* 16: 391–403.

7. Heatherton, T. F., and R. F. Baumeister (1991), "Binge eating as escape from self-awareness," *Psychological Bulletin* 110: 86–108.

8. Gross, J. J. (2007), *Handbook of Emotion Regulation* (New York: Guilford Press).

9. Kabat-Zinn, J. (2005), *Coming to Our Senses: Healing Ourselves and the World Through Mindfulness* (New York: Hyperion); see also Wallace, A. B., and S. L. Shapiro (2006), "Mental balance and well-being: Building bridges between Buddhism and western psychology," *American Psychologist* 61: 690–701.

10. Kabat-Zinn, J. (1994), *Wherever You Go, There You Are: Mindfulness Meditation in Everyday Life* (New York: Hyperion), 4.

11. For a review, see Kabat-Zinn, J. (2003), "Mindfulness-based interventions in context: Past, present, and future," *Clinical Psychology: Science and Practice* 10: 144–56.

12. Segal, Z. V., J. M. G. Williams, and J. D. Teasdale (2002), *Mindfulness-Based Cognitive Therapy for Depression: A New Approach to Preventing Relapse* (New York: Guilford Press).

13. Miller, A. C., J. H. Rathus, and M. M. Linehan (2006), *Dialectical Behavior Therapy with Suicidal Adolescents* (New York: Guilford Press).

14. Schwartz, J. M., E. Z. Gulliford, et al. (2005), "Mindful awareness and self-directed neuroplasticity: Integrating psychospiritual and biological approaches to mental health with a focus on obsessive-compulsive disorder," in S. G. Mijares and G. S. Khalsa, eds., *The Psychospiritual Clinician's Handbook: Alternative Methods for Understanding and Treating Mental Disorders* (New York: Haworth Press).

15. Dahl, J., K. G. Wilson, and A. Nilsson (2004), "Acceptance and Commitment Therapy and the treatment of persons at risk for long-term disability resulting from stress and pain symptoms: A preliminary randomized trial," *Behavior Therapy* 35: 785–802; see also Blackledge, J. T., and S. C. Hayes (2006), "Using acceptance and commitment training in the support of parents of children diagnosed with autism," *Child & Family Behavior Therapy* 28: 1–18.

16. Schwartz et al., 2005.

17. Davidson, R. J., Kabat-Zinn, et al. (2003), "Alterations in brain and immune function produced by mindfulness meditation," *Psychosomatic Medicine* 65: 564–70.

18. For a compelling introduction to the new science of neuroplasticity, I recommend Sharon Begley's 2007 book, *Train Your Mind, Change Your Brain: How a New Science Reveals Our Extraordinary Potential to Transform Ourselves* (New York: Ballantine Books).

19. I also highly recommend the book *Natural Childbirth: The Bradley Way,* by Susan McCutcheon-Rosegg, which is highly compatible with Buddhist psychology and mindfulness awareness.

20. Aspinwall, L. G. (1998), "Rethinking the role of positive affect in self-regulation," *Motivation and Emotion* 22: 1–32.

21. I draw here from James Gross's framework for describing "antecedent-focused emotion regulation techniques." See Gross, J. J. (2001), "Emotion regulation in adulthood: Timing is everything," *Current Directions in Psychological Science* 10: 214–19.

22. This finding emerged in the classic work by George Gerbner and colleagues. See Gerbner, G., L. Gross, et al. (1980), "The 'mainstreaming' of America: Violence Profile No. 11," *Journal of Communication* 30: 10–29.

23. Huesmann, R. L., and L. D. Taylor (2006), "The role of media violence in violent behavior," *Annual Review of Public Health* 27: 393–415.

24. American Psychological Association, Task Force on the Sexualization of Girls (2007), *Report of the APA Task Force on the Sexualization of Girls* (Washington, DC: American Psychological Association), accessed at www.apa.org/pi/wpo/sexualization.html. See also Fredrickson, B. L., and T. Roberts (1997), "Objectification theory: Toward understanding women's lived experience and mental health risks," *Psychology of Women Quarterly* 21: 173–206.

25. Ueshiba, Morihei (1992), *The Art of Peace,* translated by J. Stevens (Boston: Shambhala Publications).

26. Gottman, J. M. (1994), *What Predicts Divorce: The Relationship Between Marital Processes and Marital Outcomes* (Hillsdale, NJ: Lawrence Erlbaum).

27. Drigotas, S. M., C. E. Rusbult, et al. (1999), "Close partner as sculptor of the ideal self: Behavioral affirmation and the Michelangelo phenomenon," *Journal of Personality and Social Psychology* 77: 293–323.

CHAPTER 10. INCREASE POSITIVITY

1. Rosenberg, E. L., P. Ekman, et al. (2001), "Linkages between facial expressions of anger and transient myocardial ischemia in men with coronary artery disease," *Emotion* 1: 107–15.
2. Moskowitz, J. T., and E. S. Epel (2006), "Benefit finding and diurnal cortisol slope in maternal caregivers: A moderating role for positive emotions," *Journal of Positive Psychology* 1: 83–91.
3. Seligman, M. E. P., and M. Csikszentmihalyi (2000), "Positive psychology: An introduction," *American Psychologist* 55: 5–14.
4. To read the *Positive Psychology Manifesto* crafted in Akumal, Mexico, in January 1999, visit the Positive Psychology Center website at www.ppc .sas.upenn.edu/akumalmanifesto.htm.
5. Bonanno, G. A., and D. Keltner (1997), "Facial expressions of emotion and the course of conjugal bereavement," *Journal of Abnormal Psychology* 106: 126–37.
6. Stein, N., S. Folkman, et al. (1997), "Appraisal and goal processes as predictor of psychological well-being in bereaved caregivers," *Journal of Personality and Social Psychology* 72: 872–84.
7. These questions about big meaning are inspired by the work of Jim Loehr. See his book under Recommended Resources.
8. Bryant, F., and J. Veroff (2007), *Savoring: A New Model of Positive Experience* (Mahwah, NJ: Lawrence Erlbaum Associates).
9. Wood, J. V., S. A. Heimpel, and J. L. Michela (2003), "Savoring versus dampening: Self-esteem differences in regulating positive affect," *Journal of Personality and Social Psychology* 85: 566–80.
10. Lyubomirsky, S., L. Sousa, and R. Dickerhoof (2006), "The costs and benefits of writing, talking, and thinking about life's triumphs and defeats," *Journal of Personality and Social Psychology* 90: 692–708.
11. John and I know how powerful his efforts to savor were because he conducted a formal experiment on them as part of a class assignment. Just as I suggest you do, he recorded his emotions each day for several

weeks. After a baseline period during which he lived life as usual, he began his efforts to savor. He reported his results in his final term paper and then later gave me permission to share them here.

12. Gable, S., H. Reis, et al. (2004), "What do you do when things go right? The interpersonal and interpersonal benefits of sharing positive events," *Journal of Personality and Social Psychology* 87, no. 2: 228–45.

13. Folkman, S., and J. T. Moskowitz (2000), "Positive affect and the other side of coping," *American Psychologist* 55: 647–54.

14. McCullough, M. E., S. D. Kilpatrick, et al. (2001), "Is gratitude a moral affect?" *Psychological Bulletin* 127: 249–66.

15. Emmons, R. A., and M. E. McCullough (2003), "Counting blessings versus burdens: An experimental investigation of gratitude and subjective well-being in daily life," *Journal of Personality and Social Psychology* 84, no. 2: 377–89.

16. Lyubomirsky, S., K. M. Sheldon, and D. Schkade (2005). "Pursuing happiness: The architecture of sustainable change," *Review of General Psychology* 9: 111–131.

17. Otake, K., S. Shimai, et al. (2006), "Happy people become happier through kindness: A counting kindnesses intervention," *Journal of Happiness Studies* 7: 361–75.

18. Lyubomirsky, et al., 2005.

19. Boezeman and Ellemers (2007), "Volunteering for charity: Pride, respect, and the commitment of volunteers," *Journal of Applied Psychology* 92: 771–85.

20. Brown, S. L., R. L. Nesse, et al. (2003), "Providing social support may be more beneficial than receiving it: Results from a prospective study of mortality," *Psychological Science* 14: 320–27.

21. Csikszentmihalyi, M. (1990), *Flow: The Psychology of Optimal Experience* (New York: Harper Perennial).

22. Csikszentmihalyi, M., and J. LeFevre (1989), "Optimal experience in work and leisure," *Journal of Personality and Social Psychology* 56: 815–22.

23. Sheldon, K. M., and S. Lyubomirsky (2006), "How to increase and sustain positive emotion: The effects of expressing gratitude and visualizing best possible selves," *Journal of Positive Psychology* 1: 73–82.

24. Ganis, G., W. L. Thompson, et al. (2004), "Brain areas underlying visual mental imagery and visual perception: An fMRI study," *Cognitive Brain Research* 20: 226–41. For a compelling review, see Begley's 2007 book, *Train Your Mind, Change Your Brain: How a New Science Reveals Our Extraordinary Potential to Transform Ourselves* (New York: Ballantine Books).

25. Cooperrider, D. L. (1990), "Positive image, positive action: The affirmative basis of organizing," in S. Suresh and D. L. Cooperrider, eds., *Appreciative Management and Leadership: The Power of Positive Thought and Action in Organizations* (San Francisco: Jossey-Bass), 91–125.

26. Fredrickson, B. L. (2000), "Why positive emotions matter in organizations: Lessons from the broaden-and-build model," *Psychologist-Manager Journal* 4: 131–42; see also Buckingham, M., and D. O. Clifton, (2001), *Now, Discover Your Strengths* (New York: Free Press); Peterson, C., and M. E. P. Seligman (2004), *Character Strengths and Virtues: A Handbook and Classification* (New York: Oxford University Press).

27. Roberts, L. M., J. E. Dutton, et al. (2005), "Composing the reflected best-self portrait: Building pathways for becoming extraordinary in work organizations," *Academy of Management Review* 30: 712–36.

28. Roberts, L. M., G. Spreitzer, et al. (January 2005), "How to play to your strengths," *Harvard Business Review* 83: 75–80.

29. Seligman, M. E. P., T. Steen, et al. (2005), "Positive psychology progress: Empirical validations of interventions," *American Psychologist* 60: 410–21.

30. It is not, however, a sufficient condition for flourishing. That is, some people who are doing less well are also comparably social. See Diener, E., and M. E. P. Seligman (2002), "Very happy people," *Psychological Science* 13: 81–84.

31. Fleeson, W., A. B. Malanos, and N. M. Achille (2002), "An intraindividual process approach to the relationship between extraversion and positive affect: Is acting extraverted as "good" as being extraverted?" *Journal of Personality and Social Psychology* 83: 1409–22; see also McNiel, J. M., and W. Fleeson (2006), "The causal effects of extraversion on positive affect and neuroticism on negative affect: Manipulating

state extraversion and state neuroticism in an experimental approach," *Journal of Research in Personality* 40: 529–50.

32. Watson, D. (2000). *Mood and Temperament* (New York: Guilford Press).

33. Woodcock, A., and A. Custovic (1998), "ABC of allergies: Avoiding exposure to indoor allergens," *British Medical Journal* 316: 1075–78.

34. When the weather gets too hot, say above 67 degrees Fahrenheit, the positivity-boosting effect of going outside begins to diminish. Keller, M. C., Fredrickson, B. L., et al. (2005), "A warm heart and a clear head: The contingent effects of weather on mood and cognition," *Psychological Science* 16: 724–31.

35. Franklin, H. (2001), "Beyond toxicity: Human health and the natural environment," *American Journal of Preventive Medicine* 20: 234–39.

36. Openness unlocks positivity for a host of reasons. Beyond the fact that openness and positivity go hand in hand, each sparking the other, another key is to consider the natural landscape of good and bad experiences. How frequent is each? Recall that people's pleasant experiences outnumber their unpleasant ones by at least 2 to 1. Scientists call this the positivity offset. Knowing this, you can be fairly certain that when you open yourself more fully to your current stream of experiences, that stream will be offset to the positive side to some degree. Also, being open expands your awareness so much that you notice things you'd totally miss otherwise, like that bright green patch of moss almost completely obscured beneath the freshly fallen snow. As your recognition of beauty and oneness grows, self-transcendent positive emotions like awe, gratitude, and love naturally follow.

37. Davidson, R. J., J. Kabat-Zinn, et al. (2003), "Alterations in brain and immune function produced by mindfulness meditation," *Psychosomatic Medicine* 65: 564–70.

38. Easterlin, B. L., and E. Cardeña (1998), "Cognitive and emotional differences between short- and long-term Vipassana meditators," *Imagination, Cognition and Personality* 18: 69–81.

39. Wilson, T. D., D. B. Centerbar, et al. (2005), "The pleasures of uncertainty: Prolonging positive moods in ways people do not anticipate," *Journal of Personality and Social Psychology* 88: 5–21.

40. Also called "metta" practice, introduced to westerners by Sharon Salzberg. See her book under Recommended Resources.

CHAPTER 11. A NEW TOOLKIT

1. Dutton, J. E. (2003), *Energize Your Workplace: How to Create and Sustain High-Quality Connections at Work* (San Francisco: Jossey-Bass); see also the offerings of the Center for Positive Organizational Scholarship at the University of Michigan's Ross School of Business: www.bus.umich.edu/positive/.

2. Reivich, J. J., and A. Shatte (2003), *The Resilience Factor: Seven Essential Skills for Overcoming Life's Inevitable Obstacles* (New York: Random House); see also C. Peterson (2006), *A Primer in Positive Psychology* (New York: Oxford University Press).

3. Seligman, M. E. P. (2002), *Authentic Happiness* (New York: Free Press); Peterson, C. (2006), *A Primer in Positive Psychology* (New York: Oxford University Press).

4. Visit www.bus.umich.edu/Positive/ and look for POS Teaching and Learning Tools.

5. At first it may seem awkward to turn your palms up, but I suggest you give it a try. Laboratory experiments demonstrate that having your hands palm-side up can spark positivity, whereas having them palms down can spark negativity. See Cacioppo, J. T., J. R. Priester, and G. G. Berntson, (1993), "Rudimentary determinants of attitudes. II: Arm flexion and extension have differential effects on attitudes," *Journal of Personality and Social Psychology* 65: 5–17.

6. Wegner, D. M. (1989), *White Bears and Other Unwanted Thoughts: Suppression, Obsession, and the Psychology of Mental Control* (New York: Viking Penguin).

7. Seligman, M. E. P., T. Steen, et al. (2005), "Positive psychology progress: Empirical validations of interventions," *American Psychologist* 60: 410–21.

8. I trace my fascination with endings back to a seminar I took from my undergraduate mentor, Neil Lutsky, called "The Psychology of Endings." That course shaped my research over the next decade, including my dissertation "Anticipated endings: An explanation for selective social interaction" and several of my early publications: Fredrickson, B. L.,

and L. L. Carstensen (1990), "Choosing social partners: How old age and anticipated endings make people more selective," *Psychology and Aging* 5: 335–47; and Fredrickson, B. L., and D. Kahneman (1993), "Duration neglect in retrospective evaluations of affective episodes," *Journal of Personality and Social Psychology* 65: 45–55.

9. King, L. A. (2001), "The health benefits of writing about life goals," *Personality and Social Psychology Bulletin* 27: 798–807; see also Lyubomirsky, S., L. Sousa, and R. Dickerhoof (2006), "The costs and benefits of writing, talking, and thinking about life's triumphs and defeats," *Journal of Personality and Social Psychology* 90: 692–708; for Jim Loehr's work, see Recommended Resources.

10. See www.PositivePsychology.org.

11. Marty Seligman, director of the Positive Psychology Center at the University of Pennsylvania, was in this trying situation when he and his colleagues, James Pawelski and Debbie Swick, christened James's earlier use of reassuring words and objects as a Positive Portfolio.

Recommended Resources

Brantley, M. and Hanauer, T. (2008). *The Gift of Loving-Kindness: 100 Mindful Practices for Compassion, Generosity, and Forgiveness.* Oakland, CA: New Harbinger.

Burns, D. D. (1999). *Feeling Good: The New Mood Therapy* (revised and updated). New York: Avon Books.

Cameron, K. S., Dutton, J. E., & Quinn, R. E. (2003). *Positive Organizational Scholarship: Foundations of a New Discipline.* San Francisco, CA: Berrett-Koehler.

Csikszentmihalyi, M. (1990). *Flow: The Psychology of Optimal Experience.* New York: HarperCollins.

Hayes, S. C. and Smith, S. (2005). *Get Out of Your Mind and Into Your Life: The New Acceptance and Commitment Therapy.* Oakland, CA: New Harbinger.

Loehr, J. (2007). *The Power of Story: Rewrite Your Destiny in Business and in Life.* New York: Free Press.

Lyubomirsky, S. (2008). *The How of Happiness.* New York: Penguin Press.

Mipham, S. (2003). *Turning the Mind Into an Ally.* New York: Berkley Publishing.

Nolen-Hoeksema, S. (2003). *Women Who Think Too Much: How to Break Free of Overthinking and Reclaim Your Life.* New York: Henry Holt Co.

Peterson, C. (2006). *A Primer in Positive Psychology.* New York: Oxford University Press.

Reivich, K. and Shatte, A. (2002). *The Resilience Factor: 7 Keys to Finding Your Inner Strength and Overcoming Life's Hurdles.* New York: Broadway Books.

Salzberg, S. (2005). *The Force of Kindness: Change Your Life with Love and Compassion.* Boulder, CO: Sounds True, Inc.

Seligman, M. E. P. (2002). *Authentic Happiness: Using the New Positive Psychology to Realize your Potential for Lasting Fulfillment.* New York: Free Press.

———. (1991). *Learned Optimism: How to Change Your Mind and Your Life.* New York: Knopf.

Vaillant, G. E. (2002). *Aging Well.* Boston, MA: Little, Brown & Company.

Williams, J. M. G., Teasdale, J. D., Segal, Z. V., and Kabat-Zinn (2007). *The Mindful Way through Depression: Freeing Yourself from Chronic Unhappiness.* New York: Guilford Press.

Acknowledgments

With all the words of this book now in line, here's my opportunity to voice my appreciation for those who've helped me along the way. Although I take full responsibility for the ideas in this book, science—like life itself—is always a communal endeavor.

First, I'd like to thank my mentors—Neil Lutsky, Laura Carstensen, and Bob Levenson—for helping me find and clear my own path in psychological science, and for showing me the proverbial ropes.

Second, I'd like to recognize the past and present members of my Positive Emotions and Psychophysiology Laboratory (a.k.a PEPlab). Each has worked tirelessly by my side to test the ideas that run through this book, sharpening my thinking and often inspiring me with their own bold ideas. I've enjoyed their intellectual companionship and am grateful for their many key contributions. They include Sara Algoe, Christine Branigan, Stephanie Brown, Tracey Callison, Lahnna Catalino, Lisa Cavanaugh, Kimberly Coffey, Michael Cohn, Anne Conway, Stéphane Côté, Jose Duarte, Kareem Johnson, Matt Keller, Bethany Kok, Greg Larkin, Yi-Chen Lee, Alysson Light, Roberta Mancuso, Elizabeth Meier, Joe Mikels, Keiko Otake, Jolynn Pek, Janice Templeton, Eddie Tong, Michele Tugade, Tanya Vacharkulksemsuk, Tor Wager, and Christian Waugh.

I'd like to gratefully acknowledge my other scientific collaborators who've made the research studies described in this book more persuasive and engaging, especially Mary Brantley, Michael D. Cohen, Sandra Finkel, Melissa Gross, Ahalya Hejmadi, Thomas Joiner, Daniel Kahneman, Oliver Schultheiss, Steve Taylor, and Jon-Kar Zubieta. I owe special thanks to Marcial Losada for the brilliant mathematical work that led to our discovery of the positivity ratio.

My sincere appreciation to the hundreds of people who have volunteered their time and honest self-reflections as participants in my research studies. They are the lives behind the numbers that inspired this book. I especially thank Nina, for taking the chance to meet with me and share her story. Likewise, I appreciate the many students of positive psychology who've shared their experiences with me, especially their efforts to build their own positivity portfolios and raise their ratios.

For their inspiration and support over the past decade, as well as their contributions to the field, I appreciate those who've led the way toward creating a more positive approach to the human sciences, especially Wayne Baker, Kim Cameron, Mihalyi Csikszentmihalyi, Ed Diener, Jane Dutton, Christopher Peterson, Robert Quinn, Martin Seligman, Gretchen Spreitzer, and George Vaillant. Special thanks to James Pawelski for working with me to hone my discussion of positivity portfolios, as presented in chapter 11.

Most of the scientific publications upon which this book rests would not have been possible without federal funding from the National Institute of Mental Health. I'm grateful to have been deemed worthy of their investment over the past decade. I've also been fortunate to have additional financial support from the Templeton Foundation and the Kenan Foundation for Distinguished Professors at UNC–Chapel Hill. More generally, the University of Michigan and the University of North Carolina have each invested in and supported my research program in innumerable ways over the years. I am sincerely grateful to my colleagues and champions at these two superb public institutions.

My agent, Richard Pine of InkWell Management, has been phenomenal, right from our first conversation. He's a true master at helping shape academic ideas for broader consumption and finding them the right home. This book wouldn't be in your hands without his behind-the-scenes efforts. For that, I'm immensely grateful. And I thank Susan Hobson, also of InkWell, for helping bring *Positivity* to international readers.

I appreciate the dedicated crew at Crown Publishers for shaping and promoting *Positivity,* each in turn, including Christine Aronson, Patty Berg, Cindy Berman, Tina Constable, Laura Duffy, Shawn

Nicholls, Heather Proulx, and Penny Simon. My editor, Heather Jackson, warrants special heartfelt praise. Her gentle wisdom and honest assessments helped me discover better ways to arrange my thoughts within the pages of this book. She made my task of revising the book not only painless but fun.

To my many dear friends for creating time, space, and energy for me to test-drive and refine the ideas in this book, in both academia and life, I offer my abiding gratitude. Although they very well know who they are, I'd like to call out a few in particular, namely Lisa Feldman Barrett, Rita Benn, Jane Dutton, Vivian Foushee, Harry Gallaher, Julie Harris, Corey Keyes, Laura King, Jim Loehr, Yun Lu, Sonja Lyubomirsky, John Mader, Batja Mesquita, Judy Moskowitz, Susan Nolen-Hoeksema, Erika Rosenberg, Wendy Treynor, Terry Vance, and, of course, my Wednesday chocolate-loving friends. Their warmth, insights, challenges, and most of all—their shining example—have inspired me to new heights.

And ginormous thanks go to my sister, Jeanne Gallaher, who read several early versions of this book and talked with me about every page and then some—a true gift. After all these years, there's still nobody who can make me laugh better than Jeanne can.

Above all, I am forever and deeply grateful to my husband, Jeff Chappell, and our two amazing sons, Garrett and Crosby. They've each, in their own way, been enthusiastic about this book project from the start, even though it too often drew me to hide away in my home office. Atop all his love and support over the years, Jeff has provided immeasurable practical advice as he responded to countless early drafts of this book and graciously allowed me to work out my ideas through our extended and lively dinner conversations. Every day, I thank my lucky stars for him.

Last, although a scientist to my core, my own scientific evidence gently reminds me to acknowledge the broader context in which I live and work. In that spirit, I wish to voice my appreciation for the sun, for rising and inspiring me each day, and for the earth, for nourishing us all, giving us each the precious opportunity to flourish.

Index

About the Author

BARBARA FREDRICKSON, PH.D., earned her undergraduate degree from Carleton College and her doctorate from Stanford University. She is currently Kenan Distinguished Professor at the University of North Carolina at Chapel Hill, with appointments in Psychology and the Kenan-Flagler School of Business. She has received numerous honors for her research on positive emotions, including the American Psychological Association's inaugural and highest Templeton Prize in Positive Psychology and the Society for Experimental Social Psychology's Career Trajectory Award. Her work has also received more than ten consecutive years of research funding from the National Institute of Mental Health. Beyond her research and writing, she enjoys cooking, dancing, walking on the beach, and exploring the world with her family. She lives in Carrboro, North Carolina, with her husband, her two young sons, and their beloved cat, Spike.

10